Pop Music, Pop Culture

To LB

Pop Music, Pop Culture

Chris Rojek

polity

First published in 2011 by Polity Press

Polity Press
65 Bridge Street
Cambridge CB2 1UR, UK

Polity Press
350 Main Street
Malden, MA 02148, USA

ISBN-13: 978-0-7456-4263-5
ISBN-13: 978-0-7456-4264-2(pb)

A catalogue record for this book is available from the British Library.

Typeset in 10.5 on 13 pt Quadraat
by Servis Filmsetting Ltd, Stockport, Cheshire
Printed and bound in Great Britain by MPG Books Group Limited, Bodmin, Cornwall

The publisher has used its best endeavours to ensure that the URLs for external websites referred to in this book are correct and active at the time of going to press. However, the publisher has no responsibility for the websites and can make no guarantee that a site will remain live or that the content is or will remain appropriate.

Every effort has been made to trace all copyright holders, but if any have been inadvertently overlooked the publisher will be pleased to include any necessary credits in any subsequent reprint or edition.

For further information on Polity, visit our website: www.politybooks.com

Contents

Tables and Figures

Tables

Figure

Introduction: Why 'Pop', Not 'Popular'?

This is a book about *pop* music and *pop* culture. In recent years, some authors, especially traditional musicologists, have objected to the use of 'pop' as a synonym for 'popular'. The reasons for this are complex. For Simon Frith (2001) the question essentially turns upon two matters.

Firstly, while the terms 'pop' and 'popular' both refer to well-favoured or widely liked practices and commodities, the former is held to bear derogatory connotations. On this reckoning, 'pop' is an inherently dismissive term signifying disposability and inferiority. This is part of an older cultural studies tradition which maintains that elite culture is impervious to, or contemptuous of, the practices of the folk in traditional society and the masses in industrial society.

Secondly, with respect to well-favoured music, pop is held to designate a specific, territorialized genre: that is, music defined by the Tin Pan Alley tradition of the three-minute song formula structured around narrative typifications, basic chord structures, harnessed to powerful commercial interests.[1] To identify the people's music with pop is judged to be too limiting. Other widely liked genres, such as rock, progressive, heavy metal, country, indie, reggae, hip hop, rap, electronica, and so on, are organized differently. In particular, they are regarded as having purer aspirations to articulate the customs, practices and values of the people. This is very different from the blind worship of Mammon in which pop is held to indulge. As a result, traditional musicologists generally prefer the term 'popular music' as an umbrella term to cover the people's music as a whole.

The division between pop and what might be called 'the people's music' has influenced a generation of traditional musicologists and permeates the analysis of popular music. It holds that composition, production and marketing in pop are commercially driven. By implication, the musical texts that make up the people's music are held to be more authentic. Categorically speaking, they are less tainted by commerce and truly reflect the people's concerns, practices, traditions and aspirations.

The present book seeks to break with this convention. It does so for three reasons. In the first place, in terms of a simple head count, pop reaches a lot of people. By definition, pop is a well-liked genre. The analysis of the people's music must necessarily address it and consider the reasons why it is well liked, how it is composed, produced, represented and distributed, and why judgements of low taste do not hinder its mass appeal. In a word it is important to understand accurately why pop is popular. To separate pop from the rest of the people's music because it is attached to strong commercial objectives is, I believe, arbitrary. It is the widely favoured nature of pop, as against other 'popular' genres, that is the issue. In sum, pop is more well liked than many examples of so-called 'authentic' popular forms, like blues, folk, country, heavy metal, rock, rap and techno. Must we fall back on tired old arguments that yoke the people's likes, of which a few progressive academics disapprove, with 'false consciousness'? Surely it is right to propose that nowadays we are dealing with a more literate pop audience than was the case when Adorno (2009) was writing in the 1940s and 1950s? People like pop despite being alive to its associations with commercialism, manipulation and low taste. The question is, why?

Secondly, to suggest that pop exemplifies commercial values whereas folk, blues, country, rock and other genres of the people's music are immune does not carry water. Popular music texts are not independent of commercialized communication highways. The pop of Abba and Westlife reaches mass audiences by the same gateways as Bob Dylan and 2Pac. 'Unbreakable' by Westlife (2006) and 2Pac's 'To Live and Die in L.A.' (2007) are popularized by essentially the same commercialized information highways. These highways may not have the *same* commercial effect on the texts, but that they exert *an* effect is not in doubt. An approach to the people's music that omits to balance the aesthetics and politics of songs with the mechanisms of popular communication is naïve and unacceptable. Pop music uses the same mechanism as other branches of the people's music to influence mass opinion.

Thirdly, to imply that pop can be separated from the people's music is to mistake today's leaky boundaries between genres, idioms, association and practice in music and much else besides. The production, exchange and consumption of the people's music have undergone tectonic movements over the last twenty years. As a result, huge fissures and major schisms have emerged in boundaries. This has changed traditional ideas of musical hierarchies, corporate power, authorship and the docility of the audience. These movements have made music ubiquitous and instantaneous. The abbreviation 'pop' appears to be better suited as a descriptor than 'popular' because it is more direct and informal. For me, this accurately parallels the profound social and technological changes that are making the production and exchange of music more direct, and the settings in which music is consumed more informal. Before spelling out these arguments at greater length, it is necessary to go into more detail about what traditional musicologists and the majority of sociologists mean by 'pop'.

Make no mistake, there are problems with the term. Frith (2001: 94) himself describes the descriptor 'pop' as 'slippery'. In an effort to resolve the issue, he submits that pop music ought to be regarded as a type of music harnessed to commercial rather than artistic imperatives which is designed to attain maximum public access (2001: 94–6).

To consolidate the argument, Frith offers four identifying characteristics of pop music:

(1) *General appeal.* Pop aims to generate a general cultural response. It is not tied to communal or subcultural experience. Instead it seeks to appeal to everyone. As examples, Frith lists Euro-pop (Abba /Boney M), with its 'family music' pitch, and the assembly line of hits produced by the Stock, Aitken and Waterman songwriting and production team in the 1980s. A more contemporary example would be the music format showcased by Simon Fuller's *Idol* and Simon Cowell's *Got Talent*

franchises: that is, songs and middlebrow performers who, in the majority of cases, aim for the lowest common denominator of emotions.

(2) *Light entertainment.* Historically, pop grew out of a light entertainment/easy listening tradition. Generally, it holds no brief to challenge audiences socially or to inspire political activism. Unlike folk, blues and country traditions, which often include expressions of resistance and opposition, pop is conservative. This imposes tight restrictions upon narrative content, musical composition and the packaging of performers. The best pop songs carry a powerful emotional payload, but they are ultimately decorative aural wallpaper for urban-industrial life.

(3) *Commercial imperatives.* The main purpose of pop music is to generate revenue. It is a business rather than an art form. As such, it places ultimate value on professional songwriters, slick production values and overwhelming star-images. Pop tries to mould public reception. It does not constitute the free articulation of the people. Rather, it is an imposed form of well-liked music, designed by business, in order to shift units.

(4) *Personal identification.* Pop is an industrial type of music aimed ro appeal to the masses. However, the medium of expression is typically organized around achieving instant empathy with personalities rather than the public. Pop works with clichés, stereotypes and melodrama to connect with individual listeners. When the singer sings of a boy with a cheating heart or a girl left crying at the altar, the composition, production and performance are organized to 'speak' directly to you. This raises a separate set of questions about the nature of the individual desire that pop seeks to supply. These questions generally culminate in the conclusion that pop is ideological since it is unable, or has no wish, to generate general criticisms or social and psychological alternatives.

Upon this basis most musicologists and sociologists conclude that pop must be treated as a differentiated genre. It is part of the people's music, but its content and mode of production must be kept separate from other genres that have emerged from the people and are favoured by them.

In contrast, the present study runs against the grain. New technologies, revised systems of mass communication and grassroots resistance have combined to transform the postwar business model of the people's music. Sampling, sequencing, social network sharing and unauthorized downloading have become general forms of practice. Miniaturization has produced high-quality playback systems that are slimmer and lighter than a cigarette packet. The old conventions linking training and practice with musical proficiency, and consumption with paying, no longer obtain. For the under-30 demographic, the *normal* ways of producing and consuming music are microchip-based.

These transformations are not modish. It is important not to confuse a revolutionary aesthetic genre, such as glam, punk or rap, with a radical technological and cultural transformation in the production, exchange and consumption of pop music. Aesthetic genres influence only a segment of the market, albeit often an appreciable one; and they also date as new genres challenge and replace them. In contrast, a revolutionary cultural transformation in production, exchange and consumption constitutes a tectonic shift which may last for many decades and, in some cases, for centuries. It changes the way in which music is composed, distributed and experienced. I maintain that we are in the midst of such a shift today.

What does it mean to propose that, over the last twenty years, the people's music has undergone a *tectonic* change in production, exchange and consumption which makes general responses more immediate and fragmented? Sampling, sequencing, the internet and the emergence of various countercultures to capitalism have dislodged old concepts of authorship, accumulation and power. The main consequences that follow from this are fourfold:

(1) *Spatial distribution*. The laptop and mobile phone have replaced the bedroom Dansette and the Grundig transistor radio as the main focus for individuals to listen to the people's music. In the days of mods and rockers, soul, grunge and electronic, the club, the coffee bar, the high street record store and the ever-changing rave venue were the primary spatial settings for the collective consumption of recorded music. Over the last twenty years these primary locations have been seriously eroded. The high street record store is arguably the biggest casualty. It has all but disappeared, to be replaced by legitimate file distribution sites like iTunes, multiple unauthorized servers for peer-to-peer (P2P) exchange, subscription models of streaming and free internet blogging and exchange sites, such as MySpace, YouTube, Spotify and Last.fm. The exchange of recorded music is now instant and weightless. Because of this, the focus of consumption and exchange is today often mobile, through hand-held devices like laptops, mobile phones and iPads, or the sound playback system in automobiles.

(2) *Subcultural formation*. Fixed spatial settings were propitious for the development of communal responses to music that ultimately strengthened subcultural formation. Music subcultures still exist – think of goth, metal, country, trance, punk and emo traditions and practices. But the internet encourages more diffuse and contradictory forms of reception. The weightless and mobile character of exchange and consumption militates against subcultural formation because it removes the principle of visible collective experience, the urgency of collective organization and the necessity of collective practice. This results in much weaker notions of collective consciousness. This does not mean that network society is unable to make connections between people and build recognition of collective interests and initiatives (Castells 1996, 1997). Rather, it means that the way in which collective recognition and action now operate is less transparent than in the days when the people's music was centrally consumed in fixed spatial settings. For example, internet exchange makes it unlikely that regional subcultures, like the Mersey and Madchester scenes of, respectively, the 1960s and late 1980s, or the Compton rap scene in Southern Los Angeles of the 1990s, will emerge with the same force and influence in the future. Scenes depend upon physical locations. The effect of the internet is to disembed listening and the production of music from primary spatial locations like the neighbourhood or the city and spread them out electronically.

(3) *Authorship and co-operative labour.* The postwar music business model identified authorship with the composition and performance of popular music. This elevated composers and performers as stars or potential stars and positioned listeners as passive consumers. Sequencing, sampling and the internet have radically challenged this hierarchical model of production, exchange and consumption. They have recast the rules of composition and performance by reducing the need for technical training to make music. All that is necessary to do this now is basic keyboard skills. Admittedly, this imposes limits upon the virtuosity and range of what is produced. Even so, it represents a fundamental transformation from the days when learning an instrument and music composition were prerequisites. In addition, sampling and sequencing enable producers of music to engage with old traditions of pop music as well as contemporaneous forms. Samples of mod classics and soul standards can be easily spliced into new rhythms to produce multi-layered sounds. In effect, the only limits on appropriating recorded music from the past or the present are copyright restrictions.

Not only this, but sampling, sequencing and the internet increase the power of ordinary consumers to engage creatively with recorded music. There is no seal around it. New digital technologies allow consumers to hack into recorded sounds, amend arrangements, transform rhythms, strip out (or insert) layers of sound and change lyrics. The old business model that positioned music fans as passive consumers is now redundant. The situation today is closer to a system of co-operative labour in which the recordings of stars are not simply played and listened to but also reassembled.

(4) *The power of the record corporation.* Widening access to illegal downloading and ineffective systems of policing have combined to produce a haemorrhage in the revenues accruing to record corporations. Traditional A&R (Artist and Repertoire) scouting functions have been outpaced by exchange on MySpace, YouTube and Twitter. Artists themselves do not necessarily regret this weakening of corporation ties. The idea of the omnipotent corporation and the heinous recording deal has long had immense resonance in the industry. In 1977, The Eagles released 'Hotel California'. Superficially, the song dealt with a noirish storyline of abduction in California. In reality the song was an attack on the Los Angeles record industry and the tyrannical moguls and business executives who sought to imprison artists in punitive record deals. Performers like The Clash, David Bowie, Prince, George Michael and The Rolling Stones are all well-known victims. However, new technologies are increasing the artist's independence from record contracts.

Record corporations are being squeezed in a pincer movement. Revenues are being decimated by unauthorized downloading and streaming, which creates a hole in profits and research and development income. At the same time, digital technologies and the commercial opportunities of the internet are liberating artists from studio control. Beyoncé's producers may still work in highly sophisticated studios, but the laptop has become an indispensable device for composition. In the long run it will weaken the capacity of record corporations to make demands on future royalties as the price paid for leasing studio space and personnel for recording, pressing records and retail distribution.

Initially, the record corporations dealt with the threat of unauthorized downloading by litigation. The law was applied against both unauthorized servers and consumers. On the part of illegal servers this produced a lively, prolonged exchange of counter-litigation in which peer-to-peer downloading was defended with reference to the 1st and 14th amendments of the US Constitution, which guarantee the freedom to express information, ideas and opinions, independent of government restrictions. The record corporations have enjoyed some success in attacking servers. The pioneering unauthorized P2P exchange site Napster was a prominent scalp in 2001. However, litigation has not succeeded in eliminating unauthorized servers, since providers simply change sites when they are threatened with court actions.

With respect to the unauthorized consumption of recorded material protected by copyright law, the conventional wisdom now is that litigation is counter-productive because policing is ineffective. Litigation merely creates victims and makes record corporations look like tinpot tyrants. The bad publicity that arises is held to outweigh commercial gains and ethical victories are widely discounted as pyrrhic.

Cultural De-differentiation

The tectonic changes in the production, exchange and consumption of recorded popular music are best described and understood as a massive movement in *cultural de-differentiation*. This term refers to the collapse of boundaries and the breakdown of genres. Nothing, any longer, is hermetically sealed. Technology, mass communication and creative ambition have combined to borrow elements from one genre tradition and blend them with others.

All of the main players in the music business, from artists through to record corporations, media hubs and audiences, have been caught up in a process of de-familiarization: that is, a social and cultural process that has positioned individuals differently in relation to recorded sound and performance. Instant, weightless access and the emergence of the microchip as a standard compositional and performance device have changed the rules of the game. The present condition is a state of flux in which the new conventions and reciprocities have not settled down into customs or traditions. The production, exchange and consumption of pop are in deep transition, which makes writing about and studying the subject both exciting and demanding.

The most popular type of people's music now is rap (Rentfrow et al. 2007, 2009). Aesthetically speaking, rap both is a symptom of cultural de-differentiation and shows the way for future developments. Consider Puff Daddy's multiple-platinum single 'I'll Be Missing You' (1997). A tribute to the slain fellow Bad Boy Records artist The Notorious B.I.G., the song famously samples sections from 'Every Breath You Take' (1983) by The Police and the melody from the American spiritual 'I'll Fly Away' (1929). It is a genre piece that relies on multi-lane surfing and splicing from other music genres. It doesn't recognize boundaries or limits. It is music that purports to speak for the oppressed, but it is microscopically calculated for the purpose of economic accumulation. It plays with identities and impressions, and its public appeal rests upon overturning assumptions and forcing people out of their comfort zones.

In the midst of the tectonic changes that follow from cultural de-differentiation, one can hardly escape the conclusion that the opposition to using the descriptor 'pop', with respect to the people's music, has more to do with defending academic boundaries than engaging with cultural realities. The position taken here is that there can be no closed shop in the interpretation or making of music. The production of the people's music deliberately and unintentionally mixes references from blues, country, progressive, punk, post-punk and other genres. By the term 'unintentionally' I wish to convey the sheer saturation of music in ordinary culture. This makes it impossible to avoid boundary meltdown and genre busting simply as a result of *ordinary listening*. Instead of solid, differentiated boundaries between genres, technology, resistance and innovation now mean that the people's music is created between permeable boundaries. The centre of particular genres may be purist. But the periphery is where the action is in creating contemporary music that makes waves with the public. The definitive feature of the periphery is the mixing of styles, arrangements and traditions.

Coming to the questions of exchange and consumption, the internet makes music commodities instant and weightless. There is no financial cost in ripping music from unauthorized sites and the risk of criminal punishment is routinely assessed by consumers to be negligible. The increasing popularity of streaming, downloading tracks from albums rather than the whole album, making playlists or triggering random, shuffled playlists has changed the meaning of consumer ownership. It is no longer a question of building vinyl and CD libraries. Today the accent in exchange and consumption is on low or financially neutral access and weightless transaction. Access to files is often on a temporary, leased basis. The 'here today, gone tomorrow' character of music collections on iPods, laptops and other portable electronic devices suggests an immediate, transitory, disposable relationship to ownership for which the descriptor 'pop' is better suited.

It does not follow that the general attitude to pop is dismissive. In his notes on the concept of the popular, Raymond Williams (1976: 199) observed that the mid-twentieth-century abbreviation of the popular song and popular art to 'pop' bestowed 'a lively informality' in 'many familiar and pleasing contexts'. It is this quality of lively informality, which encompasses genre busting and captures the creativity and innovation of co-operative labour and cultural de-differentiation as a whole, that I wish to convey by applying the descriptor 'pop' to the people's music and culture.

True, Williams goes on to comment that the use of the term is historically associated with the 'trivial'. As I noted at the outset, the use of the term 'pop' is not without problems. However, it is important to recognize that the association between pop and triviality is not privileged. In the mid-twentieth century, pop art emerged and produced a culturally transforming engagement with commodity culture and consumerism which incurred the displeasure of some traditional art historians. However, the work of Andy Warhol, Richard Hamilton, Roy Lichtenstein, Derek Boshier and others is hardly regarded today as trivial.

Similarly, to use the term 'pop' to refer to songs like Nirvana's 'Smells Like Teen Spirit' (1991), 2Pac's 'So Many Tears' (1995) and Eminem's 'Love The Way You Lie' (2010) does not trivialize them. On the contrary, in doing so, the associations that I seek to privilege are ubiquity, speed, flexibility of setting, direct emotional transfer and instant access. To my mind, the abbreviation 'pop' conveys this with more force than 'popular'.

There is another reason for going with 'pop' as the most suitable descriptor to apply to the people's music and culture. The general ways in which people communicate are becoming faster and more streamlined. Think of communication via mobile phones. It privileges verbs, adjectives and nouns. Many words are rendered phonetically: 'u' for 'you'; 'r' for 'are'; 'wd' for 'would'. The emphasis is upon direct, uncluttered communication. This is reinforced by web and mobile phone technology, which makes instantaneous contact possible at all times, and in all places.

In interesting research on the increasing turn towards abbreviation in communication, Todd Gitlin (2002: 98–9) compared the top ten best-selling novels from the first week of October in 1936, 1956, 1976, 1996 and 2001. He took four sentences from each book drawn from randomly chosen pages: 1, 50, 100 and 150 (or 120 in the case of books that were shorter than 150 pages). He counted the words used in each sentence and also the punctuation marks. His findings are striking. Between 1936 and 2001, sentence length declined by 43%, and the number of punctuation marks by 32%.

Gitlin is appropriately cautious about the methodology behind these findings. He notes that his sample is small and that the sentences randomly chosen may be unusual or an aberration. However, his conclusion is confidently expressed: 'best-seller sentences have gotten briefer, simpler and closer to screenplays' (2002: 1000). He puts this down to the 'torrent' of images and sounds that, through the media, are saturating everyday life. He uses terms like 'speed addiction', 'relentless sensation' and 'nonstop stimulus' to describe the character of general culture. This draws on older accounts of the distinctive qualities of modern culture. Especially significant here are the writings of the sociologist Georg Simmel (1971, 1978), who noted the ubiquity of 'haste and hurry' in urban-industrial life and speculated on the destabilizing effects on personality and culture; and Walter Benjamin (2002) on the 'explosive' effects of new electronic technologies of cultural transmission on identity, practice and association.[2]

What seems to be true of best-sellers is also true of successful pop songs. They have become shorter, more streamlined and more like screenplays. At the time of writing, the most popular songs in the charts of the day, like Lady Gaga's 'Bad Romance' (2009), Jay Sean's 'Down' (featuring Lil Wayne) (2009) and Talo Cruz's 'Break Your Heart' (2009) conform to Gitlin's rules of abbreviated, direct, instant meaning. The technology encourages cutting, pasting, surfing and clipping. This is reflected in the practice of the people's culture and the production, exchange and consumption of the people's music. As such, I maintain that, despite the risk of running the gauntlet against established musicologists and sociologists of popular music, 'the lively informality' and easy access to music in 'many familiar and pleasing places' make the descriptor 'pop' a preferred prefix to describe the people's culture and the people's music.

Organization of the Book

The text of this book is organized into four parts. Part I situates the reader in the field of pop music study. It acknowledges the achievements of musicology. However, despite the enhanced receptivity of musicologists to work from sociology, cultural studies and media and communication studies, the book argues for an approach that locates pop in the mode of production in which it is created, produced, distributed, consumed and received. Pop culture, rather than the biography of the artist, the history of the record corporation or the values of the media, is regarded to be the crucible for understanding pop music. The idea of a 'great artist' is not necessarily discounted. What is claimed is that what we mean by the term and how it emerges are indissoluble from the mode of production in which music is produced and distributed.

In this part of the book the relationship between pop and the tradition of cultural articulation is explored, with nuances of articulation around identity, resistance and regulation duly noted and elucidated. For example, the construction and meaning of pop songs are investigated in relation to harmony and convention; language, syntax and semantics; typification and transcription; culture and genre. This relationship between pop and culture, in turn, is related to problems of the cultural meaning of popularity and tectonic changes in the production, exchange and consumption of pop.

Part II surveys the main theoretical approaches to the study of pop music. This employs what is, in sociology, a well-established and useful device of dividing structuralist and agency approaches to the study of social and cultural life. This classificatory device is not without contradictions. Chief among them is the tendency to over-egg respective questions of determinism and autonomy. Nonetheless, given the wide array of theoretical contributions to the field, it was deemed necessary to impose some categorical discipline so as to avoid giving the impression that theoretical contributions to the study of pop amount to what might be called an amorphous riddle. Our enthusiasms for pop may seem to us to be wholly a personal matter. In fact, they are patterned. The theoretical approaches examined here give us tools that help to elucidate and understand how the social patterning and psychology of music operate.

The main examples of structuralism examined here are the work of Plato and Aristotle, Jacques Attali, Claude Lévi-Strauss and Theodor Adorno. Although there are many important differences between these writers, all suggest that music has general (or universal) characteristics of production and consumption. In the case of Plato and Aristotle, these characteristics are traced back to the human species' need for *katharsis* and *mimesis*; in Attali, they go back to the species' fear of catastrophe and the use of music to provide intimations of wider social-economic and political transformations; in the writings of Lévi-Strauss, the characteristics derive from the structural arrangement of cultures, which ultimately refers to the composition of the human mind; and in Adorno's work, the general or universal characteristics of production, exchange and consumption have to do with the capitalist system of world domination.

The chief representatives of the agency perspective to the analysis of pop music are subculturalism, relationism, transcendentalism and textualism. Agency approaches allow for more autonomy or, in extreme cases, total freedom for actors to interpret and act upon the world. The differences between the four traditions are explored with reference to the writings of Willis, Williams, Hebdige, Cohen, Weinstein, Steen and Condry (subculturalism); Bourdieu, Thornton and Negus (relationism); Eliade, Sylvan and Wilson (transcendentalism); and Barthes, Hebdige, Fung and Curtin, and Kaplan (textualism).

As will rapidly become apparent to the informed reader, the aim here is to draw on a much wider range of resources in the social sciences and cultural and communication studies than is normal in the analysis of pop music. It is necessary to cover some ground that may be familiar to informed readers. For how can a book that claims to offer a comprehensive account of the main theoretical approaches to pop avoid the writings of Adorno, Middleton, Willis or Hebdige? However, in referring to these writings I hope that I have done more than merely re-state the obvious or the well known. The sections on Attali, Lévi-Strauss, Eliade, Sylvan, Wilson and, to some extent, Bourdieu are novel, at least in relation to the study of pop music. The intention is very much to demonstrate the pertinence of these writings to revitalizing the investigation of how pop works and why it has colonized pop culture.

Part III of the book moves from mapping the field and surveying the main theoretical approaches, to an analysis of the mode of production in which pop is created, exchanged and consumed. It examines the historical framework of pop music in the postwar period. This framework is characterized as a mode of industrial planning and management. The challenges presented by cultural de-differentiation in the form of increasing access to recorded music and widening participation in composition and performance through sampling and sequencing are fully investigated.

The central social institutions in the mode of pop music production are music corporations, media, managers, stars and audiences. They operate as allocative mechanisms that produce and distribute scarce economic, cultural and social resources. They bear the hallmarks of more profound structural divisions of class, gender, race and status. Each of these institutions is discussed in detail and the interrelationships between them are explored.

The role of technology and mass communications in promoting cultural de-differentiation amounts to the biggest crisis faced by the industrial planning model in the pop music industry. To date, the dominant music corporation cartel has been incapable of responding adequately to the challenges of the digital revolution. Digital rights management (DRM) strategies have not countered the revenue loss produced by unauthorized downloading. Customer relationship management (CRM) strategies and so called '360 degree deals', which extend corporate control from the areas of traditional copyright privilege over sound recordings to new areas of concert tours, celebrity endorsement and mass merchandizing, have belatedly emerged. Their capacity to revitalize corporate revenues, and restore the main corporations to a position of dominance, is examined.

Part IV of the book is the Conclusion. Here the changing balance of power relationships between artists, corporations, managers, the media and audiences is addressed. Conventional wisdom in the field recognizes a polarized relationship between producers and consumers. Broadly, the producers were viewed as a sometimes contradictory, sometimes fractious, but always imperative, amalgamation between corporations, artists, managers and the media; and the consumers were viewed as the passive, disorganized audience. The combination of new technologies of production, consumption and exchange has destabilized this model. A hierarchical view of producers, on one side, and consumers, on the other, is now untenable. Co-operative labour , in which fans use the internet, rather than the media, to communicate about performers, and interact creatively with authorized production and exchange music files for free is a more accurate term to capture what has been happening for the last twenty years. Naturally, this has elicited a reaction from authorized producers, who formerly took it for granted that they constitute the dominant force in the music business. The present situation amounts to a second enclosure movement: that is, a concerted effort by music corporations' pop managers, some performers and most of the media to appropriate the co-operative labour that has revolutionized the pop business and impose a blockade around free exchange. Peer-to-peer systems are being legally challenged, but the ideas and customs that they have developed are being gorged by a music industry that is hungry to return to the high-profit days of the 1980s and early 1990s.

Sensuous Labour is Irreducible

Pop Music, Pop Culture is intended to be a first-stop guide to the key concepts, central theoretical approaches, primary historical issues and decisive dilemmas in both the field of pop music analysis and the mode of pop music production. It gives greater prominence to questions of technology and cultural de-differentiation than is evident in other books of this type. The reason for this is that these questions are altering the nature of pop music study because they are transforming the production, exchange and distribution of pop music. The changes are far-reaching and the use of the term *tectonic transformation* to describe them is, I believe, perfectly justifiable.

Naturally, a book of this type cannot hope to cover everything. The examples of songs and albums that I use to illustrate the wider arguments that I seek to pursue bear all of the limitations of personal biography and geographical location that unavoidably obtain in the practice of writing about music, culture and society, or indeed any other form of writing. However, I have tried to adopt a global perspective, by deliberately referring to Asian and some African examples of pop to counter the self-evident Euro-centric/North American bias. That being said, Europe and North America are still, by far, the dominant players in the field and in the mode of production. As such, their eminence in the text does not really require excuses. It is simply how things are in the world at the present time.

Because of the weight I give to technology and mass communications in bringing about what I call cultural de-differentiation, it might be tempting for some critics to label me as a technological determinist. So it is necessary to state plainly that my position is that human creativity is at the heart of technology, mass communication and, of course, the composition, performance and reception of pop. This creativity is the result of the rational, emotional, sensuous engagement of humans with the natural and social world. Sensuous labour is irreducible in understanding the technological changes in the industry and the socio-cultural reactions to them.

Although I am sympathetic with many aspects of the theoretical approach, the book is not written from a Marxist position. The discussion of the mode of production is, in fact, directly and tacitly critical of many aspects of the

Marxist tradition. However, it fully concurs with Marx's (1964: 113) foundational proposition that: 'Conscious life activity distinguishes man immediately from animal life activity . . . in creating *a world of objects*, by his practical activity, in *his work upon* inorganic nature, man proves himself as a conscious species being' (emphasis in the original). Like Marx, I hold that the products of this conscious activity have the power to become estranged from man's control and to stand above him, and dominate him, as an alien presence.[3] In the mode of pop music production some aspects of technology and music corporations may certainly be said to play this role. However, the rational, sensuous engagement with nature and society that brings about this adverse state of affairs is also the means through which alien domination can be exposed and elucidated. Creativity is at the centre of pop, as pop has become central to ordinary culture.

Part I

The Field

1

The Field of Pop Music Study

Musicology is defined as 'the branch of knowledge that deals with music as a subject of study rather than as a skill or performing art'.[1] It is a long-established, lively field that has generated many enduring traditions and insights about the organization and effects of music. Nonetheless, from the standpoint of sociology and media, communication and cultural studies, it is like studying a fish without water. For music is not just a combination of notes and silence, it is a social and cultural phenomenon inscribed with the flourishes of particular histories, types of creativity, cultures and emotions. It has the capacity to delineate the form and repertoire of emotions, provide sonic pick-me-ups for reflection, action and practice and create a sense of belonging between strangers (DeNora 2000: 110–11; Miller 2008: 47). As the structuralist anthropologist Claude Lévi-Strauss (1979, 1981) tells us, music is a medium of communication, like myth, via which, at its most imposing, we have the sensation that everything momentarily 'fits'.

Despite the impressive and hugely informative work of ethnomusicologists like Martin Stokes (1997) and Steve Feld and Charles Keil (1994), which creatively uses the anthropological tradition to study music, musicology falls short of adequately embracing the industrial, social, political, economic and cultural dimensions of music. It does not consider the business of what music can do for you in urban-industrial society, regardless of your education, aptitude or powers of appreciation: which is to say, music that works on the gut, or the solar plexus, not the head.

That there is a deep emotional response to music is scarcely in doubt. The Musica Humana research project in Denmark, which commenced in 1998, has well-documented findings on the connection between specially designed music environments and remedial care for cardiac patients, pain treatment, stress management, post-operative treatment, neo-natal and psychiatric care. Some of the findings are dramatic. For example, the project cites ward experience that maintains that the prescription of tranquillizers and painkillers can be reduced by 50% if patients wake up after an operation with 'soft music' in their headphones (http:www.musicahumana.org; see also DeNora 2000: 71–2, 151–2).[2]

Recognition of the therapeutic and narrative power of music has culminated in its application as an adjunct of management in a variety of organizational settings.

For example, in the 1930s managers at IBM introduced a corporate songbook designed to produce a musical repertoire that was intended to achieve strong identification with company values. The IBM songbook was designed to frame social relations in the company in a positive light, reinforce collective hierarchy, promote the work ethic and shape the distribution of emotional labour in the workforce. According to El-Sawad and Korczynski (2007: 95), the songbook functioned as a managerial 'disciplinary device'.[3] Radano (1989) makes similar claims in analysing the use of muzak in consumer service environments. That is, music is an organizational method of controlling mobility, motivation and social reaction. There are many other examples of the application of music in the workplace to increase job satisfaction, productivity and consumer management (Jones and Schumacher 1992; Oakes 2000; Corbett 2003).

Some perspectives claim an elemental, transhuman connection between music and emotional reflexes. For example, Pythagoras is usually credited with the *musica universalis* hypothesis: that is, the proposition that the movement of the celestial bodies (the sun, the moon and planets) corresponds to a harmonic order which, in turn, influences our thoughts, feelings and actions. We refer to this hypothesis more commonly today as 'the music of the spheres': that is, the belief that there is a pre-determined correspondence between the movement of the heavens and the transactions of earth-bound animate forms. Its significance for us in this book is that it suggests that from ancient times, music has been associated with an elemental cosmic and healing presence.

The traditional analysis of pop music explores the production, exchange and consumption of pop music as a source of subcultural identity. Pop and rock are examined as the focus of subcultural style, embodiment and belonging. Transparent feedback loops between music and subcultures have been unearthed and sifted (Bennett 1999, 2001). Members of mod, rocker, progressive, punk, post-punk, new romantic, grunge, house, electronica, rap, hip hop, bhangra and other pop subcultures are defined by what they listen to and how they dress, and their musical taste operates as a distinctive 'poetics' for everyday life (Bachelard 1964).[4]

Today, networking, de-differentiation and deterritorialization have modified the character of production, exchange and consumption of pop music (Castells 1996, 1997, 1998; David and Kirkhope 2004; Kusek and Leonhard 2005; David 2010). Synthesizers, sampling and MIDI (musical instrument–digital interface) systems destabilize traditional models of musical competence, credibility and relevance. It is no longer necessary to be a trained or self-taught musician to be taken seriously. With no more than basic computer skills you can compose and perform, using the Garageband function on your Apple laptop or a turntable and amplifier system for scratching.

In addition, the digital revolution has transformed the orthodox model of recorded music retail distribution. Downloading is now the default mechanism for obtaining recorded music. Thompson (2009) cites research by the International Federation of the Phonographic Industry (IFPI) which estimates that nineteen out of every twenty downloads are illegal. The rise in legal downloads has not plugged the hole produced by unauthorized downloading and the contraction in CD sales. The latest IFPI data reports that, between 2004 and 2009, despite an increase of 940% in authorized digital sales, total music sales fell by 30% to $15.8 billion (IFPI 2010).

Even allowing for the industry's exaggeration of the threat, it would be unwise to dismiss lightly the challenge of illegal downloading. The interface between the web, the laptop and the mobile phone has utterly changed the music business.

Time was when pop music media networks were constructed around national or pirate pop music radio stations and key brands in the music press like *Rolling Stone*, *Crawdaddy!*, *Creem*, *Frendz*, *Sounds*, *Melody Maker* and NME. These formed the central media hubs, producing and exchanging information about established performers, tour dates, reviews and thought pieces on dominant, emerging and residual music genres. Streaming, ripping, MTV, blogging sites and illegal downloading have transformed orthodox models of media exchange, browsing and listening. Multi-media platforms are now the key conduits of data about pop music. Fans must be equally conversant with the changing platforms (servers and browsers) of media exchange as with the musical texts produced by artists.

In the course of all of this the place of pop music in the social classification of popular culture has changed. Lévi-Strauss (1979, 1981) pontificated somewhat on the comparison between music in modern society and myth in pre-modern society. He maintained that the structural function of music is to ignite neural links that mere written representations and speech cannot match. In deterritorialized, commodified network society it is difficult for claims of this order to carry water. The function of music may still include achieving neural links that make meaning possible. But the commercial motives behind popular music, the panoramic array of settings in which it is exchanged and the social and psychological uses which consumers make of it preclude the idea of a universal structure. The production, exchange and consumption of popular music is a question of human agency and interpretation, rather than a matter of a universal mechanical link between genetic feedback loops.

The proliferation of new technologies of communication has elicited the phenomenon of social media networks such as Facebook, Twitter and MySpace in which pop music is the soundtrack rather than the foreground of social practice. Web-based applications such as iLike and Last.fm allow users to exchange musical preferences and make 'public statements about who they are, what they want to be, and how they want others to perceive them' (Rentfrow et al. 2009: 329). Here, music is an accessory of lifestyle architecture. It is one of many codes, not necessarily the privileged one, that represent who you are and what you do.

These various processes have resulted in clear and transparent social effects. Pop music subcultures require face-to-face engagement and the recognition of exclusivity. They were solidified and re-solidified by responding to the music in record stores, college hops, clubs and concert arenas. The rave and club culture scenes demonstrate that pop music still operates to make and remake collective identity for some sections of the market (Thornton 1995; Jackson 2004).

At the same time, networking, deterritorialization and the miniaturization of recording and playback systems have changed the rules of the game. The immense and relentless volume of consumer commodities and commodified experience has eroded the taste hierarchies upon which traditional subcultures are based. The pop audience still encompasses subcultures that relate to music as a mark of distinction (Bourdieu 1984, 1993), but it also includes silo cultures of accumulation, in which music is used to provide a sense of grounding and security in the perfect storm of high commodity culture (Condry 2006).

New, mobile, weightless modes of consumption threaten to dilute the basis for collective organization and action upon which subcultural life is based. Old theories of social life referred to the alienation of workers and the immiseration of consumers (Marx 1864; Marcuse 1964). In the ubiquitous consumer culture, notions of alienation and immiseration have weaker torque. It is trickier to invoke the experience of injustice, inequality and exclusion as the basis for collective agitation and action when they are primarily mediated through the headphones of an iPod or the pixel content of a Blu-ray system.

The Study of Pop and Cultural Biography

The social and cultural study of popular music may be defined as the analysis of the social and cultural production, distribution and consumption of sequenced notes, usually words and intervals of silence. This encompasses the performance, recording and representation of music. What is at issue is not merely the organization of notes, words and silences, but the composers behind this arranged sequence, the musicians who perform it, the commercial impresarios, their life stories, the social and cultural networks in which they are embedded, the music corporations that sponsor and manage the financial exchange and representation of music, the technologies that facilitate new routes of musical expression, networks of musical consumption and the audiences for whom music is experienced, *inter alia*, as a source of pleasure, emotional release, comfort, abandonment, ecstasy, background noise, distraction, social inclusion and exclusion.

Nor is this all. The study of popular music is also obliged to examine the class structure in which composers, performers, managers and audiences are located and related questions of power pertaining to divisions of gender, race, ethnicity, subculture, nation, technology and religion.

From this standpoint, popular music is first and foremost a type of communication involving bargaining and transaction around types of narrative *belonging* through which performers and audiences recognize and communicate information and develop means by which to represent it. When this information takes the form of cultural biography it carries maximal emotional voltage.

By the term *cultural biography* I mean the 'structures of feeling' and identification with a cultural representative (star) and concomitant repertoire that form the basis of social recognition and markers of collective memory. That popular music has the power to mobilize these feelings is widely recognized. Simon Frith (1996: 272) comments that music 'both articulates and offers the immediate experience of collective identity'. His focus on the question of aesthetics carries with it the assumption that rhythm, metre, timbre, tone and lyrics of pop are assimilated into people's bodies and practices in strikingly intense ways. Among culturally induced experiences, music is one of the most penetrating and communicable. This presupposes a close link between music and personal and collective emotions. Following on, David Hesmondhalgh (2007: 517) remarks that one of the most important characteristics of popular music is *expressiveness*, that is, the ability to externalize and reflect emotions.

Elsewhere, I (Rojek 2004) submitted that Frank Sinatra's biography provides a cultural biography of his times. The appeal of Sinatra transcended divisions of class, race, gender and nation. As such his career and music can be said to externalize, in ways that possess collective recognition and memory, the transpersonal experience of the times. His music was an adjunct of the transpersonal experience of romance, individual striving, courage, recreation, ageing, entitlement and rights. In this sense it is legitimate to refer to his life and music as providing a cultural biography of the era.

Sinatra is hardly singular in this respect. For a variety of reasons having to do with the revolution in mass communications technology, the miniaturization of reproductive/playback devices that make access ubiquitous, the rise of youth culture incomes and much else besides, pop music attained a significantly higher profile in the late twentieth century. As such, the lives and music of stars like Elvis Presley, Marvin Gaye, Bob Dylan, Paul Simon, James Brown, Jim Morrison, John Lennon, Paul McCartney, David Bowie, Joni Mitchell, Madonna, Kurt Cobain, Bob Marley, Neil Young, Michael Jackson, 50 Cent, Jay-Z, 2Pac and many others operate as lightning rods channelling much wider questions of culture, economy, politics and society.

Technically speaking, two meanings of the term 'cultural biography' must be distinguished. Firstly, popular music has the power to characterize an historical moment and the dominant, emergent and residual political, social and cultural sentiments of the time.[5] This is because, to an unusually powerful degree, popular music communicates emotional voltage. Just as there are epochs of history, there is also epochal music. 'Psychedelia', 'progressive', 'punk', 'post-punk', 'grunge', 'rap', 'garage', 'techno', 'house', 'jungle', 'trance', 'microhouse' and 'bhangra' condense a complex brew of meanings having to do with aesthetics, politics, economics, race, ethnicity, subculture, generational cohesion, power and difference. Music is the means of communicating belonging that has the capacity to override economic, political, social and cultural divisions. But what it signifies is a matter of *reflexive* engagement at the level of both producers and recipients. By the term 'reflexive', I mean the awareness of interpreting or expressing social and economic forces and aesthetic codes.

Secondly, besides this, certain pop stars are sometimes elevated to the status of idols representing particular issues relating to wider social formations such as generation, ethnicity, class, gender, nation or subculture (Stevenson 2006). In doing so, they humanize abstract social textures, economic forces and political values. Their biographies, therefore, are not just a matter of the facts relating to their personal life trajectory. Additionally, they embrace and interact with the allegorical and metaphorical interpenetration of these trajectories with the wider 'poetics' of time and place (Bachelard 1964; Straw 1991).

One might say that Elvis Presley and, to a lesser degree, Buddy Holly, Bill Haley, Eddie Cochran, Gene Vincent and Little Richard embodied the surging social, political and spiritual values of the rock and roll generation of the 1950s. Through their iconic status they crystallized a specific poetic moment that possessed cultural meaning that was, so to speak, 'surplus' to the music they produced. Bob Dylan, The Rolling Stones, The Beach Boys, The Doors, The Byrds, The Who and The Beatles acted in this way for progressive thought and the permissive society in the 1960s; Marc Bolan and David Bowie were the leaders of the 'glam rock' era; Johnny Rotten, Joey Ramone, Debbie Harry, Siouxsie Sioux and Joe Strummer were the faces of punk; Bob Geldof and Bono were symbols of Live Aid in the 1980s and 1990s; Marvin Gaye, Bob Marley, Brenda Fassie and Miriam Makeba ('Mama Afrika') represented black consciousness and post-colonialism; Kurt Cobain personified 'Generation X'; Lebo Mathosa was the icon of the post-apartheid age in South Africa; and Coldplay provide the insignia for post-9/11 preoccupations and sensibilities. In this sense cultural biography is individualized in the career of the pop celebrity.

Cultural biography does not come out of nothing. The construction of a pop music idol involves a complex network of agents, including managers, promoters, agents, media personnel, record corporations, fan clubs and much else besides. Generally, commercial interests are integral to these processes. Thus, glam rock, punk, post-punk, garage, electronica and other modern pop music genres must be considered in terms of a combination between artistic imperatives and commercial logic. The tension between the two is a thorny issue in the pop music industry. Some pop music impresarios, such as Simon Cowell (2003), insist that artistic communication is impossible without micro-business management. But this raises a set of separate questions about who is behind the processes of representation, the nature of the objectives involved and the potential conflict of interest between artistic imperatives and commercial logic. Pop music is not born. It is *made*. This is why the book concentrates upon the intersection between production, exchange and consumption as the foundation of analysis.

The Limits of Musicology

It is an error to propose that musicology is indifferent to the influences of anthropology, sociology and cultural, media and communication studies. For example, the sub-discipline of ethnomusicology uses methods of ethnography, fieldwork and social anthropology to investigate the production and personal and group effects of music (Feld and Keil 1994; Stokes 1997). Nonetheless, the dominant approach examines music as an autonomous artistic form with immanent meanings that are privileged over popular cultural and social factors (Shepherd and Wicke 1997). For orthodox musicologists, the ideal form resides in the European tradition of classical music. By comparison, the study of popular urban-industrial social and cultural factors and their relationships to the production, exchange and consumption of popular music is confined to the margins.

Sociologists of music, radical musicologists and students of culture, media and communication challenge the power structure of orthodox musicology. Philip Tagg (1987) advances three reasons why the traditional tools of musicology developed in relation to Western music of the classical period are unable to provide an adequate perspective for the study of popular music:

(1) *Pop audience.* Unlike classical music, which is composed for sponsors and a selective chamber or concert hall audience, pop music aims at mass distribution to heterogeneous, multi-cultural and multi-ethnic groups of listeners. The pop

song is typically short and direct in its expression of emotion and information. It requires of the listener no previous knowledge or training. The metre and the beat are often organized around urban-industrial rhythms to produce consonant physical and mental responses in both performers and listeners.

Huge claims have been made for the effect of music. The phenomenologist Alfred Schutz (1982) holds that music combines the sense of spacelessness with attention to rhythm and, therefore, time. Because of this, echoing the view of the Ancient Greeks, Schutz (1982: 192–3) claims consonance between music and our 'inner duration'. That is, it is the cultural form that most closely captures our inner life.

Yet *popular* music also clearly reflects what is external, easily accessible or downright common among composers, performers and audiences. Thus, urban-industrial experience, including politics, economics and culture, is central to the production, exchange and consumption of pop music. Some writers submit that there is a direct causal link between industrial mechanics and musical metre and rhythm. For example, the Futurists studied the interaction between music and the chromatic-diatonic system associated with the machine age. According to the composer Luigi Russolo (1986: 20), writing in 1913, ancient life is 'all silence'. 'Noise' is 'born in the nineteenth century'. This is a rhetorical statement. Russolo is well aware that nature comes with noise (the sound of waves crashing on a beach, the wind through the trees, the twitter of birds, the roar of the lion). His claim for proposing the nineteenth century as the 'birth' of modern music is that the noises produced in the machine age created unprecedented sonic intensity. As one of the first experimental composers, he invented a series of *intonarumori* (or noise machines). Their purpose was to mechanically produce all of the sounds played by the traditional orchestra. This constitutes perhaps the first attempt to present music as an analogue of machine noise. As such, one can trace linkages with contemporary metal, goth and industrial music forms.

More recently, Paul Willis (1978) has claimed that there is a homology between urban-industrial subcultures, embodiment and musical genres.[6] Thus, the lifestyle and types of embodiment of motorbike gangs go with traditional and turbo-charged rock, whereas the hippie lifestyle connects up with progressive music. The same might be said about rave cultures and electronic dance music, acid house and techno.

Leaving aside the rights and wrongs of these forms of analysis for the moment, one might propose that the making and meaning of pop music are bound up with urban-industrial forms of life, and especially subcultural formations (Bennett 2001, 2008).

The audience for pop requires no schooling, no immersion in salon culture or elite circles. Pop is brazen in seeking immediate reactions to the organization of notes, words and silences. The salient knowledge required to appreciate it can be readily gleaned from the ordinary channels of mass communications. Developing a perspective on the history and structure of these forms is not something upon which orthodox musicology has placed a high premium.

(2) *Pop composition.* Typically, composers of classical music are trained in the written production and communication of musical scores. By contrast, pop

composers and performers are often self-taught and produce and exchange music in non-written form.

Through accumulation, pop music has developed traditions to which composers and performers self-consciously refer. Still, the form remains based in the exchange of unvarnished emotion, plain speaking and immediate impact.

(3) *Pop distribution.* Pop music is organized upon the principle of flexible accumulation, which makes no bones about adopting the commodity form of distribution in order to maximize market potential. The genre favours structures of harmony and lyrics that can be readily assimilated by the use of simple, direct chord progression. Practically speaking, this means that pop music generally consists of direct, simple chord sequences and lyrics that draw upon vernacular speech systems and topical issues. The simplicity of form and directness of expression are valued over adherence to the canons of classical music taste. Pop music frequently expresses raw emotions, values and other preoccupations which polite society either deflects or represses. Hence the strong associations between pop and authenticity (the telling of unpopular truths is part of this), to say nothing of the matters of political agitation, organization and practice (Grossberg 1997; Russell 1997).

Pop and Articulation

Critics of a pure musicology approach have redefined pop music as social *articulation*. Stuart Hall (1996) uses the term 'articulation' to apply to the inscription of forces that, in being expressed, change the content and form in which these forces proceed. Applying this concept to the study of pop soon reveals that many songs can be said to have a dual function. For example, a song like 'Career Opportunities' (1977) by The Clash might be said to be the band's expression of the social and economic forces of 1970s unemployment, urban decay and punk resistance; but in being articulated by the group the song both draws on a shared vocabulary of cultural resources and modifies how these resources are understood, applied and practised. A pop song can inspire direct action which comes from direct experience; but it is also the product of social and cultural forces.

In addition it is a channel of cultural memory. Anderson (2004) distinguishes between the 'involuntary memory' of music (in summing up a time, a place or a group) and 'intentional memory' (in addressing a time, a place or a group for the purposes of recall or motivation). In this sense pop is at one and the same time the articulation of wider social, cultural and economic forces and a cultural tool through which social, economic and cultural contradictions or tensions are crystallized and carried forward. The concept of articulation, then, aims to acknowledge aristic creativity (in 'making' the song) and to heed the social, economic and political forces in which composition, performance and the consumption of music is situated.

A considerable literature has developed around articulation and pop. In order to facilitate comprehension, it is helpful to differentiate between three positions:

(1) *Pop music articulates* identity. Pop music is a means by which group, more particularly subcultural, identity is located and represented (Lewis 1992; Kohl 1993;

Keightley 2001). In terms of embodiment (dress, cosmetics, hairstyle), subcultural vernacular, group beliefs and lifestyle values there is a homology between pop music and social practice (Willis 1978).

(2) *Pop music articulates* resistance. Pop music exploits and develops the possibilities of resistance and opposition. Two sub-positions in the literature can be identified. The first conceptualizes resistance primarily in political terms. Pop music chips away at the system of organized inequality and manipulation and creates a space of opposition (Chambers 1985; Grossberg 1992, 1997).The second sub-position focuses on the aesthetic role of pop music. This may involve aspects of political critique, but paramount is the mobilization of an aesthetic style that jousts with aesthetic relations that are in dominance and joined to a particular regime of authoritative power (Frith 1996; Keightley 2001).

More recently, the digital revolution has combined technology and subculture with the politics of resistance. What has come be called the Darknet refers to the aggregate of networks and technologies designed and maintained to participate freely in the anonymous exchange of copyright data (David and Kirkhope 2004: 442–3; Burkart and McCourt 2006; David 2010). Engaging with the Darknet, and appropriating elements from it, carries a cultural cachet. It is recognized as acting as an agent against the conventional order of music exchange and consumption.

(3) *Pop music articulates* regulation. Pop music reproduces organized inequality and dominant power relations by advancing compliance. On this account, pop is a type of social control. At the society-wide level, this role has been explored in relation to class inequality and oppression (Adorno 2009). But pop music has also been examined as reproducing the largely informal micro-orders of everyday life (DeNora 2000, 2003; Witkin 2003) and structured settings of work and consumption (Jones and Schumacher 1992; Korczynski 2003; El-Sawad and Korczynski 2007).

In a word, what distinguishes pop music from classical music is that the former is a strident, exuberant *demotic* form. It is the study of the people's music (MacDonald 2003). The form of this music is not constant, since different genres articulate historically specific conditions and concerns. When MacDonald (2003) collected the best of his published writings that constitute his small opus, he could reasonably assume that rock was the main expression of the people's music. As we shall see, the latest academic research suggests that things have moved on: rap has become the people's music, while the passion for rock now correlates with a middle-class audience (Rentfrow and Gosling 2007; Rentfrow et al. 2009).

The musical refrains and lyrical motifs through which pop operates privilege spontaneity, flexibility, heartfelt emotion and plain communication. The old distinction between composers and performers as active, and audiences as passive, has decomposed. Popular culture, de-differentiation and technology have weakened the division between producers and consumers. Through scratching, mixing and sampling techniques, the audience forages through recorded popular music and transforms recorded texts from different times and places. Increasingly, understanding the audience has ceased to be a matter of subcultural or generational characteristics and become a more complex matter of the relationships between production, texts and contexts (Livingstone 1998).

The Creativity Problem

This raises the difficult question of creativity, which we have already alighted upon in the discussion on reflexivity. Generally, audiences view the greatest pop stars to be supremely creative agents. Even if the intermediate roles of managers, public relations experts and the media are allowed, durable pop stardom is generally held to be a matter of unique individual talent.

This commonsense view exaggerates the autonomy of the person. This is objectionable on observational grounds. The labour of composers and performers is deeply collaborative. As agents of production they work with others, be they fellow musicians, sponsors, recording engineers and other sections of the music industry, to create music. As 'symbolic communicators' they draw on typifications of personality, narrative and predicament (Hesmondhalgh 2002). The concept of articulation should alert us to seeing that what is communicated expresses more than the creative skills of the artist. It also embraces common concerns, hopes, desires and ways of communication.

Charles Turner (2004) coins the term 'social imaginary' to refer to popular intimations, contributions and dreams of a more just, robust and inclusive society. Iconic pop stars, performers who crystallize cultural biography, are both bearers and articulators of the social imaginary. In societies in which organized religion is in steady decline, and where politics is often automatically associated with double-think and dirty dealing, pop stars have an unusually powerful connection with the social imaginary, particularly with the telling of unpopular truths (Grossberg 1997; Rhodes 2007). This is why pop superstars like Bono, Chris Martin, Jackson Browne, Peter Gabriel, Madonna and Sting have emerged as celebrity diplomats, acting without plebiscite to articulate common concerns relating to hunger, poverty, natural disasters and environmental degradation (Cooper 2008).

By the same token, the counter-view that holds that creativity is formative of social influences such as class, race, nation, generation or subculture negates or attenuates the role of personal creativity by reducing it to a dependent variable of pre-existing, conditioning, external structures. Creativity is integral to the individual. But the individual is both a natural and a social agent. That is, the individual bears the particularities of genetic inheritance and the social specifics of time and place.

This is not a matter of splitting hairs. One might say unequivocally that, for example, Elvis Presley and Bob Dylan are both specific individuals and social-historical beings who carry iconic, global social significance. They are unique creatures and subjective manifestations of the features of society as experienced and thought, with which millions of people connect at psychological, emotional and cultural levels. Composers and performers are unique individuals and cultural reeds. This connectivity may be a matter of the eternal truths that the highest expressions of pop music are purported to convey. Or it may be that songs communicate qualities that are culturally universal. The decisive question turns upon the balance between the particularities of the agent who formally articulates the songs and the place of the agent in the articulation of much deeper and wider social, economic and cultural forces.

Troubadours, Society and Copyright

We can portray the nature of this problem directly by briefly considering the historical question of troubadours, society and the growth of copyright that established legal boundaries around musical creation and consumption. In traditional society, composers and musicians are regarded as folk authorities. While they draw on history and the law, the core of their power rests in knowledge and communication about the emotions among the folk and the court. Before the emergence of counselling and therapy, popular music played the function of offering what we would now call life-coaching about the emotions and self-help resources for psychological healing. Hence, popular acknowledgement of the capacity of music to communicate true and momentous feelings was born. It long predates the era of rock and roll (the 1950s) and the various types of popular music that are properly described as its progeny.

For example, Robert Briffault (1965: 119–20) shows how the medieval troubadours produced musical statements of romantic and erotic love which manipulated the conventions of court society and provided the impression of being constitutive of wider social formations that were often marginalized by the hierarchical structure of the aristocracy. According to Briffault, one important effect of this was to transform the balance of power between the sexes. Troubadour songs of romance and erotic love augmented the power of women in social and political structures that were essentially male-dominated. They boosted the standing of 'the woman's view' and enlarged the emotional sphere of romance over staple considerations of warfare, ritual obedience and subsistence. Briffault is not saying that the troubadours *replaced* these considerations or invented romantic popular music. Rather, his point is that the music of the troubadour articulated wider social, political and economic forces that raised the transpersonal profile of the emotional sphere and developed new forms of emotional intelligence and emotional labour.[7] At one and the same time, troubadour music was also the articulation of these forces. However, this latter dimension is somewhat underscored in commonsense reactions to popular music.

Troubadour songs were associated with particular agents. Between the eleventh and twelfth centuries, Guilhem de Peitieus, Bernart de Ventadorn, Graut de Borneth and Bertran de Born were known for particular songs and genres of troubadour music. An oral tradition recognized them as composers, with cultural entitlements, but it was not exactly copyright.

The close correlation that copyright law produces between specific agents of musical production and particular instances of popular music was a product of print culture and became normalized in the eighteenth and nineteenth centuries. Copyright defines the authority of composition as the product of the author and renders it defensible by the rule of law (Goldstein 2003; Bielstein 2006). The legality of copyright increases the psychological connection between music and the personal creativity of the agent (the composer/performer). By legally presenting composition to be a matter of personal invention and ownership, it abstracts the process of creation from cultural and material relations. Composition is defined as deriving from the personal experience and unique talent of the individual 'artist'. Inferentially, this experience is submitted and popularly understood as richer, more pure or larger than that of ordinary men and women. Thus the exceptional, unique qualities of personal artistic expression are magnified. Correspondingly, the relation between specific instances of pop music and the articulation of wider social, economic and cultural forces is obscured.

What is a Pop Song?

The difficult issues involved here can be illustrated by asking the question: What does it mean to produce a pop song? If you ask the average man and woman this question, the probability is that they will commence by invoking the role of the composer. But this begs a number of related questions. In order for a song to become popular it must communicate with a wide audience. Musical communication depends upon several historical and social particulars that are independent of the artist. These derive from the predicament of shared social being linking composers, performers and audiences. Pop presupposes linguistic, historical and cultural conventions. Were this not the case, it would not be communicable to listeners. To be sure, creative artists seek to express this or that emotion, belief or value in a form that audiences will find compelling. However, the process of communication only succeeds because the particulars of social being are shared.

　　The character of the problem can be illustrated by considering the co-operative nature of composition and performance in popular music. It may be that some composers write and play for themselves. If this is the case the adjective 'pop' cannot apply to them, for the term presupposes the exchange of musical composition with a mass audience. Moreover, the process of production and exchange is typically collaborative and therefore possesses an inherently social character.

　　The point can be elaborated by differentiating between some salient variables of culture and society which bear directly and forcefully upon the production, exchange and distribution of popular music: harmony and convention; language, syntax and semantics; typification and transcription; and culture and genre.

Harmony and Convention

To make a musical statement means being conversant with accessible and communicable traditions and networks of musical notation, harmonics, metre and tonality. These traditions are hardly universal. Max Weber submitted that in the West, composition and performance are based upon the unification of rationalization of note systems with harmonization. He explained this process as the result of the distinctive rational system of musical notation developed here, the invention of Western mechanical instruments and 'the methodical conduct of life' which has its roots in the monastic tradition (Radkau 2009: 372).

　　Convention refers to an established set of relationships through which specific practices are articulated. Conventions of speech have been much studied by formalists in language. The conventions of pop music typically require songs to be no more than five minutes in duration, organized around the verse–chorus, thirty-two bar form. Melodies obey standard European notation structure, deploying rhythm as an anchor, and build to a hook that is designed to be catchy and memorable. The presentation of persons and situations in pop songs generally follows commonly understood causal relationships between emotions and standard patterns of social conduct. Common roles of personhood represented in popular music are the lover, the plaintiff, the jester, the cuckold, the scold, the dreamer and the rogue. Similarly, common life-situations represented in popular song are betrayal, desire, erotic love, jilted love, vengeance, pride, greed and forgiveness.

Theodor Adorno (2009: 327) – arguably one of the most vituperative critics of pop – contends that pop, or, to use his term, 'light' music, is conditioned by the deformation of conventions. Melodic harmony and lyrical structure are determined by compositional formulas. The standardization of composition and listening mirrors the system of industrial planning and the associated 'far-reaching' division of labour that characterizes the Western mode of production (Adorno 2009: 278).

Be that as it may, composition and performance in pop cannot be correctly understood as the simple product of personal inspiration. They entail the interaction between creative individuals and a pre-existing musical and lyrical *form* that conditions expression. Composers, performers and audiences fundamentally depend upon this form in order to communicate musically.

Language, Syntax and Semantics

Pop combines intervals of notes and silence with lyrics. To operate in a language is to submit to its characteristic syntax and semantic distinctions. English syntax and semantics are different from those of, say, Hindi, Afrikaans or Mandarin. Composition and performance rely upon socially inherited, linguistically defined notations and conventions. The absence of these notations and conventions would result in Babel.

Creativity, then, is situated in a distinctive linguistic structure and social inheritance. It is not reductive to propose this much. Any version of individualism that is indifferent to linguistic and social conditions is of limited practical value, for it displaces the social foundations that presuppose the communication of creativity.

Typification and Transcription

Songs like 'In My Room' by The Beach Boys (1963) or 'Stan' by Eminem (1999) possess impact partly because they are transcriptions of social situations. As such, they draw upon typifications of emotional intelligence and emotional labour that are common in culture. In principle, everyone – in the West at least – can comprehend the sentiments of intimacy and privacy conveyed in Brian Wilson's song, just as the themes of indifference, projection and repression articulated by Eminem are commonplace. A composer may 'create' memorable characters and situations in a song. It may be that the data are copied from real life. Or that the composer combines elements from real people and real-life situations and projects them onto an imaginative plain. Something new is added through the process of composition and performance. But it is not self-evident that what is happening can be properly described as individually 'creative', because the process depends upon typifications of character and life-circumstances and rules of language. In this sense, pop songs are activations of typifications and precedents found in real life. It goes without saying that it is not satisfactory to describe the composition of pop reductively as the simple transcription of typifications of conditions encountered in real life. Nevertheless, it is acceptable to propose that this is the *basis* of composition. Although the composer is an active force that makes of the data something greater than emulation and reproduction, what is happening here is not exactly 'new' in the sense of being unprecedented or unparalleled. The configuration of typifications of character and predicament, notation and form utilize common resources.

Drastic transformations are comparatively rare. In the mid- to late 1970s punk was a reaction to what might be said to be the *over-ripe* accomplishments of progressive rock, as exemplified by bands like Yes, Genesis and ELP. Punk groups like The Sex Pistols, The Clash and The Ramones exploited and adopted a 'back to basics' stance. Progressive music was denigrated for collapsing under the weight of its own pretensions. Unlike some variants of the progressive genre, punk and post-punk wanted no truck with the tradition of classical music. Punk sought to rebuild bridges with rock's roots: direct sentiments, simple chord structures and uncluttered arrangements. It ridiculed what it held to be the baroque pomposity of progressive music. Post-punk was more granular. Bands like Pere Ubu, PiL, Joy Division and Talking Heads embraced the energy and scepticism of punk, but they balanced them with a re-engagement with the art school knowingness of Roxy Music and David Bowie, the Dadaist experimentalism of Captain Beefheart and Frank Zappa and the atmospheric, ambient soundscapes of King Crimson, Soft Machine, Robert Wyatt and Brian Eno. In addition, while punk concentrated largely on a white, male, working-class agenda, post-punk developed an open, generous response to world music, especially African and Asian traditions.

What occurred here was the globalization of typifications and predicaments and the corresponding enlargement of the radius of transcription. White cultural idioms and motifs were redefined to encapsulate musical instruments, vocal styles, arrangements, stereotypes and narrative structures from the emerging and developing world. The post-punk engagement with world music re-politicized Western audiences, resulting in the stadium activism of politically engaged mainstream acts like Bob Marley, U2, Peter Gabriel, Annie Lennox, Bruce Springsteen and Sting. This was bolstered by the contribution of migrant multi-ethnic cultures into the metropolitan centres of the West, which transformed their own musical traditions through critical confrontation with the host culture and its self-image.

The transformation involved here *was* drastic. It became tougher for progressive music to claim relevance to popular life. Having said that, groups like Yes, Genesis and Pink Floyd survived and prospered. It might be said that they partly recast their music in response to the punk and post-punk challenge of direct, unfussy emotion. For example, Peter Gabriel's first two self-titled solo albums

(1977 and 1978) were notably more direct and simple than the rock opera format of *Foxtrot* (1972) and *The Lamb Lies Down on Broadway* (1974) by his former group, Genesis.

Be that as it may, the punk and post-punk reactions were not genuine revolutions in pop music. They ran the gauntlet against traditions which were viewed as over-blown and exhausted. In doing so, they drew on pre-progressive resources built around simple chord structures and direct emotional reflexes.

Culture and Genre

The transcription of typical personalities and predicaments in the West and the reaction of relocated migrant groups and the emerging and developing world to Western idioms and motifs reflect distinctive cultural and historical characteristics. Colin Campbell (1987: 72) holds that it is only in the modern period of Western history that people have taken it for granted that emotions spring from individuals and propel agency. Pre-modern people held emotions to be external to the individual and to intrude upon them from far away. That is, people were 'angry' or 'merry' because external infuences made them so; and not because these feelings were momentarily representative or characteristic of the individual.

What does this mean for the composition and performance of contemporary popular music in relation to the past? Paul McCartney's Beatles song 'Yesterday' (1965) recounts the response of an individual to a break-up. It is often referred to as the song that has the most cover versions of all time. There are said to be eternal, universal qualities to the harmonic structure and lyrical content. Yet, if Campbell's analysis is correct, the personal introspection of emotional content, the acceptance of personal circumstances and motivation behind the break-up recounted in McCartney's song are very Western and very modern. According to Campbell (1987: 73), what might be called the introjection of emotion and connotation of emotion with motivation and agency in the modern period derive from deep-rooted, transpersonal processes. Chief among them are: (a) the rationalization of everyday life; (b) the separation of the world from the consciousness of the human observer; and (c) increasing human knowledge relating to objective, historical, social, economic and psychological causes and patterns of behaviour. It is a matter of 'a growing consciousness of the self as an object in its own right. This is revealed in the spread of words . . . such as "self conceit", "self confidence" and "self pity" which begin to appear in the English language in the 16th and 17th centuries, and became widely adopted in the 18th century' (Campbell 1987: 73). Only such a self, subject to and formed by the modern socio-economic and political processes that Campbell recounts, can 'believe in yesterday', 'when all my troubles seemed so far away'.

Solidarity, Technology and Consumption Today

Older traditions of popular music conveyed sentiments of typical personalities, common predicaments, shared aspirations, the responsibility of common struggle and an ethos of 'we are all in it together'. Russell (1997) draws strong parallels between the music hall tradition and popular fortitude, the Empire appeal to pluck, and the reaffirmation of class, nationalism and political solidarity. As with the troubadour tradition, this music is communicated through spatial settings (the physical space in which the performance occurs) and oral and written systems of exchange. Contemporary pop is quite different.

The last century perfected electronic forms of exchange and distribution. The consumption of pop is now weightless, accessible at the flick of a switch or sweep of plastic, in the sense that, through computer technology, audiences have the capacity to intervene to change the recorded structure and create new sound values. Rap, hip hop, scratching and sampling are textbook examples of this phenomenon. They have produced a new balance of power between composers, performers and listeners.

Surprisingly, the phenomenology of pop – the spaces in which listening occurs and the actual experience of consumption, and its effects – is under-theorized and under-researched. It may be that contemporary pop still produces social solidarity. Although the ends may be very different from, say, the Empire tradition described by Russell (1997), it may be that contemporary pop still has the capacity to rouse collective emotions and build solidarity. The success of global pop mega-events like Live Aid (1985), Live 8 (2005) and Live Earth (2007) suggest that this is the case. Smaller political and cultural events like rallies, marches and group protests also frequently utilize live or recorded pop to enhance a sense of togetherness.

Nonetheless, over the last century, side-by-side with the exchange of contemporary pop in settings where groups assemble has been the *privatization* of listening experience. The development of the portable record player, the automobile sound system, the transistor radio, the Walkman, the iPod and the MP3 player has expanded the range of settings in which popular music is consumed. In the postwar period, listening to pop music in your bedroom was one of the blood-rituals required by many youth subcultures. Across the country – to be sure, across the *world* – countless individuals would listen in their rooms to Bob Dylan, The Beatles, The Rolling Stones, The Doors, Joni Mitchell and The Who, not only for pleasure, but as markers of generational belonging.

Later, listening in domestic dwelling space became a generalized mechanism that not only divided kids from parents, but generational subcultures from each other. In David Bowie's Mott The Hoople song 'All the Young Dudes' (1972) the reconstructive political and lifestyle ambitions and practices of the sixties generation are ridiculed in favour of the immediate, elusive, transitory, fragmentary experience of the post-Beatles generation. The glam rocker leaves his 'brother back at home with his Beatles and his Stones', while he strikes out into the real world – not the world of peace, love, sincere emotions and authentic identities, but a media-permeated world, saturated with codes and representations, where the rising influences of feminism and post-colonialism expose the conceits and crudities of hetero-normative, male power, fixed identity and the dogma of white superiority. This generational ritual of leaving and moving on has been repeated by successive pop music generations: the adherents of punk, post-punk, grunge, rap, trance and the rest.

The transistor radio, the Walkman, the iPod and the MP3 player made access to popular music ubiquitous. Music is everywhere. Perhaps in being so, its capacity to be a focus for generational concentration and social solidarity has diminished. It is increasingly used in conjunction with multi-media platforms, such as television, games, the web and the computer. Of course, it is still used to build identification, as with the IBM songbook. But it has a surfeit status in popular culture that makes it the background accompaniment of other forms of social activity, such as driving, walking and multi-tasking.

Articulation and Cultural Monadism

In practical terms, how do most of us listen to popular music today? With the emergence of the car stereo-system, the Walkman and the iPod, the laptop and the automobile, listening is twinned with mobility. The transitional space of the street, the highway and public transport systems has taken over from the bedroom, the kitchen or the living room as the primary social setting for listening to music. In terms of the language used in the debate about the rise of network society, popular music has become *deterritorialized* (Castells 1996, 1997, 1998). This is not just a matter of cultural references in pop songs no longer being confined by geographical boundaries.

The rise of the Darknet in the production, exchange and consumption of popular music means that supply and demand chains have become international, beyond the law and, for most intents and purposes, invisible. Mobility and speed are conjoined with illegal consumption to change the character of listening and accumulating. It is estimated that 800 million files are currently available through unlicensed file-sharing networks (David and Kirkhope 2004: 441; David 2010). Streaming, ripping and downloading create new forms of exchange and cultural solidarity. They also annihilate old ones.

For example, the high street record store traditionally acted as a spatial venue of commercial exchange and the affirmation of collective identity. It was here, in listening booths, or over the counter, that discussions, news and opinions about established and new music were exchanged and refined. These data and retail hubs are now going out of business as a result of the digital revolution. The exchange and consumption of popular music are becoming automatic, weightless and, hence, more privatized, mobile and invisible.

It may be that one effect of this is to make common dilemmas questions of public spectacle and private consumption, rather than common organization and collective action. To be sure, popular music sets agendas about common problems that it develops by reflecting on issues of social being. In consuming it we have the pleasurable experience of direct, positive action.

Yet if 'doing something' amounts to recognizing a common dilemma through one's headphones, or watching artists perform on television or at sports stadia, does it truly constitute a meaningful political action? A cultural monad is someone who distils wider cultural agendas and internalizes and applies them as a private, mobile unit in the form of gestural currency. Consumption occurs through a combination of multi-media platforms, including television, film, DVD, games and the web. Because the distillation of culture occurs along many fronts and through multiple media, social unity and collective focus are more elusive. In order to be regarded as credible, competent and relevant agents, cultural monads need to be well versed in popular culture. This includes knowing about the deceptions of solidarity as well as the social and cultural potential of togetherness. In sum, the main characteristics of cultural monadism are as follows:

1   *Articulation*: knowledge about cultural data and associated powers of expression.
2   *Mobility*: an ease of movement along many layers and between many fronts of popular culture.
3   *Dramaturgy*: the competence and credibility to translate political, cultural and economic issues into *gestural culture*. By this term I mean a form of cultural articulation that expresses commitment and solidarity as cultural representation rather than a basis for action. So the cultural monad, unlike the activist, listens to 'Feed the World' (1984), approves of the sentiment with respect to global inequality and the complacency of the advanced industrial countries and uses it as cultural capital to achieve identification, without engaging in any form of concrete action to transform things.

Might it be that mobility, access (including unlawful access) and privacy are now the primary characteristics of the consumption of pop, so that the main consumer type is the cultural monad?

Without doubt, the theme of pop music as an accessory of consumer culture producing a fake sensation of 'doing something' rather than a spur to raising collective consciousness and achieving transcendence occurs repeatedly in the literature. Adorno (2009) famously categorized the entire pop genre as bolstering conformity, social compliance and pseudo-individualism. His view of Tin Pan Alley mirrored that of his friend and sometime associate Siegfried Kracauer (1995) with respect to the Hollywood of the 1920s: it is a distraction factory. It diverts the creative, sensual energy of the masses into clichéd representations of romantic love, the politics of justice and brotherhood and leaves the fundamentals of organized inequality intact. Capitalism damages individuals. Pop elicits subconscious conditioning that provides damaged individuals with the illusion of time off and escape through music in the midst of a system that requires everyone to finally accept obedience to the rule of capitalism as fate.

Adorno's argument remains pertinent, but today it is widely criticized as too bleak and sweeping. Make no mistake, pop has the capacity to radicalize listeners. The Rock Against Racism movement that developed in the 1970s combined music with anti-racist speeches and rallies. It was politically significant in changing youth attitudes to multi-ethnic society and institutionalized racism. Live Aid, Live 8 and Live Earth exploited the global television network to raise consciousness about, respectively, Third World hunger, injustice and global pollution. Similarly, singers like Bob Dylan, John Lennon, Bob Marley, Marvin Gaye, Curtis Mayfield, James Brown, Joe Strummer, Bruce Springsteen, Bono, Randy Newman, Jackson Browne and Billy Bragg, to name but a few at random, have an extensive back catalogue of recordings which address social and political questions.

Yet the probability is that the majority who listen to this music never attend a rally or join a political organization. Even rap and hip hop are symbolic articulations of place and social divisions rather than theme music for revolution. You can identify with the sense of metropolitan disempowerment and social injustice expressed by rap artists in Compton, or South Central, LA, from the safety of your bedroom or kitchenette in the suburbs.

In the age of universal mass communications, where pop music is ubiquitous, the political effect of radical popular music is different in kind from the political education that follows from protesting against a labour lock-out, a lynching or a case of police corruption. In being everywhere it is simultaneously nowhere. Its capacity to operate as a rallying point for solidarity or catalyst for social action cannot be assumed, because the effect of music is culturally diffused.

It may no longer be appropriate to critique pop primarily as a form of organized distraction designed to achieve compliance. If it is correct to propose that the cultural monad is the pre-eminent listening type in the West, it may be that pop supports role-play and the acting out of structural problems in capitalism that are judged, on rational grounds, to be intractable.

In this vein, Ian Condry (2006) has castigated Pierre Bourdieu's (1984, 1993) approach, which, when applied to pop, identifies music as a bearer and marker of social distinction. Instead, he points to *otaku* culture in Japan as evidence of the contemporary importance of silo culture in pop. As we shall see in more detail later (pp. 172–4), while there is no precise English synonym for *otaku*, the word is associated with home, boundaries, safety, security and obsessive interest. An *otaku* accumulates data about music, film, comics or games as an end in itself. There is no aspirational sense of transcendence or subcultural superiority. What, then, is the purpose of accumulation in this silo culture?

Acting out dilemmas of sexual inequality, racial oppression, generational difference. economic subordination and psychological abuse depends upon information. Listening to pop songs on iShuffle or your car stereo-system may provide the means to emotionally assuage and ameliorate some of the effects of these structural divisions in real life. However, the practice is fully compatible with the perpetuation of an economic, social and political system based upon organized inequality.

Pop music has been exceptionally inventive in widening the repertoire of protest songs. The rap and hip hop traditions have gone much further than the Rock Against Racism and pop consciousness movements in mobilizing the people against authority and racial injustice. Grandmaster Flash's 'The Message' (1982), and Ice-T's 'Cop Killer' (1992) deal, respectively, with overturning racial oppression and glamourizing violence against the police. Both songs, especially 'Cop Killer', were criticized for crossing the line between social criticism and racial incitement. The questions are: Have they changed racism and police corruption? Or do they operate as placebos of positive change, consumed *en masse* by cultural monads who make no political or socal commitments that would affect the central levers and transmission belts of the system of organized inequality and mystification in power? This is Adorno's (2009) problem. It has not yet been resolved by empirical research or theoretical debate.

Other questions are thrown up by the study of how pop is articulated today. Why and how do genres of popular music change? Why does genre recycling occur? Are the meanings of songs universal, or culturally coded and represented? In an era in which there is no viable macro-political alternative to capitalism, is radical pop doomed to parody? What are the organizational chains between composer, performer and audience? Can one truly speak of a homology between music and embodiment? Is a textual approach to popular music preferable to one that situates music in political economy? Or should an amalgamation of some kind be sought between the two? Does copyright over music (defined as intellectual property) have any validity in the digital age? Will illegal downloading and streaming eliminate the CD and music DVD? Is the decisive battle in the future of popular music now waged over the question of access rather than the issue of property ownership?

These questions provide the main springboards for the material presented in the rest of the book.

The Urban-Industrial Backbeat

Pop music is fascinating to study, but difficult to write about. Three reasons stand out for this, and these concern the questions of production, exchange and consumption, the notion of 'the popular' and the issue of technology. This chapter will address each in turn.

To address the first of these areas of difficulty, today it is, in practice, impossible to separate the development of pop from the economics and technology of music production, exchange and consumption. You might say there is nothing genuinely new in this. The indie labels of the late 1970s and early 1980s, such as Stiff, Cherry Red, Chiswick and Factory, were, after all, explicitly anti-corporate and aspired to the ideal of free music. From the standpoint of the consumer, however, the results were limited because the labels retained control of the technology of production and distribution. This is quite different from today's situation with the downloading revolution. The Darknet of hand-held devices and laptops makes distribution ubiquitous and, practically speaking, detection-free. Webcasts, ripping, streaming and unauthorized file-sharing provide a serious new challenge to established distribution networks.

There are two categories of legal online distribution. The first is *downloading*, to a computer or a phone. Consumers legally purchase copyright material over the internet and pay fees to the copyright holder. Currently, the market leader is iTunes. Founded in 2003, it offers the largest catalogue of music. Other major providers include Amazon, emusic, Play.com and Napster. Recently, this legal output has been supplemented by providers offering free downloads, supported by advertising. For example, in 2008 Qtrax launched with a reputed catalogue of 25 million songs. We7.com, backed by Peter Gabriel, offers 80,000 free downloads. Both servers adapt peer-to-peer (P2P) technology developed by networks such as Gnutella and LimeWire, but claim to eradicate viruses and spoof tracks and comply with the entitlements of copyright holders.

The second category of legal online distribution is *streaming*. This is a mode of accessing copyright material. Essentially, it involves turning the internet into a radio. Songs are provided either for free or for nominal subscription and supported by advertising from companies like Burger King, Ford, H&M and Virgin

Media. They can be played indefinitely on a repeat basis. The biggest provider is the Swedish-based company Spotify. This is supplemented by servers like Last. fm, Blip.fm, Twitter and Pandora, who additionally offer link 'social' playlists to registered users.

Legal on-line provision is, of course, a reaction to the unauthorized downloading revolution. Accessible P2P file-sharing was initiated by Napster (founded in 1999). It supplied an output of free music, without advertising, and applied a policy of inflexible neutrality with respect to the rights of copyright holders. Napster was subject to protracted legal challenges from many sources. The most notable plaintiff was the Recording Industry Association of America (RIAA). Initially, its law suits boosted traffic to the Napster site. Eventually, however, in 2001 an injunction was issued against Napster to cease trading in music unless it observed copyright fees. The company was directed to repatriate backdated royalties. It regrouped as a legal downloading supplier, but it traded in a diminished market as the result of massive consumer loyalty to the illegal providers that had since emerged.

At the time of writing, notable illegal suppliers include Gnutella, Pirate Bay, Rapidshare, isoHunt.com and Soulseek. It is estimated that in 2006 worldwide, 5 billion songs (38,000 years' worth of music) was downloaded illegally on P2P sites, compared with 5,079 million songs that were purchased legitimately (Black 2009).

Sociologically speaking, the practice of illegal downloading has been normalized. That is, it does not carry the stigma of criminal conduct. One reason is that consumers judge policing to be ineffective – so much so that it is practically discounted as a risk. On top of this, many illegal downloaders believe that their behaviour is legitimate resistance against the profits enjoyed by what they take to be the pampered fat cats of the popular music industry. Unauthorized access and the reactions to it which have established legal channels of distribution comprise an unprecedented challenge to traditional networks of production, exchange and consumption. This may be further illustrated on a variety of fronts.

The web is now used by many performers, such as Simply Red, as a more direct and profitable way to sell music to consumers: that is, by eliminating the overhead that would otherwise accrue to record companies and conventional retailers. In 2007 Radiohead controversially made their new album *In Rainbows* available on the internet for an outlay freely determined by the customer. The average payment was £2.90. Although this may seem low, bear in mind that artists signed to major music labels are fortunate to achieve a return of 5% on CD sales. The do-it-yourself internet model may shift fewer units, but because the overheads are radically lower, the rate of return to the performer is appreciably higher. Many performers with scant public profile have lucrative careers from legal web trade in their music. AWAL (Artists Without A Label) cites the case of Ingrid Michaelson, who has sold 250,000 albums and over 800,000 digital downloads (*www.awal.com*). Other independent web-based successes include Oberst, Dragon Force, Kate Walsh and Kimya Dawson.

At the peak of singles sales in the 1980s a single had to sell 250,000 copies to occupy the number 1 spot in the UK market. By the 1990s, this plunged to 100,000 copies. In 2006, Orson's 'No Tomorrow' gained the number 1 spot in the UK with the lowest number of weekly sales recorded since the early 1960s: 17,694. In the past, chart success was supported by TV slots on prestige shows like *Top of the Pops*, *American Bandstand*, *Soul Train*, *Shindig*, *The Old Grey Whistle Test*, *The Tube* and national and international tours. Now the metric of success is no longer defined by record sales or television appearances. Synchronization (placing music onto TV ads, TV series and movies), product endorsement, merchandizing, internet streaming, ringtones and magazine cover mounts have transformed the pop music business model. Musicians like Kimya Dawson and Ingrid Michaelson gained an internet audience when their songs were respectively featured in the 2007 Academy Award-winning movie *Juno* and the TV series *Grey's Anatomy*.

Before the advent of the web, musicians had to reply upon the A&R (Artists and Repertoire) personnel of music multinationals to be discovered and promoted. A&R personnel performed a scouting function in pubs, night clubs, dance halls and all of the other venues where popular music is played for free. Traditional routes of building a band through the A&R machine persist. However, things are very different today. MySpace, YouTube, Facebook, Twitter and other sites have emerged as global popular music platforms in which unknown artists make their music available for free. Several popular artists, notably the Arctic Monkeys and Lily Allen, have acknowledged the role played by these sites in breaking them with the public.

Blog sites and social networks are now significant channels of data exchange that supply a contrast to the more traditional fan routes of pop music data. They do not exactly replace the popular music press or TV and radio pop music transmission. More accurately, they provide an unprecedented counterpoint, which may be more penetrating precisely because it is unstructured by manifest commercial considerations.

The internet has revolutionized the retail system for selling CDs. Many of the big brand record stores have closed. In addition, retail outlets have diversified. Coffee stores like Starbucks and broadsheet newspapers like *The Sunday Times* have negotiated exclusive deals in which the CDs of mainstream artists are available for purchase with your latte or stock exchange report. In 2005, Bob Dylan released *Live in the Gaslight in 1962* exclusively through the Starbucks chain. The move was followed by free downloads from Starbucks from acts such as Joss Stone, Genesis, Paul McCartney, Dave Matthews and Annie Lennox. Likewise, Ray Davies and Prince bolstered ticket sales by releasing their new albums as freebies in newspapers.

However, despite the considerable gains in access and flexibility that now exist in the production, exchange and consumption of popular music, it is fanciful to posit that these combined circumstances herald the dawn of a new era of creative capitalism in the music industry, in which commercial considerations play second fiddle to the supposedly pure, financially neutral exchange of music. Squeezed between declining revenue from vinyl, CD and DVD sales and under-performing authorized digital sales, musicians and multinational record companies are exploring new ways of reaching consumers. This involves co-opting and appropriating the supply networks that ostensibly provide music for free on the web.

Consider the case of Sandi Thom. In 2006 UK media reports portrayed her as a self-made internet superstar. Drawing comparisons with Janis Joplin and KT

Tunstall, she was portrayed as a penniless and struggling troubadour who secured a £1 million recording contract from RCA Records after webcasting twenty-one gigs from her South London basement that purportedly generated an on-line audience of 70,000. Subsequently, investigative journalism revealed that Thom had been represented by the Quite Great PR company, which admitted placing articles about her in the national press and using 'street teams' to spread the word in target groups such as the student press. It emerged that one million virtual flyers had been distributed to publicize her webcasts. In short, Quite Great utilized the web as a public relations rumour mill to generate an audience.

The attempt to massage public interest was reminiscent of the 1970 concert by the unknown British group Brinsley Schwarz in New York's Fillmore East. Dave Robinson, the manager of the group, presented them as the next big thing. It was a publicity stunt that back-fired, cruelly exposing the hiatus between hype and a genuinely spontaneous reaction between an audience and performers.[1]

Web innovations in the music industry are creative responses to the threat of illegal downloading to copyright holders. The point to underline here is that none of them quite dissolve the relationship between the economics of production, exchange and consumption. Rather they are business responses to the new communication technologies of file exchange and webcasting. This is not to say that the pop music industry can carry on with a 'business as usual' philosophy.

The framework to apply to the study of pop is in need of drastic revision. Despite the home taping scare of the 1970s, before the popularity of illegal downloading, it was acceptable to consider the fields of production, distribution and consumption in terms of a finite number of interlocking agents located in secure territorial boundaries. The most common agents identified in the literature were copyright holders (musical performers and music corporations), the media, retail outlets and consumers. Subterranean cultures of piracy and illegal reproduction were acknowledged, but the industry generally viewed them as containable. The regulatory role of the state was significantly under-played.

With the rise of web technology, the exchange of music has become weightless, deterritorialized and, practically, detection-free. The regulatory role of the state in policing intellectual property has correspondingly augmented. The Digital Millennium Copyright Act (DMCA), passed in the USA in 1998, attempted to criminalize file-sharing. At the levels of both legislation and policing, the principles have been widely adopted throughout the Western world.

Despite this, copyright infringement remains rife (David and Kirkhope 2004; Burkhart and McCourt 2006; David 2010). In the last decade, the strenuous efforts of the industry to outlaw P2P file-sharing have won scarcely a pyrrhic victory. Music multinationals have stood aghast as millions of dollars of revenue have been pumped away from their business through the lesion in the music business cut by illegal downloading. Appeals to voluntary restraint and the introduction of legal exchange sites like the Apple iTunes store amount to no more than a band-aid over the revenues lost by copyright holders.

So far, the substance of the reaction of the music industry to the threat of illegal downloading has chiefly been posturing. How could it be otherwise? In a wired-up world the holders of copyright, and the agencies responsible for representing their interests, lack the means to apply the letter of the law to daily practice. The RIAA might have high-profile campaigns to eradicate illegal file-sharing in Cedar Rapids and Tribeca, but what about Seoul, Johannesburg, Beijing, Jakarta and Delhi?

Globally, illegal downloaders are simply maximizing the potential offered by computers, hand-held devices and the web to gain access. The RIAA flails about issuing this or that injunction against the infringement of copyright in the USA. For every schoolgirl, or senior, reluctantly brought to the courts in Cedar Rapids or New York, however, there are millions of 'invisible' Americans and Europeans using mobile phones and laptops to download music illegally with nary a care for the rights of copyright holders. Widen the aperture to take in the global market in Asia, Africa and Eastern Europe, where policing of unauthorized downloading is often erratic and unstable, and the numbers involved in infringing copyright become uncountable, but surely prodigious.

All of this has many significant and far-reaching consequences for the study of pop, the most important of which is that questions of production, exchange and consumption can no longer be conceptualized as overwhelmingly a matter of territorial legal exchange of copyright material. The perspective must be extended to include illegal, cost-neutral forms of consumption organized around the deterritorialized points of exchange consistent with computer, the mobile phone and the web. Three significant consequences follow, relating to the point of exchange, the relationship between performers and fans, and the balance of power between copyright holders and consumers. These will be addressed below.

While the legal consumption of copyright material currently retains dominant market share, illegal downloading and cost-neutral forms of streaming are widely accepted alternative forms of owning that supplement legal CD and DVD consumption. Owning is no longer simply a question of possessing a vinyl or CD pressing of copyright material. Additionally, it is a matter of possessing access to flexible outputs of (illegal) delivery, ripping and streaming. Nor is this the end of the matter. Cost-neutral access to recorded material enhances the status of live performance and magnifies the attraction of webcasts and blogging sites for fan cultures. Indeed there is an inverse relationship between the declining cost of recorded music and the rising price of concert tickets. As the point-of-sale price of recorded music gravitates to a zero margin (via unauthorized downloading/ streaming), the premium that audiences put upon seeing live acts has soared.

In 2008 the biggest live acts in the world were Bruce Springsteen and Bon Jovi. Madonna's 'Sweet & Sticky' tour (2008), with ticket prices from £80 to £160 ($128 to $256), was the biggest grossing tour by a solo artist. The Police's reunion tour, which ended in 2008, grossed £242 million ($340 million). Tour income is made up of merchandizing sales (licensed programmes, T-shirts, commemorative mugs and other memorabilia), endorsement fees and synchronization as well as concert arena ticket sales. Despite declining CD sales, concert revenue in the USA leapt from $1.3 billion in 1998 to $2.1 billion in 2003 (Kusek and Leonhard 2005: 7).

The value generated by concert ticket sales is altering the relationship between headline artists and record labels. In 2007 Madonna announced that she would leave her long-time record label, Warner Music, to sign with the special event promoter Live Nation for $120 million (£59 million). Live Nation organized the Live 8 events. Under the terms of their agreement with Madonna, they have exclusive rights to distribute her future recordings and promote her concert tours. *Billboard* estimates that Madonna's 2006 'Confessions' tour grossed $260.1 million, including eight sell-out concerts at London's Wembley Arena, which is managed by Live Nation.

U2, the headline money-making tour act of 2009 (see Table 2.1), have a twelve-year multi-rights contract with Live Nation. It covers worldwide touring, merchandizing and the band's U2.com website. They named their 2009–10 global concert run 'The 360 Degree Tour', an ironic reference to the so-called '360 degree deals' now struck by record and multi-media entertainment corporations with new or established acts that are designed to cover all facets of creative labour, including composing, performing, touring, merchandizing, franchising and ancillary rights income.

In addition, the relationship between copyright holders is undergoing extensive reformulation. Traditionally, musical performers transferred commercial rights to the music corporation in return for contractually specified production, promotion and distribution services. The situation is very different in an era of advanced computer technology in which an iBook, PC or laptop can reproduce the essential standards of a recording studio and where low-cost servers can be established to distribute recorded material. The traditional relationship between the music corporation and the consumer is attenuated by a do-it-yourself approach to music production and exchange. Additionally, the relationships between musicians and corporations are de-differentiated. Corporations may provide specialist functions in marketing and public relations, but, from the artist's point of view, why cede copyright to multinational rights agencies and music corporations if they do not command adequate means of revenue retention? These are extremely pertinent issues in the contemporary pop music industry. We will have recourse to them again at several points in the book.

At this stage, it suffices to note that the various relationships between the production, consumption and exchange of pop are in a state of flux caused by increased global access to web technology. In no way is it evident how matters will settle. Nor is it clear that the metaphor of 'settling' is quite appropriate to describe what is currently happening. We are already living through a moment of transition in which conventional thinking about the production, retailing and consumption of popular music is becoming obsolescent.

Table 2.1 Top grossing tour acts, 2009

Act	$US
1 U2	108,601,283
2 Bruce Springsteen	57,619,037
3 Madonna	47,237,774
4 AC/DC	43,650,466
5 Britney Spears	38,885, 267
6 Pink	36,885,658
7 Jonas Brothers	33,596,576
8 Coldplay	26,326,562
9 Kenny Chesney	26,581,141
10 Metallica	25,564,234

Source: Billboard 01.03.2010

What Do We Mean by 'Popular'?

The second difficulty that students face in studying pop has to do with the concept of the *popular*. Common sense renders the term 'popular' naturalistically as 'of the people'. As such, pop is often understood naïvely to mean the expression of what is widely practised or well favoured by the majority. Social Darwinism regards popularity as evidence of social adaptation. So what is popular does not simply express what is characteristic. It also indicates what has been most successful in the struggle to survive. In this sense what is common is that which has prevailed over other ways and traditions of being because it possesses superior evolutionary fitness. These interpretations have been subject to many provisos, the most important of which is that to correlate what is common with evolutionary fitness is a naturalistic fallacy.

Raymond Williams (1976: 198–9) elaborates upon the point by noting that the concept of the popular derives from the Latin word *popularis*, a term with legal and political roots meaning belonging to the people. In the high tide of the Roman era, orators and intellectuals like Cicero and Tacitus were openly attacking popular culture as subject to the depredations of corrupt leadership. They proposed that supplying people with bread and circuses is not merely popular, but *populist*. That is, it employs demagogy and manipulation to curry favour and degrade the body politic. Contrary to naturalistic interpretations of the term 'popular', populism suggests that what is widely practised and well favoured reflects social and political interests, which are conceived as distinct from common sentiments. The inference is that what is popular is partly a matter of cultural manipulation and imprinting designed by the cunning of leaders.

Not surprisingly, at the same time, the term 'popular' acquired derogatory connotations as a synonym for 'common' or 'base'. For if what is well liked or widely favoured is partly the result of leadership intent upon currying favour, a reasonable inference is that it is valid to regard the mass as, to a degree, plastic, unsophisticated, their sentiments frangible and subject to the taste or cunning of leaders and other agents of influence. As we saw in the opening lines of the book, this association carries over today in the view of some musicologists and sociologists of music that the term 'pop' is inherently associated with inferiority and triviality (Frith 2001).

The eighteenth century witnessed an influential reaction to these various constructionist readings of the popular. It was stoked by the famous distinction made by Johann Gottfried Herder between the *Kultur des Volkes* and the *Kultur des Gelehrten*: that is, the culture of the folk and the culture of the elite. The German Idealist tradition, as exemplified through what we would now call the 'ethnographic' work of Clemens Brentano and the Brothers Grimm (who collected folk tales and folk songs), conflated the sense of the popular with the real. According to the German Idealist tradition, the culture of the elite is detached from everything that is genuine, natural, real and sincere. It perseveres as an essentially elliptical, self-absorbed realm of artificial, abstract relations. At the heart of these relations is what might be called representations about representations: that is, privileged talk about privileged talk or perpetual, self-referential coded responses to inscrutable codes signifying rank and superiority. This constitutes a reality of sorts, since many people base their lives upon it. But its fabricated, synthetic character contrasts pointedly with the realm of production in which tradition, mutual support and fellowship are widely held to prevail.

The world of the *Volk* offered an alternative self-image to German intellectuals. It was associated with a repertoire of heartfelt emotion, pure fellowship and sincere, organic relations. The *Kultur* of the *Volk* was portrayed as direct, uncluttered, frank and honest.

It might be objected that embedded in this reaction is a sentimental view of *völkisch* culture. The simplicity, honesty and unity of the *Volkes* is an exaggeration that expresses the distaste of German Idealists with the pretensions of court society. On this account, the world of the *Volks* does not refer to an actual society. It is an allegory that the rising bourgeois industrial class fashioned and deployed in order to acquire privilege and influence in German society.[2]

Be that as it may, from the late eighteenth century this Idealist view of the culture of the *Volk* coloured thought and discussion about the popular, and spread far beyond the borders of Germany. In the twentieth century, traces of it are evident in the condescending attitude of elite culture to Tin Pan Alley in the 1920s and 1930s, during the age of sheet music and radio; the outrage among many traditional, conservative circles against rock and roll and youth culture in the 1950s and 1960s; and the moral panics against punk music in the mid-1970s, and electronica, trance, techno, grunge and hip hop after the 1980s.

In all of this there is disdain for what is taken to be the fleeting, clumsy, raw nature of pop in contrast to the alleged polish and sophistication of high art or salon music. At its most lofty, this is fully reproduced in musicology.

Yet, far from suppressing pop music, this disdain is incorporated into the form itself. For example, during the punk moment of the 1970s, it was fashionable for groups and performers to boast of their musical *incompetence* (Reynolds 2006: 58–69). Punk presented itself as a heartfelt, direct emotional form of musical communication that contrasted sharply with the self-absorbed, *grand guignol* pretensions of prog rock and classical/jazz fusion. The pleas of Johnny Rotten and Joe Strummer for real emotion and direct action in music in the 1970s would have been understood by Herder, who rejected the ornate flummery of German court civil society in favour of the raw, uncluttered emotion of the people.

An important point is raised here. The concept of the popular may have been inflected by the cunning of leaders, but it also constitutes the aesthetic and political basis of resistance, opposition and the construction of the 'imaginary': the dreams, poetics and political forces that represent a superior counter-world (Taylor 2004). Pop figures like Michael Jackson, Johnny Rotten, Joe Strummer, Kurt Cobain, 2Pac, Ice-T and Jay-Z became popular idols with a cultural significance that stretched far beyond music. This line of thinking connects the pop music of self-questioning, inspiration and protest with the radical salon culture of the French Revolution, the Dadaist and Surrealist avant-garde and 1960s movements like Fluxus and Situationism that highlight the arbitrary nature of social and economic order. It takes the divide between politics and pop to be artificial (Marcus 1989).

Grossberg, Pop/Rock and Resistance

Within the field of pop music analysis, the connection of pop and rock with empowerment and resistance is most fully accomplished in the work of Larry Grossberg (1992, 1997). This work is firmly located in the Birmingham School tradition of contemporary cultural studies,[3] which reacted against the social control theories developed, most notably, by the Frankfurt School. Instead it emphasized the role of popular culture in challenging and subverting class domination and political authority. Grossberg accepts that pop/rock music can follow the end of social control, but he also insists that it is a front of challenge and resistance that may not result in collective salvation or transcendence, but indubitably makes connections between individuals and groups, and supports a sense of generic commitments and solidarity.

For Grossberg (1997: 109–10), pop/rock music is more than the mere textual conjunction of music and lyrics. The identity, meaning and effect of pop/rock are products of context. Musical practices are treated as the articulation of specific and complex sets of relations that condition their meanings and effects. What Grossberg has in mind here is the balance of forces that both buttress and destabilize hegemony, including, *inter alia*, the shifting alliances between classes, interest groups and territorializations of power and the influence of new technologies of production and consumption and the socio-technic networks that arise from them. Pop/rock music constitutes the articulation of these forces, and, through the process of inscription, it elicits 'moods, passions, organizations of will' and 'mattering maps' that influence the operational logic of articulation (Grossberg 1997: 113).

In the course of his argument, Grossberg reformulates the concept of the popular, loosening its anchor from theories of social control and endorsing its capacity to generate affective agency. His work captures the contradictions and tensions involved in the use of the concept of 'popular' in relation to the production and reception of music.

For Grossberg (1997), the term 'popular' is *over-determined*. That is, its meaning can be validated in a variety of ways. The main distinctions are that it is:

(a) characteristic of the people: that is, a trait or practice that defines the majority from others in society;
(b) well favoured or well liked by the majority;
(c) base or coarse, in the sense of being less refined, developed or sophisticated;
(d) manipulated by the agenda and cunning of leaders;
(e) honest and true, in the sense of being untainted by the values of high society; and
(f) resistant and progressive, in the sense of opening the curtain on a world of brotherhood, justice and, in the words of John Lennon, 'no possessions'.

The popular is a challenging subject not because it combines aesthetics with description. Most cultural categories involve the same combination. The special difficulties of the term derive from the natural predisposition to connote the popular with that which is *characteristic*. It is a short hop from this to assume that what is characteristic is always natural and right. This is the step taken by Social

Darwinists. Yet this is nothing but a natural fallacy that confuses that which is commonly distributed with that which is necessary or true.

Grossberg's (1997: 21) thought on the relationship between rock and popular music makes a crucial distinction between what might be called *general, collective resistance* and *niche, eclectic resistance*. The distinction corresponds to two successive, historical stages of ascendance in postwar youth culture.

According to Grossberg (1997: 21), between the 1950s and the late 1980s the production, exchange and consumption of pop/rock music were dominated by the cultural formation of *general, collective resistance*. The principal characteristics of this formation are generic commitments, a common sense of temporal and generational solidarity, and a labour market based in full employment or the sure prospect of a return to full employment in times of economic recession.

Elsewhere, Todd Gitlin (1987: 201–4) coined the evocative and useful term 'communard utopianism' to refer to the 1960s and early 1970s instantiation of this formation: that is, the moment of the hippies and the generic commitment to socio-economic transformation. The 'communard' element of the phrase can be extended to the punk and post-punk generations of the late 1970s and 1980s. For while their utopianism was not especially evident, both musical and subcultural genres evinced a strong sense of generational and political solidarity. They were communards after their fashion.

Deploying the terminology of Raymond Williams (1977, 1980), Grossberg (1997: 21) submits that after the late 1980s this pop/rock formation became 'residual' and was replaced by an 'emergent' *niche/eclectic* form. The main features of this formation are hybrid composition, a shift in adherence from music to a multi-media apparatus (consisting of music, television, film, computer and digital games), and a move from binary ('Them' and 'Us') opposition to more flexible and less exclusionary sites of affective agency (plural fronts of resistance and multiple alliances). For Grossberg, this emerging formation is now dominant.

As Williams (1977, 1980) explained, a residual formation is not necessarily bereft of influence. It is merely no longer in a position of cultural ascendance. With respect to the new dominant formation, Grossberg (1997: 21, 119) writes:

> It is a formation that operates without the mediations of the ideology of authenticity; hence it willingly and simultaneously embraces the global megastar and the local rebel. . . . there is a change not only in the way scenes and alliances are formed, but also in the forms of mobility between them. In other words, differentiation – the production of differences – seems not less important or less effective, but rather to have a different sort of effectivity and a different sort of importance.

'We want the world and we want it now,' proclaims Jim Morrison in The Doors song 'When the Music's Over' (1967). This is the voice of the general/ collective formation. It struts over barriers of class, race and gender to invoke communard solidarity and declare imminent transcendence. In contrast, the music of the new dominant formation does not observe territorial boundaries of embodiment or space. It is deterritorialized. Via the internet it operates as an affective agent globally and along multiple media fronts. Criticism and polemic are still integral to this formation. Grossberg notes that rap and hip hop are part of it. But it is expressed along many fronts. Besides music, film, television, games, social network platforms, blog sites, politics, graphics and fashion are involved. Pop has ceased to be the *core* of generational consciousness. This is one reason why revenues to record corporations have been declining in the last decade. Youth markets are spending their money on many different fronts rather than concentrating resources in popular music. It is not a matter of pop music losing salience. More accurately it is a matter of salience being recast along multiple media platforms, some of which are interlocking and others which are not.

Technology

The third difficulty facing anyone who studies pop is to separate artistic creativity from technology in musical performance. In the beat and rock revolutions of the 1950s and 1960s success and popularity could be achieved with a drum, bass guitar, rhythm and lead. Musical reproduction was concentrated in youth culture, the teenage bedroom, the coffee bar and the discotheque. Today, both musicians and audiences widely regard this combination of production and consumption to be quaintly retro. Pop production has been colonized by technologies of digital reproduction (Goodwin 1993; Gracyk 1996). Synthesizers and samplers created a postmodern turn in pop because they meant that non-musicians could be competent and credible in making music. Hip hop undermined the orthodox division between the consumer and the commodity by re-commodifying recordings and transforming what they signify. The emergence of MIDI (musical instrument–digital interface) and VST (Virtual Studio Technology) have revolutionized the home software studio, permitting professional standards of arrangement and recording to be achieved at low cost. Hip hop, house, techno and post-techno rely upon turning a system of communication (the turntable) into an instrument. This has reformulated the conventional notion of authorship and made producing popular music through electronic apparatuses more accessible than ever.

Strictly speaking, there is nothing truly new about this. As early as the 1920s, the experimental artist and alternative theorist Lászlo Moholy-Nagy experimented with reformulating the Grove Script lines on mechanically produced recordings in order to create new sounds. Historically speaking, this is the forerunner of the scratching and sampling technique that is at the heart of DJ club culture today. In effect, Moholy-Nagy proposed the redefinition of the phonogram as an instrument of production as well as a means of reproduction.

Electronic technology is hardly incidental to pop; it constitutes the historical and practical prerequisite for production, exchange and consumption (Gracyk 1996). The radio and analogue and digital recording were path-breaking in the experience of pop music because they transported the listening experience from the concert hall or club to, in principle, *any* public or domestic setting. It was no longer necessary to confine musical production to dedicated space or segregate it from other activities, notably work and transport. The same is true of the consumption of pop. The Walkman, the iPod, downloading, streaming and ripping effectively make consumption ubiquitous. Pop has entered every aspect of popular life because the technology that makes its reproduction possible is miniaturized, elastic and light enough to fit comfortably into the breast pocket of your jacket or blouse. By widening access and flexibility, the social and cultural significance of popular music has vastly increased.

In the twentieth century, pop evolved into the urban-industrial backbeat of daily life. Nearly every home and vehicle has a sound system of some sort. Canned music is a standard feature of shopping malls, call centre waiting lists, fast-food places, elevators, hotel lobbies and most forms of advertising. Sports arenas play popular music during half-time intervals and before and after fixtures. The Super Bowl intermission has become one of the pre-eminent stages for live music in the world.

Pop music supplies the idiom and vernacular for many forms of emotional expression that are intrinsic to our sense of wellbeing, truth and identity. We declare our love, group identity and disaffection with this or that subject or object by means of the lyrics of hit songs. In private life pop is used to express love, and in public life it is applied to provide a sonic script to individual and group identity, as, for example, when bars and lyrical refrains are chanted by crowds in sports stadia and at political rallies and other public meetings. At its best, the harmonic-contrapuntal and rhythmic qualities of pop can speak beyond words to communicate a shared sense of cultural depth, absorption, social inclusion and cultural biography. This does not just apply to staged crowd events. It also relates to the *zeitgeist* through which collective memory is categorized and replayed. The baroque pop of Coldplay's song 'Viva la Vida'(2008) and the anthemic opening riffs of Bruce Springsteen's 'Born in the USA' (1984) or The Rolling Stones' 'Brown Sugar' (1971) summon up the sensation of a time and place beyond individual and group preoccupations or memories. This is often referred to colloquially as a spirit of 'togetherness'. As with Williams's (1961) concept of 'structure of feeling', and Grossberg's (1997) identification of pop music with the politics of domination and resistance, it is impossible to conceive of this spirit of unity in popular culture without recognizing the part played by technology. Collective emotions do not emerge spontaneously. Rather they are transmitted and amplified via electronic media.

Because we are accustomed to privilege intentionality in behaviour, we commonly regard the operation of technology to be neutral. We think of technology as the mere tool through which human motives are realized. In fact, as Steve Woolgar (1997) and others have submitted, the relationship between technology and users is complicated. Technology configures users and the patterns they use. For example, the 'shuffle' function on iPods is not programmed by users. It is a random selection function. Upon activation, it is debatable whether you are playing the iPod or the iPod is playing you.

Electronic technology is a source of social propulsion, cultural recognition and bonding and a catalyst of resistance. It triggers dance, arguing, eating, drinking, exercise, sex, reflection and sleep. The technology of popular music is not only a code of representation through which group identity is acknowledged and exchanged (Hebdige 1979). It is also a network by means of which social groups are constituted. It is as much a building block of group identity as sex, nation, age and race.

Paul Willis's (1978) famous ethnography of motorbike and hippie subcultures was one of the first studies to explore the 'integral circuiting' between subjective consciousness, technology and popular music as an external form. In both groups music is crucial in making and reproducing individual and group identity. The motorbike boys were deeply attached to the rock and roll created by the likes of Elvis Presley, Buddy Holly, Little Richard, Fats Domino, Chuck Berry and The Dave Clark Five. They favoured the scratchy, static, harsh qualities of the reproduction of singles, especially vinyl 78s, because they regarded them as 'authentic'. In contrast, they were intolerant of the technical and aesthetic innovations of long-players. As with their motorcycles and style of dress, the motorbike boys preferred uncluttered music which eschewed 'progressive' posture and pretence of any kind. There was a spit and sawdust quality to the music that they listened to which both reflected and carried over into the no-nonsense relations that they cultivated in the exercises, jokes, sexual relations, friendship ties and power struggles in the group.

For their part, the progressive music favoured by the hippies rejected the conventions of the single in favour of a more textured, multi-layered type of music. The exemplar was The Beatles' 1967 record *Sgt Pepper's Lonely Hearts Club Band*. This, together with the consciousness-expanding work of other progressive artists of the 1960s and 1970s, such as Pink Floyd, Frank Zappa, Cream, Jimi Hendrix, The Doors, Van Morrison, Jefferson Airplane and Country Joe and the Fish, was lauded as the highest popular form of music. Hippie society saw itself as the exponent of 'head culture' and grabbed musical taste as a sieve to separate 'heads' from the 'straight' population.

Theorists of later pop culture, such as Dick Hebdige (1979), insert the structuralist concept of *bricolage* into the analysis of popular music in order to reveal the promiscuous admixture of form, the play of style and the deliberate juxtaposition of contradictory elements. In contrast, Willis's hippies fetishized the purity of musical form. They insisted upon maintaining clarity in notes and chords. Their sound systems and vinyl collections were state of the art, consistent with their cultural capital and subjective sense of group identity. In the words of Willis (1978: 160):

> Their music was trusted because its complexity and difficulty held logocentric meaning at bay and suggested something in their spiritual meanings without clarifying them in a way that was bound to reduce them . . . . the exhilaration produced occasionally by the music gave credence to some kind of general belief in transcendence as well as implying the impossibility of realizing it directly in normal life.

Of course, this relationship between pop, embodiment and social patterning was not the invention of Willis's sample groups.

Historians of music have made strong connections between industrial technology and pop music form. The Futurist artist and theorist Luigi Russolo (1986) boldly argues that the evolution of music is related to the multiplication of machines. Musical polyphony has become more complex in its combination of consonance, dissonance, cadence, timbre, pitch and rhythm in direct proportion to the expansion of the machine age.

Russolo's Futurist manifesto *The Art of Noises*, written in 1913, calls upon musical composers to seize the noises of the industrial era and bring pop into closer correspondence with them. Specifically, quartets, quintets, sextets and larger ensembles like chamber groups and orchestras are urged to mechanically realize the sound of roars, thunderings, hissing, bangs, booms, whistlings, whispers, murmurs, mutterings, screechings, creakings, clankings, hammerings and human and animal sounds such as screams, shrieks, wails, hoots and howls. The manifesto makes the important observation that in the machine age, music is not only about pleasurable cadence and harmony. It is also about sheer noise. Futurism is dissonant, disturbing and destabilizing. It awakens us from the somnambulism produced by bland consumer culture.

European industrial metal and digital hardcore have utilized some of these ideas to challenge popular notions of harmonic integrity and community pastoralism. The inference is that these notions are complacent, ideologically impregnated and emotionally subdued. *Neue Deutsche Härte* bands like Oomph!, Fleischmann, ASP, Megaherz, Unheilig and, most successfully of all, Rammstein build and perform noise soundscapes that operate as the antithesis of meaning and the annihilation of compliance. The industrial black metal scene, revolving around groups like Mysticum, Blut Aus Nord, Aborym and The Axis of Perdition, follows broadly similar musical objectives. In respect of aesthetics and subculture, these musical forms bear the birthmarks of the industrial era – in particular, the ubiquity of machines and the regimentation of the urban-industrial order. They are curt, concentrated musical genres that, in most cases, strive to make common cause with political nihilism and artistic expression.

Other historians of music have focused on less uncompromising musical statements about the industrial era. They have pointed to the connections between industrial regime and musical tempo, machine syncopation and harmonic arrangement and assembly-line automation and musical improvisation.

Thus, Stephen Kern (1983: 123–4) observes that the emergence of ragtime in the Mississippi, Missouri and Ohio River valleys around 1890 was both a reaction to, and extension of, the relentless drive of the factory system through the American South. Kern draws a direct parallel between modern life and the style of pop music. He repeats it in his brief discussion of jazz, which was born around 1900 in New Orleans. Unlike ragtime, which followed a regular tempo, jazz made recourse to constant interruptions in harmony and rapid variations in score. As Kern (1983: 124) puts it:

> Wild squawks of the saxophone and squealing cries of muted horn accentuated the strangeness of unfamiliar cross-rhythms, polyrhythms, or other unidentifiable rhythms. While jazz had its slow parts, the early Dixieland bands especially seemed to keep to the quick step of modern life. One of the many speculations about the origin of its name was that 'jazz' was a slang term for speed.

The jagged, transient character of Dixieland arrangements directly paralleled the hydraulic motion of the machine age. They provided a form of entertainment and consumption culture that was homologous with the battery pump and internal combustion engine.

In addition, I have always been struck that Paul Willis, who was the first structuralist author to identify a 'homology' between music and embodiment (Willis 1978), was born and raised in the English West Midlands. Before the onset of de-industrialization in the 1980s, along with the North of England, this was an economic region based in heavy engineering, industrial foundries and assembly-line factory production. It is surely no accident that this was also the home of the heavy metal revolution involving bands like Black Sabbath, Judas Priest, Saxon, Def Leppard and Led Zeppelin (or at least drummer John Bonham and vocalist Robert Plant). The iron forges, mechanical pistons and steam hammers of the West Midlands were surely paralleled by the power riffs, pounding drums and wailing vocals that were the hallmark of heavy metal music. Thus, the industrialization of production found its counterpoint in the industrialization of music.

Pop music, then, is not correctly studied as little more than the relationship between creative musicians and a receptive audience. Technology is fundamental in the production, exchange and distribution of popular music. The separation of music from the concert hall and the emergence of portable data devices such as pocket radios, mobile phones, iPods, MP3 players, microphones, samplers, MIDI and VST systems are as significant in the study of popular music as the aesthetics of musical genres or particular songs.

Nor is this all. Willis's (1978) study proposes that pop performs central ends of bonding and identity for youth subcultures; and Kern (1983) hypothesizes a causal relationship between the mechanization and acceleration of everyday life through industrial development and the coherence of popular music content and form. But what exactly are these ends and causal relationships? It is one thing to propose that progressive music fulfils the hippie goal of expanding consciousness or that syncopation in New Orleans jazz is an extension of the pulley–piston motion of the machine age. But can we speak of pop music as having structures of feeling to which common functions are attached in pop culture? And if we cannot speak of this, must we see pop as an incomprehensible pot-pourri of musical forms that apply in disconnected fashion to an elusive plurality of niche markets?

These questions bring us to the question of the nature and range of theoretical approaches to the study of pop. The entire second part of the book is devoted to these considerations. It constitutes the platform for leaping off to explore the mode of pop music production which occupies the third part of the book.

Part II

Theoretical Perspectives

3
Structuralist Approaches

Conventionally, pop is twinned with personal creativity. But what does it mean to be creative? The production and reception of music imply a common language of communication. We are used to thinking of pop music as the product of culture. Banda, rock, salsa, rai, house and techno are clearly inscribed by quite narrow cultural dimensions (Lipsitz 2007). Yet some songs in these traditions clearly have the power to transcend cultural boundaries and resonate universally. If Led Zeppelin's 'Whole Lotta Love' (1969) articulates music that connects with listeners in London, Lagos, Laos and Los Angeles, does it not imply the presence of a structural base for reacting to music in humankind?

In sum, this is the argument that structuralism makes. As we shall see in the next chapter, the proposition that pop music is based in universal structures is quite contrary to ascendant thinking in the field (Hebdige 1979; Negus 1996; Bennett 2001; Longhurst 2007). The latter supports a *relativistic* type of analysis that differentiates pop in accordance with specific variables. Among the most commonly studied are history, nation, gender, culture, class, generation, subculture, ethnicity and race. This type of analysis explores the production and consumption of pop in relation to the meaning that it possesses for individuals and groups. The emphasis is upon viewing musical producers and consumers as agents who make meaning through playing, performance and interpretation. These meanings are not universal. That is why, typically, a fan of a Latin pop act like Shakira or a commercial diva like Beyoncé is indifferent to the lo-fi, indie music of Gomez or the late Elliott Smith. These variations are explained as a consequence of diverse social, economic and political factors.

In contrast, the structuralist approach proposes that music is universalistic. That is, it posits that pop music is a universal type of communication. Not only this, structuralism seeks to unearth the universal elements in the organization and practice of musical production, exchange and consumption. These elements are not held to be reducible to the intentions or interpretations of individuals or groups. Genre difference is explained as a matter of variation in the underlying rules governing the production and reception of music. The structure of these rules is ultimately located in the mechanisms for processing information in the human cortex.

Middleton (2002) offers a template of four dimensions that must be addressed as a preliminary to understanding where the structuralist approach is coming from and where it is leading.

(1) *Generative.* This is the so-called 'deep level' of music production and reception. It proposes that the creation and appreciation of music reflect a combination of how the human brain is ordered, cultural patterns (such as time frames, note frames, systems of tonal and harmonic relationships), the rules of musical genres (such as scales, intervals and rhythm) and the specific manifestations of these influences in combination, performance and reception.

(2) *Syntagmatic.* This refers to the ordering of links that form the chain of meaning by which a pop song is composed and received. Syntagmatics makes the lyrics or chords of a song seem to 'go together', to obey an order that seems natural and logical, but which in fact reflects the work of the four generative structures listed above. Thus, G/D/C/G/Em/Am/Cmaj7/D is the march tempo that informs the opening couplet of 'Yellow Submarine' (1967) by The Beatles. This syntagmatic chain is the product of the brains of the composers, John Lennon and Paul McCartney. But the 'choice' that they make in this respect reflects the predispositions of cognitive structure (how the human brain is organized), cultural patterns and the rules of musical genres. These are the resources that precondition the manifestation of the syntagmatic chord sequence that opens the song.

(3) *Paradigmatic.* This level of structure refers to the syntagmatic sequences that were not pursued in a particular composition. Thus to begin with the choice of G in 'Yellow Submarine' rules out all of the other major chords. The point being made here reflects Saussure's distinction between *langue* and *parole*: namely, that every utterance or inscription both excludes other utterances and inscriptions, while at the same time having no meaning without the existence of the whole system of language of which they are a part.

(4) *Processual.* Syntagmatic chains are not static. They exist in time. The meaning of a song like 'People Are Strange' (1967) by The Doors or 'River Man' (1969) by Nick Drake is changed by the premature deaths of Jim Morrison (lead singer of The Doors) and Nick Drake. What was once whimsical becomes redefined as a sign or prologue, a foretelling of the death not merely of an individual but of a generation.

Similarly, the Freddie Perren and Dino Fekaris number 'I Will Survive', which was a hit for Gloria Gaynor in 1978, was redefined in the 1980s from being an anthem of female empowerment into a sign of HIV/AIDS awareness. My use of the term 'sign' here is perfectly deliberate, for Middleton's fourth dimension cannily carries with it the suggestion that structural meanings are not monolithic or fixed, but are transformed through the interchange between production and reception.

Middleton's (2002) work directly follows from structuralist presumptions and ambitions. At the same time, it offers a bridge into textual and semiotic forms of analysis, which we will examine in the next chapter.

Briefly, structuralism presupposes that syntagmatic chains ultimately reflect the universal neural and cognitive framework of the human species. Cultural practice may modify this framework, especially as it relates to musical performance and reception, but only within *determinate* limits.

In contrast, textual or semiotic analysis grants that structure elicits syntagmatic chains of musical production and reception. But once the music is out in the world, once an achieved syntagmatic chain has excluded other paradigmatic options, the meaning of notes, silences and lyrics ceases to be *confined*. In being communicated, its meaning is inflected by human agency, especially the power of interpretation, and, of course, spatial location. Against this, structuralism holds that agency is ultimately subject to structural generators, such as the neural characteristics of the species or the mode of production, over which agency possesses only secondary powers.[1]

In this chapter I will examine the main contributions of the structuralist case as it applies to popular music. I will begin with Plato, Aristotle and the Ancient Greeks. In many ways this perspective set the bar for structuralist treatments of popular music. Plato and Aristotle argued that music is *mimesis* – the continuation in representational, harmonic form of the music of the spheres created, and ulimately governed, by the gods. Music possesses an emotional connection with the listener because it represents that which is integral to the world and the heavens that surround it.

Traces of this conception of music carry over into the neo-Marxist/Freudian approach of Jacques Attali (1977). He relates music to the mode of production, with the former both anticipating and reflecting changes in the latter. Yet Attali does not see the origin of music in the neural reflexes of the human species. For him, it is the consequence of the mode of production. Through all known cases in human history, one of the primary identifying characteristics of the mode of production is the primal fear of catastrophe and annihilation. No sooner do humans discover the forces of production and devise the means of production that, in unison, generate surplus value than they are beset with a primal fear that all of this will be taken away from them. The forces and relations of production that produce subsistence and luxury will cease to function, through either war or natural catastrophe. For Attali, the art of music is to sublimate or repress the universal fear of personal and collective disintegration.

Claude Lévi-Strauss (1970, 1979, 1981) takes over the Ancient Greek idea that music is a universal form of communication. In tribal and pre-industrial societies, myth occupies a pre-eminent place in playing out questions of birth, life, death and the mystery of creation in allegorical and metaphorical form. The process of playing out is often drenched in ritual. Anthropologists have regularly noted that shamanic rites of re-birth, healing and collective remaking are frequently accompanied by music. As Mircea Eliade (1964: 223) remarks:

> Among the Yenisei Ostyak healing requires two ecstatic journeys. The first is more of a rapid survey; it is during the second, which ends in trance, that the shaman enters deep into the beyond. The séance begins, as usual, with invoking the spirits and putting them in the drum one after the other. During all this time the shaman sings and dances.

Similarly, Dale Olsen (1975: 213) observes of the Warao Indians of the Orinoco Delta in the tropical forest of Venezuela:

> Music, combined with cultural conditioning, produces, I believe, a 'pure' trance, similar to the meditative trance state achieved by Buddhist monks while using music to reach enlightenment. Music is the vehicle, or shamanic tool, among the Warao that induces this so-called 'pure' trance state during the shaman's benevolent curing role and even, perhaps, during his malevolent role as an inflictor of destruction and illness.

The link between music and ecstatic experience persist into our own day. Robin Sylvan (2002) proposes that certain forms of rock, techno, house and heavy metal are universal forms of communication with a transcendental function. That is, they provide us with intimations of inclusion, transcendence and the sacred. In the 1960s and 1970s, Jim Morrison, Jimi Hendrix, Mick Jagger and Robert Plant consciously played with the motif and idiom of the shaman in the form of the Rock God. The punk and post-punk eras parodied this manoeuvre by brutally stressing the link between the Rock God and corruption. In doing so they implied that the Rock God was not the embodiment of popular urges but, rather, the grotesque distortion of them in the form of a being composed in equal parts of self-absorption, vanity, priapism, amorality and empty excess.

For Lévi-Strauss, there is correspondence between the structures of myth and music. The organization of each bunches meaning in clusters of tales and notes that only possess full significance when performed as a whole. Like myth, music is exchanged and replayed continuously to provide allegories and metaphors for the rest of life. Music is the sonic analogue through which we play and re-play the joys and dilemmas of existence. The pleasure that we derive from it is like completing a crossword puzzle or game of sudoku when everything, fleetingly, 'fits'.

The final structuralist position to be examined here is, with respect to the field of popular music study, the most influential. Theodor Adorno's (1941, 1947, 1967) analysis of pop conjoins it with social control, standardization, pseudo-individualization and cultural regression. As with Attali (1977), the structural unit at the centre of analysis is the mode of production, specifically the capitalist mode. The performance of pop music is analysed as subordinate to the music corporation, just as the process of consumption is theorized as producing passive compliance to a wider social and economic system based upon organized inequality. Adorno (1998) approvingly cites the work of Duncan MacDougald (1941), which, long before the 'Payola' scandal of 1960, revealed the crucial roles played by high-pressure advertising and plugging in achieving 'incessant repetition' in radio play. However, his critical analysis of pop is more trenchant in proposing that manipulation and the capitulation of the consumer are inherent in the technology of the modern pop song. The technology of composition, the arrangement of instruments, the construction of lyrics and the stereotypical characters and lifestyle issues that they portray are designed to produce universal responses of distraction and, finally, submission.

Structurally speaking, pop music is theorized as a constituent of the culture industry: that is, the various branches of the capitalist mass communications industry that include television, film, radio, advertising, newspapers and periodicals. These discharge the outward functions of innocuously informing and entertaining the masses (Adorno and Horkheimer 1979). Yet their deeper role is to establish the horizon of cultural fatalism that finally makes the masses, with resignation, accept their lot.

All of these structuralist positions explicitly propose that music is a universal form of communication, although of course they differ markedly in their analysis of what music communicates. The pivotal proposition that they share is that music exerts universal effects and springs from universal needs and capacities that transcend social divisions and cultural distinctions.

Plato and Aristotle: Music as *Mimesis* and *Katharsis*

Plato (2005), in the *Laws*, submits that music is intimately related to ritual. The *Laws* include precise rules for the use of music in festivals. Plato (2005: 240, 257) stresses the relationship between music, control and 'welcome pleasure'. The gods give music and control to humanity through Apollo, Lord of the Muses, and Dionysus, Master of the Feast, as a respite for sorrow. This endowment exists from birth. Plato's famous discussion of play observes that all young people move, jump and take delight in making noise. All animals are aware of the distinction between order (rhythm, harmony) and disorder (cacophony, discord). Yet only humans possess the faculty of perception that enables them to objectify, calibrate and manage this distinction as a source of pleasure. For Plato, music belongs to the mimetic arts. It mirrors and extends the music of the spheres that surrounds it. As such, it is neither true nor false, beautiful nor ugly, useful nor painful. It is simply the continuation of the truth, falsity, beauty, ugliness, usefulness and pain that are givens in the world and engrained in the human experience of existence.

In today's language, we may think of the special mimetic quality that Plato identified in music as expressing *chunks of sentiment*. These chunks do not necessarily clarify or reconcile sentiments, but they are extremely potent in articulating them. As Johan Huizinga (1949: 162) explains:

> The Olympian melodies rouse enthusiasm, other rhythms and melodies suggest anger, sedateness, courage, contemplation, etc. Whereas no ethical effect is associated with the sense of touch or taste, and only very feebly with that of sight, the melody of its own nature expresses an *ethos*. The various *modes* in particular are of ethical significance. The Lydian mode makes sad, the Phrygian quietens; likewise the flute excites, etc., each instrument having a different ethical function.

Aristotle (2000) in the *Politics* takes over many aspects of Plato's discussion of music and *mimesis*. However, he is much plainer in attributing discrete technical, psychological and moral functions to music. Thus, he sees it as a desire that is as natural as the requirements for sleep and drink. Technically, it is part of the arsenal of instruments in life that we use to dispel care and produce enjoyment. Psychologically, it is a source of enthusiasm, relaxation and a remedy for pain. Through it we gain a sense of balance and fitness in life. Morally, it is a means of education and a source of learning and understanding. For Aristotle, music is a blessing that the gods give to humanity. He approvingly quotes Musaeus, who says, 'Song is to mortals of all things the sweetest' (Aristotle 2000: 308).

Although Aristotle recognizes the power of music over character and the soul, he does not see it as necessarily important in itself. Rather, he again stresses the relationship between music and *mimesis*. That is, music represents all that is serious, potent, playful, joyful and harmful in the world and the heavens, ruled by the gods. The cultural importance that it possesses arises from its power to arouse the sentiments that it emulates. As he writes:

> When men hear imitations, even unaccompanied by melody or rhythm, their feelings move in sympathy. Since, then, music is a pleasure, and virtue consists in rejoicing and loving and hating aright, there is clearly nothing which we are so much concerned to acquire and to cultivate as the power of forming right judgements, and taking delight in good dispositions and noble actions. Rhythm and melody supply imitations of anger and gentleness, and also of courage and temperance and of virtues and vices in general, which hardly fall short of the actual affections. (Aristotle 2000: 309)

Because of the mimetic power of music, Aristotle (20002: 310) advocates that it should be a staple part of the education of the young so as to form character.

In addition, and crucially, Aristotle identifies a cleansing or purgative function to music, which he call *katharsis*. He introduces this concept in the context of a discussion of the effect of Tragedy on the audience (Aristotle 2000). It refers to the pleasurable, positive release of powerful emotions of fear, foreboding, delight and joy. In the *Poetics* he directly claims that music functions to produce education, amusement and purgation (Aristotle 2005: 669–71). The effect is not unlike medicine. As he puts it: 'Under the influence of sacred music we see people, when they use tunes that violently arouse the soul, being thrown into a state as if they had received medicinal treatment and taken a purge' (Aristotle 2005: 671).

Aristotle's proposition that music has an innate capacity to trigger cleansing emotional responses is widely shared. For example, Friedrich Nietzsche (1858), a lifelong devotee of music, writes of the experience of the form. According to him, music 'elevates' the human spirit, 'cheers us up', brings 'delight', 'deeply moves us', 'delivers us from boredom' and provides 'beautiful enjoyment'. The point to note is that this line of thought implies that human beings possess the same structure of *emotional* responses. That is, for Nietzsche, emotional responses to music are intrinsic to the species and transpersonal.

Is it acceptable to proceed on the assumption that popular songs produce a set of finite emotional responses among listeners? Is my response to Johnny Cash's version of Trent Reznor's song 'Hurt' (2005) or Erykah Badu's 'Bag Lady' (2000) the same as yours? Or is the emotional response which the songs evoke for me so conditioned by codes of biography, age, gender, class, ethnicity, nation and generation that it is qualitatively different from yours? Plainly, we do not all like the same pop music.

While there is sparse academic research into the question of the emotional stimulus that pop carries for listeners, it is sensible to proceed on the assumption that pop music produces common emotional reactions. Besides Nietzsche's fragment on the experience of music, which clearly suggests a transpersonal, emotional network that connects to music, there is good reason for believing that music has transpersonal powers. At its best, pop *connects*, swiping through barriers of nation, class, gender, race and subculture. Nor is it a matter of a powerful emotional or political lyric that overcomes social divisions or soothes frictions. Just as Plato and Aristotle's accounts suggest, songs that deal with commonplace experience have the capacity to create a common cultural *ethos*, to become standards in the genre, to be recognized and appreciated by all races, classes and ethnicities and to evoke a sense of a greater whole, a human harmony beyond political differences and social divisions.

Consider a song like Ralph McTell's 'Streets of London' (1968). In an interview, McTell recalls that he wrote the song when he busked in Paris in 1965. It deals with poverty, drugs, love and redemption. The geographical and historical setting is incontrovertibly local in place and time: London in the 1960s. But the lyricism of the tune and the power of the words have made it a global contemporary classic. Over 200 cover versions have been recorded. It is sung in schools and used in English lessons all over Europe, even though, as McTell wryly notes, the grammar of the lyric is faulty. He gives an anecdote to illustrate the song's power of global transcultural inclusion: 'A friend was hitch-hiking around the Himalayas ten years ago, and they asked him to sing them a song, and in return they sang him a song in English that they'd learned from another hitch-hiker – it was "Streets of London". I don't know why or how it happened but there you go' (*Time Out*, October 17–24, 2006: 36).

The Himalayan villagers hardly prove the case that there is a universal structure to music. What they do is lend credibility to the proposition that music is transcultural. The appreciation of music is not confined to East or West, Muslim or Christian systems. The density and grain of musical stimuli produce responses that are widespread in the human species. Whether this structure inheres ultimately in humans as a gift of the gods, the genetics of the neural cortex or the mode of production that humans make is, to some extent, beside the point. Music, one might say, is intrinsic to the human condition. It exists wherever human beings subsist because it is an extension and elaboration of the world *as it is*. In sum, this is the practical import of the case made by the Ancient Greeks.

Jacques Attali: Music, the Art of Noise

Attali (1977) submits that pop music must be understood not as a combination of notes and silence, nor on the level of aesthetic pleasure. For him, it is, first and foremost, a type of power. It is a form of ordering that governs not merely noise, but populations. As such, it is indissoluble from the mode of production in which it is situated and out of which it grows. Societies can be understood not only by their systems of warfare, structures of religion and means of production but also by the noises they make, the soundscapes they choreograph and orchestrate.

For Attali, in principle, pop music provides intimations of shifts in the tectonics of society, economy, politics and culture. Soviet communism appreciated the change-inducing capacities of Western popular music. This is why the music of The Beatles, The Rolling Stones, The Doors, Bob Dylan and The Sex Pistols was regulated and banned. But Soviet suppression did not prevent this music from circulating in an unofficial, underground capacity. As such, within the Soviet bloc, pop music operated as an intimation of system incapacity that was just as revealing as the political cronyism of the one-party state, the repression of poitical dissidents and the absence of essentials and luxuries in the shops.

Attali is a consistent dialectical structuralist in positing that pop music is dichotomous. Through melody and harmony, music produces a sense of order and wellbeing; but by means of clamour and dissonance it speaks a different kind of language – one concerned with interference, interruption and rupture. To be sure, for Attali the primal condition of humankind is fear about the immanence of universal catastrophe or destruction in the face of nature or through warfare. This fear arises out of low conditions of control over the mode of production that humans create, the volatility of the natural environment and the differences between humans. Attali regards music as a way of managing and assuaging this fear. At its best, pop allows humankind to forget that life is lived in the midst of inevitable decline and death.

Although he considers music to be the result of the mode of production, Attali claims that changes in music occur far more rapidly than in the social, economic and political infrastructure. Hence, changes in the organization of noise and in the nature and technology of music clarify comprehension and prediction in relation to the evolution of society as a whole (Attali 2002). In Attali's work, pop is assigned a *prophetic* quality. In this sense 'All You Need Is Love' (1967) by The Beatles prophesied Gorbachev's policies of *glasnost* and *perestroika* in the Soviet Union two decades later. Music has the capacity to prefigure changes in the concrete social totality.

A problem with Attali's discussion is that the dialectical functions of pop that he addresses are expressed conceptually and thus are very abstract. Nor are they specific to pop. They apply just as well to politics, ethics, painting, sculpture and much else besides. All of these areas involve the reproduction of systems of power and the transformation of power regimes through resistance and opposition. In order to demonstrate the distinctive qualities of the dialectics of pop music in specific detail a historical perspective is adopted.

Attali contends that society has passed through four distinct modes of production or orders of power. In each, noise operates through a different, concrete set of functions organized around four separate codes: sacrifice, representation, repetition and composition. In all of these regimes music acts both as part of the 'monologue of power', maintaining the durability of the power structure, and, conversely, as a tactic and practice of subversion.

Drawing on the thought of Michel Foucault, René Girard and Mikhail Bakhtin, Attali makes the following observations with respect to the functions of music in each regime:

(1) *Sacrifice.* Pre-capitalist, tribal societies are organized around oral culture. Because written culture is minimal, the primary setting for listening is social, just as the chief mechanism for remembering is the oral tradition. Popular music is tied to fixed social settings such as the church or festive occasions. In a questionable imaginative leap, which we will come back to review later, Attali argues that the Festival/Carnival involves music that accompanies a real

or simulated sacrifice.[2] He proposes this as the defining quality of music in this regime. The sacrifice of a scapegoat symbolizes the renewal of the social group and the symbolic defence against the collective fear of disintegration. The music that ritualizes sacrifice is therefore automatically linked to violence. Hence, Attali's use of the term 'sacrificial' to describe the general features of pop music in this period.

The use of the term 'sacrificial' is somewhat laboured. It has a double meaning. Attali wants it to signify the primitive link between music and violence. Music is the sonic setting which is the ritual context for sacrifice. However, since sacrifice also signifies the renewal of the social group, it also conveys defence and security against the natural forces that threaten to annihilate humankind: death, chaos and natural catastrophe.

For Attali, the musician and the sacrificial scapegoat are intimately connected. Both occupy an ambivalent place in the social order. They assuage natural fears of destruction and mayhem, but in doing so they remind us that these natural forces are just around the corner, always biding their time to uproot and decimate human achievement and stability. We see here the first concrete expression of the dialectical character that Attali attributes to music. Music reproduces the power hierarchy, but it also symbolizes the contingent, frangible nature of the social order.

At this time, music has no exchange value. It is performed as part of the traditional rituals of the social group. As such it is socially inclusive. It extends to the whole of the group and does not depend on a division between specialists and generalists. Outwardly, it expresses the immoveable force of tradition. Yet it also represents surplus energy. This applies not only to the power of music to go beyond the cares and routine of everyday life, but also to its capacity to hint at a counter-world in which fulfilment, satisfaction and plenty cease to be confined by privation and want and, instead, become generalized life experience. This is another argument that Attali uses to make the case that a compelling feature of music is its prophetic quality, its capacity to anticipate transitions and shifts in the mode of production that the routine framing of life fails to recognize.

(2) *Representation.* In this period, roughly from the 1500s to the early 1900s, music becomes connected to financial exchange. The presupposition of listening and playing becomes *paying*. This assumes a division between specialists (composers, professional musicians) and generalists (the audience). Music becomes ever more subject to the cash nexus. The long road to becoming context-free begins with the separation of musical performance from religious and festive settings to special events in the concert hall and the development of the music score. The harmonic elements of composition are slowly more dictated by rational consideration. This results in the inevitable commodification of music performance and consumption. Attali associates this era with the decentralization of control of music from the monarch and his court to a market form of organization.

The decisive move here is the assertion of copyright by musical composers. This is eventually guaranteed by the state, and solidifies the links between composing, playing and paying. The liberalization of copyright from the producer to the sponsor extends the opportunities for deploying popular music as a vehicle of social criticism and, in some cases, subversion. It also creates the basis for the elaboration of niche markets in the mass audience for whom popular music is a key channel for the mass communication of specialized emotion. A by-product of this is the production of various layers of distinction between high and low culture, elite and mass values. Attali sees distinction as a device to elaborate control over the fear of collective disintegration. For in purportedly 'knowing' more, high culture is in a privileged position to manage uncertainty and chaos. By comparing themselves to the so-called grubby world of the masses, the elite use the ideology of cultural superiority as a defence mechanism to assuage anxieties about decay and annihilation.

(3) *Repetition.* This era is defined by the twentieth-century industrialization of popular music. New technologies of recording permit the expansion of exchange of popular music on a massive scale. The phonogram and the jukebox replace the concert hall. Music becomes subject to the logic of industrialization. The cash nexus colonizes the experience of consuming music. Vinyl, CD formats and 'nomadic' listening systems (the Walkman, the iPod) lend themselves to turning listening into a private experience. The collective emotional charge that music produced in the sacrifice era is reduced to an erratic, often entirely private experience. The main reason for this is that, typically, we do not listen to music together, except in the regimented setting of the concert hall, the chamber room or the jazz café.

Universal access results in the decline of music's power. Attali makes a distinction between two processes here. Firstly, the rise of mass music turns listeners into a herd who are reduced to consuming formulaic tunes from the hit parade. Secondly, serious musicians react to this cultural order by striving to create challenging new sounds that oppose the standard harmonic formula behind hits and canned music. The result is an elitist art form that is rejected by the mass because it is viewed as depersonalized and meaningless.

At the crux of Attali's analysis is the proposition that the surplus in recorded music produced by vinyl, CD and nomadic forms makes owning and possessing more important than listening. His argument here anticipates contemporary audience research into the *otaku* and fan silo cultures (Condry 2006; see also pp. 170–3). He introduces the term 'stockpiling' to refer to the experience in consuming music. That is, we accumulate music from the ever-expanding catalogue of recorded music but we don't truly engage with it through listening. For Attali, this fodder form of consumption anticipates parallel developments in entertainment, junk food and health care. Stockpiling makes us kings of the musical universe since we can dictate what we buy and when we listen to it. As such it is a further iteration of the defence mechanism that humans require to combat fears about decay and annihilation, for accumulating and owning give a sense of presence and security. But our castle is built on sand, since a moment's critical analysis exposes presence and security as delusions.

Music is not exactly bereft of its capacity to shock or transport the listener away from regimented order. However, this capacity is confined to the avant-garde, who fiddle at the margins while society succumbs to principles of calculability, efficiency and external regulation.

(4) *Composition*. Attali's discussion of the 'repetition' regime is strongly reminiscent of the bleak assessment made of mass society by Critical Theory (Adorno 1941, 2009; Marcuse 1964). Pop has essentially become a key sub-system of social control. Resistance and opposition are confined to the margins (the avant-garde). The subversive qualities of pop music have been co-opted into the system. Primal fears of decay and annihilation are managed by the treadmill of work and the distractions of commodity culture. Both operate to prevent humans from dwelling on the meaninglessness of existence in the faces of natural and social forces that no-one can control.

The first edition of Attali's book was published on the threshold of what Simon Reynolds (2006) has called post-punk: that is, the period between 1978 and 1984 when a variety of bands, notably Joy Division, Gang of Four, Wire, The Fall, The Birthday Party, Talking Heads, The Human League and Cabaret Voltaire, sought to renew the emancipatory, anti-capitalist exuberance of punk. Although it used technology, especially sequencers and samplers, a prominent theme in post-punk is the disconnect between human control and technological progress. One of the first synthesizer bands, The Human League, sang of 'Empire State Human' (1979), while Kraftwerk envisaged 'Computer Love' (1981) and Joy Division released 'Transmission' (1979). The original punk explosion played on the theme of a human reaction to a mode of production that had ceased to treat people in humane ways. 'Get pissed, destroy', urged Johnny Rotten in the volcanic 1976 single 'Anarchy in the UK'. The relationship of one prominent strand of post-punk to technology and power was more ambivalent, however. It speaks of acceptance and using popular music as a sort of critical conformity: that is, a way of acknowledging the dehumanizing effects of technology and power without nurturing much hope of opposition or transcendence.[3]

The cultural anti-climax of the times undoubtedly influenced Attali's pessimistic reading of the production, exchange and consumption of pop music under the regime of repetition. Yet as a consistent dialectical thinker, against the stream of acceptance that one finds in a good deal of post-punk, he finds a structural pretext to challenge and overcome dehumanization.

To be specific, he proclaims the emergence of a new regime which he calls composition. Under this regime, pop is again used to 'compose' or orchestrate lifestyle just as it did in the era of sacrifice, when it signified a counter-world of exchange and inclusion beyond hierarchy. Illegal downloading, ripping, sampling and scratching herald a world in which the production, exchange and consumption of music move beyond the cash nexus to the principle of *gratuity* (Attali 2002). Performance and listening will no longer be subject to payment and stockpiling and there will be an end to the dependence of pop upon the global music corporation. The internet gives you synchronization and product placement which amount to a de-commodified business model of popular music since payment and ownership are no longer central at the point of exchange. Attali (2002) predicts that widening access to recorded music will translate into the growth in popularity of the live event. For in a world of ubiquitous access the ultimate scarce resource is not this or that commodity, but *time* itself. Time spent in the presence of the live act will grow in value just as the crystallized form of time embodied in the CD or streamed broadcast, which can be repeated *ad infinitum*, diminishes in value. Once again pop prefigures deeper changes in the organization of society, culture and economics.

Despite its many virtues, there are considerable problems with Attali's line of argument. Evidently, it is plausible to propose a common reaction to music. But to rationalize this as a universal defence against fear of destruction is gratuitous.

Nietzsche (1858) used the term 'ineffable' to describe the effect of music. He did so because he held a view of music as being a polyphonous entity. That is, it carries meanings that are greater than the sum of its parts. If this is the case, might it be profitable to examine music as a type of descriptive and analytic language rather than a defence mechanism against the fear of destruction? Such a mode of analysis embraces the universal character of pop. It gives credit to the capacity of music to overcome social divisions and provide intimations of transpersonality and transcendence (Attali's mode of 'Composition'). It acknowledges music's power to convey textures of meanings that are beyond the capacity of words to encapsulate. This is the core of the most durable popular music. This capacity has nothing to do with a fear of destruction. It has everything to do with social articulation, and, in particular, the ability of music to express what words and images cannot match.

When David Bowie was asked to explain the meaning of his ground-breaking Berlin trilogy of albums *Low* (1977), *Heroes* (1977) and *Lodger* (1979), which anticipated much of the alienation and synthesized, dislocated atmospherics of the post-punk wave, he responded that the music was a reaction to 'seeing the Eastern bloc, how Berlin survives in the midst of it, which was something that I couldn't express in words. Rather it requires textures' (quoted in Reynolds 2006: 5).

The general functions that Attali claims for pop music are also *textured* between control/reproduction and resistance/subversion. Different types of music can be studied to reveal how these ends are organized and pursued. Basic to Attali's argument is the proposition that the dialectic between each set of functions is integral to popular music *as a social form*.

In the hands of other neo-Marxist writers, the concept of totality has culminated in cultural suffocation (Lukács 1971): that is, the conclusion that the concrete reality of the capitalist order and its manifold support network produce a context of power and control which is, in the words of Marcuse (1964), 'one dimensional'. Meaningful resistance and the mobilization of opposition are discounted because protest and permissive lifestyle are examples of 'repressive desublimation': that is, tolerated qualitative easings in the system of control and reproduction that ultimately serve to reinforce the cash nexus and the rule of capital.

In contrast, Attali's insistence on the dialectical character of pop has no truck with the hypothesis of cultural suffocation. The balance of control and reproduction may be heavily weighted in favour of vested social interests. This is clearly the case in the analysis of the regime of Repetition, where stockpiling, private ownership and nomadism are presented as evidence of the innate stability of the dominant order. Still, for Attali, in principle, the concrete reality of totality always carries with it the possibility of resistance. For example, the regime of Repetition gives rise to the avant-garde, who challenge the commercial values that colonize popular music. The regime of Composition develops through avant-garde improvisation and the use of new technologies of electronic distribution.

Rave culture's dependence upon word-of-mouth happenings, cottage industries of organization and spontaneous expression seem to confirm certain aspects of Attali's analysis of Composition. So, too, does sampling and scratching, in the celebration of consumer sovereignty and its reframing of the music market as a free-for-all.

On the face of it, these practices certainly challenge commodification and the rule of capital. Yet whether or not they can be rightly described as prophetic is far from conclusive. Rave culture lost its vitality in the noughties and now survives as a retro genre. Similarly, the battle for the illegal use of copyright material is far from won. Sampling and scratching are subject to court injunctions. The prices paid by audiences to see star turns like Radiohead, Madonna, Eric Clapton, Coldplay, U2, Bob Dylan and Bruce Springsteen play, and the money spent on recordings by these professional musicians, hardly support the proposition that the era of Repetition is over.

In Attali's (1977) book, the examples he gives have been widely criticized as shallow and untenable. Improvisation has a long history in pop music. But it has not succeeded in fully rejecting the cash nexus or the rule of capital. Not-for-profit jazz organizations like the short-lived Jazz Composers' Guild (founded by Bill Dixon in New York in 1964) and the Chicago Association for the Advancement of Creative Musicians (AACM) have not really broken with established power relations. Despite real achievements in training musicians from poor backgrounds in the Illinois area and beyond, and providing resources for musical experimentation and performance, the Chicago AACM has received aid from the MacArthur Foundation and has strong links with Columbia College. In fairness to Attali, the book was written before the advent of the worldwide web and the new opportunities for P2P exchange and streaming and ripping that have followed. Even so, his arguments that music is emerging into a populist regime that he calls 'Composition' seem more like wishful thinking than solid prophecy.

There are significant additional difficulties with Attali's argument. The proposition that the origins of pop are bound up with ritualized violence and the sublimation of anxieties about chaos, disaster and collapse is arbitrary. Attali's main source is Pieter Bruegel the Elder's painting The Fight Between Carnival and Lent (or Carnival's Quarrel With Lent) (1559). Bruegel portrays the familiar struggle between the Apollonian emphasis upon the value of order and restraint and the Dionysian urge for excess and freedom. The canvas is divided diagonally between figures observing the regimentation and sacrifice of the normalized order of Lent and a counter-world of Carnival in which noise, disruption, violence and ritual sacrifice rule.

A single sixteenth-century canvas is a slender pretext upon which to construct an entire theory of noise, music and power which is intended to bear upon two millennia of experience and practice. Bakhtin (1968) covered similar ground on ritual in his discussion of the medieval Carnival. But he does not make the mistake made by Attali in reading Carnival as a metaphor for the imminent demise of an entire socio-historical regime. In Bakhtin's work the period of Carnival is finite and subject to external controls if it threatens to over-run or get out of hand. The proposition that Sacrifice defines the entire character of the regime would have struck Bakhtin as misplaced and gross. For Bakhtin, what defines medieval society is order achieved through class domination, religion and the licensed, ritualized release of repressed emotions through Carnival and other play forms.

The arbitrary nature of Attali's discussion can be illustrated from another angle. Noise is fundamental to the case that he makes about the dialectic between control/reproduction and resistance/subversion. However, his definition of noise is peculiar. 'A noise', he writes, 'is a resonance that interferes with the audition of a message in the process of emission' (Attali 1977: 26). This is the basis upon which he formulates the proposition that popular music functions, as he puts it, to 'tame' anxieties of dread and disturbance that arise from the painful and 'violent' character of noise. It does so by sublimating this energy through harmony and melody.

But what does it mean to proclaim that noise is 'violent'? There is no basis for this in nature. In German phenomenology, *Dasein* refers to an original, eternal state. The word is a combination of *da* ('there/here') and *sein* ('to be'). 'Being there' is foundational to the concept of existence. Heidegger (1984), with whom the concept is closely associated, favours it because it refers to the fact of existence without committing the reader to confine the concept of existence to (a) a biological entity, (b) consciousness and (c) rationality. *Dasein* carries emotional and spiritual connotations that go beyond the material facts of personal embodiment and concrete totality (in the sense of a social, economic, political and cultural order).

What, then, is Attali's rationale for privileging noise as the original auditory condition? There is none. If we examine noise from the perspective of *Dasein* it is quite consistent to propose an original auditory harmony arising from nature, or more precisely the relationship between being and nature. The sound of a forest, the waves of the sea or the stillness of the desert possess recognizable sonic characteristics. It may be acceptable to use the term 'violence' with respect to the relationship between being and nature in each of these settings, providing certain preconditions are met. The sound of lightning or of storm rains may be legitimately described as 'violent'. However, this is not, in itself, a basis for submitting that violence is in some way a privileged synonym to describe noise.

In classical music we know that there are examples that seek to represent the order of balance in the relationship between being and nature: Beethoven's Symphony Number 6 in F Major 'The Pastoral' (1808), Sibelius's *Finlandia* (1899), Debussy's *La Mer* (1905) and Stockhausen's *Stimmung* (1968) all come to mind. Popular music has also produced innumerable examples of its own: Paul McCartney's 'Blackbird' (1968), Canned Heat's 'Going Up the Country' (1968), Pink Floyd's 'Fat Old Sun' (1970), Bob Dylan's 'New Morning' (1970) and Coldplay's 'Strawberry Swing' (2008). In these cases is it not more viable to read the structure of music as a system of expression reflecting the relationship between being and nature than as a project to tame violence and assuage the primal fear of collective annihilation?

Lévi-Strauss: Music and Myth

For Lévi-Strauss (1970: 15) myth and music 'transcend articulate expression'. The roots of both are in language (Lévi-Strauss 1979: 51–3). The key to the hold which music exerts may be unlocked if we compare its structural elements with those of language.

The structure of language consists of three elements:

(a) *phonemes*: the sounds that we use to represent different letters;
(b) *words*: the combinations of phonemes which represent concepts about the relationship between being and nature; and
(c) *sentences*: the combinations of words to make meaning.

In contrast, the structure of music consists of two elements:

(a) *notes*: A, B, C, D, E, F and their major and minor variations; and
(b) *sonemes*: the combinations of notes which create music.

Musical expression is a concrete way of communicating about the world. Like language, it is a means of thinking and feeling. But its structural composition is quite different. Music eliminates the level of words in language. It moves straight from sound (notes) to sonemes ('sentences' of meaning).

Fundamental to Lévi-Strauss's position is the hypothesis that music supplies states of consciousness and communication that language is unable to furnish. If one eliminates words from language, communication stalls. Words assemble phonemes and turn them into signs. The arrangement of signs in a sentence produces meaning. Music moves directly from the individual note simple soneme level to more complex arrangements. The result is the translation of meaning to enriched levels that words and sentences cannot accomplish. In fine, music fills the silence left by words and produces a sense of 'fit' or 'flow' (Csikszentmihalyi 1990): that is, the state of pleasurable, energized involvement in which a person is immersed in an experience of being 'out of time' or 'in a groove'.

The parallel is slightly diminished in the case of pop music. This is because pop songs generally involve a combination of lyrics with music. Nevertheless, at its best, the intertwining of verse with music produces levels of meaning that sentences or music alone cannot accomplish. In the urban-industrial milieu the well-tempered combination of verse with music is capable of producing a 'sound' that defines the structure of feeling in a particular time and place.

Consider Bob Dylan's 'Like a Rolling Stone' (1965). This was deliberately conceived as extending the pop song formula. It broke the conventional wisdom of what a pop song is by clocking in at over 6 minutes 34 seconds, using a variety of instruments beyond the guitar/bass/drum combo (organ, piano, electric guitar, bass, drums and tambourine) and employing a complex rhyming structure in lyrical phrasing (aaaab; ccccb; ddeefg; gghhh). The lyrics are accusatory, as is standard in a particular genre of pop song dealing with failed relationships, revenge or thwarted desires. In comparison with the pop songs of the day, however, what is striking is that the accusatory tone is subsidiary to the analytic master-theme. The song narrator is not just trying to explain why a relationship has foundered; he seeks to humanely relate this particular human failure to much wider themes of illusion, temptation, the personality culture of spray-on emotions and the meretricious social world. These ambitions are supported by the musical arrangement. It is a song that sums up the rearrangement of snakes and ladders in sixties culture, in which the sons of busmen became cultural icons and heiresses slummed in squats.

Greil Marcus (2005) makes a field-day out of the drum-beat that opens the song, claiming that it is without precedent in the genre of popular music. Be that as it may, the reason why 'Like a Rolling Stone' produces an uncanny sense of recognition irrespective of class, gender, ethnicity and generation is because the sound creates a landscape of consciousness and communication that articulates the cultural disaggregation of the day. The song articulates a combination of diverse and loosely connected elements that makes everything fleetingly 'fit'. Other songs have done this. One thinks of the punk *cri de coeur* of The Sex Pistols' 'Anarchy in the UK' (1976), the noirish homage to Calfornia of The Eagles' 'Hotel California' (1977), Nirvana's grunge anthem 'Smells Like Teen Spirit' (1991) or rap classics like Big Punisher's 'Still Not a Player' (1998) or Nas's 'One Mic' (2002). These songs connect and condense cultural, political and generational relations that articulate the structure of feeling or, more widely, the spirit of the times in ways that mere words are unable to match.

How does the work of Lévi-Strauss help us to understand what is going on here? In *The Savage Mind*, he argues that native societies classify thought on concrete objects in a logically consistent structural framework of nature and experience (Lévi-Strauss 1966: 17–19). They develop myth as a 'matrix of magical meaning' that operates through what are, frequently, outwardly perceived by strangers as opaque analogies and contrasts. Myth allows for 'totemic classifications': that is, a system of thought and classification that 'works rather like a kaleidoscope, an instrument which also contains bits and pieces by means of which structural patterns are realized' (Lévi-Strauss 1966: 36). Music performs the same function in the modern world. It concentrates and condenses a kaleidoscope of images and data and weaves them into a recognizable structural pattern. The purpose of this pattern is to articulate ties of social inclusion and exclusion. If you relate to 'One Mic' or 'Hotel California' you instantly 'say' to others a good deal about who you are and where you are coming from.

The totemic principle is very evident in the relationship between pop, cultural biography and the 'structure of feeling'. Thus, for example, The Beatles, with *Rubber Soul* (1965), *Revolver* (1966), *Sgt Pepper's Lonely Hearts Club Band* (1967), *Magical Mystery Tour* (1967) and *Abbey Road* (1969), to say nothing of their major single releases of the same time, transformed the pop song. Rather than mere entertainment, this music became a front for channelling the myths, dreams and popular politics of the day. The Beatles were not alone in doing this. Bob Dylan's *Bringing It All Back Home* (1965), *Highway 61 Revisited* (1965) and *Blonde on Blonde* (1966) performed much the same function, as did albums by The Rolling Stones, The Who, Leonard Cohen, and Joni Mitchell for their respective subcultural audiences. These works brought together a myriad of different elements, including components of politics, youth culture, fashion, lifestyle and the social imaginary, and appeared to magically resolve wider social, economic, political and cultural contradictions.

For Lévi-Strauss, the mechanics of musical scores work by suggesting an absence or lack in meaning. This induces the listener to fill the gap with an affirmative response. To repeat an analogy already used in this book, the pleasure of listening to music is akin to completing the clues in a crossword puzzle and so acquiring a momentary sense of 'fit'. As Lévi-Strauss (1981: 647) puts it: 'Music is language without meaning; this being so, it is understandable that the listener, who is first and foremost a subject with the gift of speech, should feel himself irresistibly compelled to make up for the absent sense.' Later, he refers to music as 'a concrete form of union' between the composer and the listener wherein, with respect to the latter, the individual is carried to 'a place . . . inside him for the music: he is, then, like the reverse, hollowed-out, image of the creator, whose empty spaces are filled by the music' (Lévi-Strauss 1981: 654) . When this emotional and psychological sense of 'fit' is achieved, the audience responds with an affirmative reaction of a 'concrete union' with different components.

In postulating the analogy between music and myth, Lévi-Strauss is intent upon observing that myth also performs this function. But whereas music employs sound to accomplish the goal of expanding consciousness, myth uses oral and visual codes. Both employ stereotypical formulae and gestures. They operate as bundles of images and notes that only possess complete meaning if they are apprehended as a totality.

Structurally speaking, musical composition is the manipulation of sonemes and lyrics in order to construct calculated, concentrated emotional responses. In pop music this manipulation is blatant in the sequenced repetition of riffs combining front-loaded bass and rhythm guitar underpinned by compact drum-beats. The classic pop song is less than five minutes in duration. It employs traditional chord and rhythm structures and a verse–chorus–bridge formula. The thirty-two-bar form was refined by Tin Pan Alley in the mid-1920s and adopted and developed by pop composers after the 1950s. Typically, this consists of a regular harmonic structure which begins with the main melody and verse (the A section), builds to the bridge or middle eight (the B section), and closes with a reprise of the A section. Examples include 'From Me to You' (1963) and 'I Want to Hold Your Hand' (1963) by the Beatles; 'Surfer Girl' (1963) by the Beach Boys; 'You've Lost That Lovin' Feelin'' by the Righteous Brothers (1964); and 'Whole Lotta Love' (1969) by Led Zeppelin.

The verse–chorus–bridge structure is a standardized formula that aims to cluster the emotions around modulated sound climaxes focused on the rhythm guitar (Middleton 2002). Black Sabbath's 'Paranoid' (1970) is a classic exemplar of the verse–chorus–bridge structure based upon a power riff. Nirvana's 'Smells Like Teen Spirit' (1991), which echoes the power motifs of Black Flag, the Detroit sound of The Stooges and The MC5 and seventies punk, uses the same method. This music unleashes chunks of primal emotion in verse sequences built around pronounced power-riff bursts to create a string of intense associations that build to a climax. The effect is closer to the 'spoon feeding' mode of composition discussed by Lévi-Strauss (1981, 1997). The structure of musical composition and performance is intensely ritualized.

John Castles's (2008: 49–52) analysis of the rock concert as ritual behaviour takes the structuralist argument in the analysis of popular music a stage further by applying it to the performance arena. For him, far from constituting unique events, rock concerts follow structurally patterned codes of behaviour that resemble ritual conduct in native societies. Fans assemble in a stadium, conscious of participating in a collective life event that constitutes a break with routine and is designed to take one out of everyday experience. Pre-performance recorded music is used to settle the fans in their seats; the lights are dimmed in graduated movements as the expectations of the fans gather pace and all eyes are focused on the stage; in the semi-darkness, chants, whistles and cheers accompany the entrance of musicians onto the stage. As soon as the first chords are struck, and the lights come on, the audience explodes into a sort of programmed ecstasy. The 'concrete union' between the audience and performers is enhanced by electronic amplification and lighting, which are sequenced to 'recreate the ecstasy of the first revelatory moment' (Castles 2008: 65). The relationship between the concert star and the audience is one of co-operative labour. The emotional energy between the star and the audience is both festive and feast-like. The image of the star is the basis for positive affirmation, but successful pop and rock concerts demand a co-operative energy spiral between the star and the fans that celebrates 'concrete union'. As Castles (2008: 66) puts it: 'The crowd constitutes itself as a single entity so that . . . the star on stage can become the one who absorbs its power . . . the star [becomes] the embodiment of all of them. The "super self" made by the crowd is then imaginarily re-appropriated. Repossessed by each of its members.' The best concerts are recalled as magical resolutions where everything 'comes together'.

The use of musical rhythms, tones and textures to build clusters or, to use a term employed by Castles (2008: 65–6), 'plateaus' of emotion that require listeners to fill 'absences' or make connections is even more pronounced in progressive rock. In the 1970s and 1980s groups like Genesis, Yes, The Jimi Hendrix Experience, The Moody Blues, King Crimson, Van der Graaf Generator, Pink Floyd and Jethro Tull extended the verse–chorus–bridge structure by inserting interludes and tangents. The extension of musical space allowed for experimental passages often built around improvisation. These experiments often drew on motifs from classical music, folk and jazz. In many cases, the bass, lead, rhythm and drum structure of the standard pop band was radically expanded with the deployment of more instruments, notably synthesizers, flutes, violins, cellos and saxophones.

The lyrical content of progressive rock utilized elements from fantasy and science fiction to provide a magical narrative. Good examples are *Tarkus* (1971) by ELP (1972); *The Lamb Lies Down on Broadway* (1974) by Genesis; *Tales from Topographic Oceans* (1973) by Yes; and *The Wall* (1979) by Pink Floyd. The narrative content of these rock operas was often deliberately oblique which expanded the scope for listeners to participate in 'filling in' the gaps in the meaning of the music.

For Lévi-Strauss (1981), myths and musical scores are approximations of universal, species-specific categories of thought and emotion. They offer a model of life that uses not only techniques of *mimesis*, but also cultural ordering which accelerates and concentrates a diffuse ensemble of sensations and memories and brings them to a satisfying, 'magical' resolution.

This brings Lévi-Strauss (1981: 659–60) to his most concise formulation of the function of music:

> The musical work, which is a myth coded in sound instead of words, offers an interpretative grid, a matrix of relationships which filters and organizes lived experience, acts as a substitute for it and provides the comforting illusion that contradictions can be overcome and difficulties resolved . . .

it is inconceivable that there should be any musical work that does not start from a problem and tend towards its resolution – this word being understood in a broader sense, consistent with its meaning in musical terminology.

Music only performs the function of totemic thought because it relates to subconscious strings and networks of association that are distributed in culture. These strings/networks are common to the species because they are cultural articulations from the deep structure of the human brain. In principle, Lévi-Strauss considers music to be a universal language. But there are problems with this line of analysis.

It is one thing to propose that a Kalahari bush man and a metal fan in Birmingham, Antwerp, Melbourne or Chicago have a similar emotional and physical response to Zeppelin's 'Whole Lotta Love'. But it is a big leap from this to posit (a) that this is the *same* response and (b) that it derives from the deep structure of the human brain. Neural responses are not finite. They depend upon the relationships between individuals and natural phenomena. These relationships are infinite. So there are immediate difficulties with the hypothesis of 'standard neural reponses' to music or anything else.

Lévi-Strauss's evidence for the parallel effect of myth and music to achieve the alchemy of 'concrete union' is inconclusive. To be sure, it yields a fruitful way of thinking about how music *might* work and an equally rich line of speculation about the *possible* affinity between music and myth. However, this is very different from proceeding on the basis that music really does have a universal response because of structural, species-specific features in the human brain which ultimately override cultural barriers and codes.

Adorno: The Hammer of the Backbeat

Adorno's study of the structure and functions of music divides into a story of extremes. In *The Philosophy of Modern Music* (1973: 15) he gives due to the capacity of music to reflect and elicit 'enlightenment'. However, this function is strictly confined to the genre of serious music: that is, a critical form that endeavours to break the mould of emotional repression and economic subordination that governs mass emotional and psychological reflexes. Adorno's application of structuralist arguments, then, postulates standardized human responses to pop music. However, unlike Lévi-Strauss, he traces them back to the capitalist mode of production rather than the neural structure of the species.

In the atonal compositions of Arnold Schoenberg, Alban Berg and Anton Webern, Adorno cites examples of what he takes to be serious music. According to him, this music demands 'the renunciation of the customary crutches of listening . . . [it requires] not mere contemplation but praxis' (Adorno 1967: 149). Such music wrests consciousness and conventional practice from what Adorno understands to be servitude to the pseudo-individualism and social conformity that dominate the capitalist mode of production.

For Adorno (1978, 2009), the contrast between serious music and light music could not be starker. The latter is the popular form that pervades the hit parade, commercial radio and the concert trail. The beat of the pop song hammers out the standard thirty-two-bar verse–bridge–chorus formula based upon hackneyed typifications of character and stereotypical narratives of human interaction. It is constructed around a regimented repertoire of harmony, rhythm and verse narratives. In this line of reasoning, light or pop music works on the same principles as industrial planning and factory management. In deploying limited musical stimuli to elicit tightly controlled emotional reactions, it is the mirror of the industrial division of labour.

The functions of pop music are to (a) reproduce social conformity, (b) achieve compliance with organized economic inequality and (c) divert attention from social conditions.

What is the pretext for Adorno's argument? More or less without qualification, he accepts Marx's theory of surplus value and the associated Marxist idea of false consciousness. Briefly, as the theory has it, under capitalism, the worker, having no other means of subsistence, is forced to sell his labour power (creativity and energy) to the owner of the means of production: the capitalist. As a result the worker is deprived of (a) control over the labour process, (b) rights of distribution and (c) matters of industrial strategy and policy. Adorno shares Marx's view that the main social and psychological consequence of this state of affairs is alienation. The worker is divorced from the labour process and the results of production; and the capitalist is dehumanized by the business of treating the worker as a commodity, to be set to this or that task like a mule pulling a wheel, in order to make a profit.

By Adorno's day, the relationship between the capitalist and the worker was complicated by the replacement of the *laissez-faire* state with the interventionist state and the rise of consumer culture. The welfare state offers a measure of relief and protection to wage labourers in the form of centrally administered pensions, schooling, the provision of recreation and health care. Adorno portrays it as a central piston extending the logic of capitalist accumulation from the sphere of production to the realm of consumption. By enhancing the rights of the worker at play, at school and in ill health and old age, the interventionist state does not so much protect the powerless as increase the general propensity to consume. Consumption provides individuals with the illusion of freedom, for their capacity to consume is determined by their position in the labour market. This position presupposes subjection to the discipline of the extraction of surplus value. What individual consumers see as an act of freedom is, in reality, an act of control and compliance. Hence, Adorno's (2006) thesis that freedom under capitalism is unfreedom and the related conclusion that the worker lives in a state of false consciousness.

Where does this leave pop? Adorno views pop music as a major cog in the culture industry. Concomitantly, specialized branches of the culture industry reinforce social control. For example, the 'incessant' plugging and 'repetition' of hit songs on the radio combined with pop television shows and magazines enhance the compulsion to consume (Adorno 1998: 229). In this way, 'the culture industry concretely and utterly dominates and controls both the conscious and unconscious of the people at whom it is directed' (Adorno 1998: 174).

The core of Adorno's argument about popular music may be distilled into one sentence: 'The whole structure of popular music is standardized, even where the attempt is made to circumvent standardization' (Adorno 2009: 281). So the efforts of punk, grunge, rap and electronica to beat the system fail because their commercial value attracts cultural entrepreneurs who co-opt the music and transform it from a front of resistance into a new branch of cultural consumption. Thus, 'alternative' bands like The Sex Pistols and The Arctic Monkeys eventually signed, respectively, with major labels Virgin and EMI. In this way, the resistance and challenge integral to the most exciting genres of rock and pop are choked off by the system and reabsorbed by capitalist entrepreneurs as an additional source of revenue (see also Grossberg 1997: 102–21).

Producers of pop music are fond of presenting themselves as creative artists and audiences value discernment as a primary asset of consumption. Adorno is scathing about these social and psychological responses. He prefers to see them as reflexes that are required by the capitalist mode of production to pursue the goal of accumulation. According to him, creativity and discernment in popular music amount to what he terms 'pseudo-individualization': that is, personal and group variations upon the planned, programmatic standardization of production, distribution and consumption. In his words:

> By pseudo-individualization we mean endowing cultural mass production with the halo of free choice or open market on the basis of standardization itself. Standardization of song hits keeps the customers in line by doing their listening for them, as it were. Pseudo-individualization, for its part, keeps them in line by making them forget that what they listen to is already listened to for them, or pre-digested. (Adorno 2009: 288)

This passage sharply exposes Adorno's error in proposing a dependent relationship between the economic extraction of surplus value under capitalism and the standardized cultural and social response that it theoretically produces. The economic mechanism consists of the appropriation of wealth and the exploitation of the worker. From a Marxist perspective the cultural, social and psychological consequences of this are as clear as night follows day. Pseudo-individualization both presupposes and ends in false consciousness. However, what Marxism claims to demonstrate is, in fact, imputed.

From the perspective of the concerns addressed in this book, the question is: In what sense is it plausible to regard successful pop songs like John Lennon's 'Imagine' (1971), Grandmaster Flash's 'The Message' (1982), Bob Marley's 'Redemption Song' (1980) or Nirvana's 'Smells Like Teen Spirit' (1991) as exercises in engineering compliance? In response, Adorno reasserts, but does not demonstrate, the three central propositions upon which his analysis of pop music is based. That is:

1 Pop music defuses, and diffuses, political energy.
2 Passive consumption is the standard response of audience reception.
3 Resistance music reinforces manipulation and social control.

We know that songs like Charles Albert Tindley's 'We Shall Overcome' (1947), Bob Dylan's 'Blowin' in the Wind' (1963), The Wailers' 'Get Up, Stand Up' (1973), Erykah Badu's 'Bag Lady' (2000) and Peter Gabriel's 'Biko' (1980) have been adopted as anthems which are played at concerts, rallies and other collective meetings of a political nature to represent and engender solidarity. The evidence suggests that they are intended to heighten awareness of social exclusion, disempowerment and inequality, and are received by audiences as such. Far from producing a standardized response, the minimalism of the pop song (plain lyrics, simple, regular note structure and power chords) has the capacity to make cogent political statements that carry the potential to demystify ideology and inspire direct action. 'I fought the law, and the law won' and 'Ruben Carter was falsely tried' are not motifs that operate to defuse consciousness. On the contrary, they are compact musical contributions that articulate injustice, engender dissent and, in a word, *raise* consciousness. It is simply untenable to maintain that these songs result in acquiescence. They clearly inspire resistance and opposition. This may not bring down the entire capitalist mode of production. However, as Thomas Frank (1998) and Jim McGuigan (2009) demonstrate, cultural interventions of this type cannot be dismissed as mere aesthetic flim-flam. On the contrary, these songs require reformulation in the mode of production and, indeed, change the context in which power relations are articulated.

It might be objected that these readjustments are negligible. After all, sixty years of rock and roll has not delivered 'power to the people'. Elsewhere (Rojek 2007), I have argued that 'neat capitalist' corporations like Apple, Body Shop, Virgin and Microsoft have co-opted selected practices of the counterculture to make their businesses more informal, socially conscious, environmentally aware and user-friendly. The argument may be extended to the wider readjustment of neat capitalism to popular music of dissent and protest. Neat capitalism with a rock and roll backbeat is more penetrating in achieving consumer control because it utilizes the rhetoric of resistance music and turns it into the soundtrack of relevant, credible modern business practice.

However, to posit that capitalism has a strong track record in readjusting the challenges of the music of dissent and protest is very different from proposing that these readjustments are negligible. Good pop always produces a 'surplus' that cannot be eradicated merely by setting it to franchised commercial ends. 'Street Fighting Man' (1968) by The Rolling Stones carries a sense of 'fit', even if it is now used to promote designer jeans or a sports car.

Shusterman (2000) develops these points in a philosophy of popular aesthetics. He maintains that Adorno's rejection of the significance of popular art is Romantic in origin. It fails to engage with the altered aesthetic and cultural conditions of urban-industrial society, which are, in part, the result of the articulation of this art. More generally, Shusterman (2000: 199) rejects Adorno's distinction between art and life. Urban-industrial society creates a new aesthetics, having to do with the body, that the Romantic division between body and soul cannot encapsulate. The combination of rhythm and lyrics produce a new cultural and aesthetic order that cannot be reduced to Romantic precedents. Pop is incommensurate with fine art standards (see also Baugh 1993; Gracyk 2007). It is a qualitatively new medium that can be neither comprehended nor evaluated by recourse to traditional aesthetic categories.

For Shusterman (2000), a pop music art form that is regularly derided by elite musicologists is rap. They see rap as jungle music, possessing low levels of sophistication and crude insights. In contrast, Shusterman invites us to read rap as verbally complex and philosophically rich. It engages with postmodern material realities of recycling and branding. It also gives value to the cultural periphery which elite culture defines condescendingly as marginal.

The allegation that Adorno's division between art and life is redolent of an obsolete aesthetic framework that is of limited value for understanding any aspect of cultural practice today points to a major defect in his structuralist approach. As Theodore Gracyk (1996: 165) expresses it: 'If Adorno is concerned that the mass audience vulgarizes great music with a fetishization of its parts at the expense of the larger whole, his own fetishism lies in focusing on structure at the expense of other musical values.' The question of structure points to difficulties in Adorno's capacity to discriminate. In particular, Adorno was wrong in assuming a singular structure and function to the culture industry and a standardized reflex among audiences to pop. Today, most students of culture prefer to use the term *cultural industries* (Miege 1989: 9–12; Hesmondhalgh 2002: 16–17). The plural is intended to convey two things. Firstly, it is intended to convey the *limited* success in engineering compliance of corporations and state agencies that specialize in culture. As Attali (1977) reminds us, music occupies an emotive envelope that cannot be mechanically stamped with the logic of the mode of production. It articulates contradiction and provides intimations of different human relationships and, by extension, a better type of society. Secondly, the plural form *cultural industries* denotes the variable nature of the ends of cultural production. Record labels like Aftermath, Rough Trade, EMI and CBS and bands like Simply Red and Take That are as much a part of the culture industry as Gang of Four or The Fall. But to treat the means and ends of their respective activities and music as like for like is to reveal illiteracy about what pop actually is, and how it works with audiences.

Today, the dominant position in the analysis of pop music holds that Adorno's thesis is important in making explicit the link between commodification, control and consumption. Just as Adorno submits, many music corporations, and songs in the hit parade, are transparently concerned to reproduce social control through cultural distraction and the diffusion of energy. Yet to assign a monolithic function in this respect to all aspects of the culture industries and every song that becomes popular is now generally considered to be unacceptable. Hesmondhalgh (2002: 17) prefers to analyse the culture industries in terms of *complexity*, *ambivalence* and *contestation*. This is now par for the course.

It is itself not merely a reaction to Adorno's thesis, but a characteristic of the so-called 'cultural turn' in the social sciences that started in the late 1970s and rapidly gathered momentum thereafter. The cultural turn recognizes the central antagonism between the dominant and subordinate classes, but also emphasizes the creativity of social actors in social action, the situated character of meaning and the importance of coding and representation in social practice. These analytic traits signal a move from what is widely held to be the inflexibility of the structuralist perspective and the embrace of an agency approach to the study of pop culture and pop music. The key questions of the contribution and significance of this approach are the next focus of this book.

4
Agency Approaches

This chapter addresses what I take to be the four most significant agency approaches to the analysis of popular music: subculturalism, relationism, transcendentalism and textualism. To understand what they are we must begin by outlining the key general features of the agency perspective. These are:

(a) the proposition that individuals are situated actors who possess the capacity to interpret the conditions in which they are located and have the power to act upon them;
(b) the methodological principle that meanings and values reflect the circumstances of time and place and the capacities of individuals and groups to decode and communicate these conditions; and
(c) the proposition that social action and interpretation are coded and represented. The *systems* in which action and interpretation are culturally articulated are of equivalent analytic moment to concrete divisions of economic, political and social power.

Whereas structuralism foregrounds the desiderata that are alleged to condition or determine individual and group action, the agency perspective launches from the position of the knowledge, motivation and action of social actors to transform history and socio-economic contexts. It takes for granted that the central defect of the structuralist approach is to deny creativity, variation and cultural difference. The criticism that structuralist approaches are unable to handle producers and consumers of pop music as reflexive, creative actors, responding variously to rhythm, tempo, melody, metre, rhyme, harmony, texture, lyrical content, production and packaging, might be levelled at the writings of Attali, Lévi-Strauss and Adorno.

Against this, agency approaches emphasize the creativity and aesthetic contribution of artists and audiences and their attempt to make meaning and act upon society and history. The caveat here is that subjective choice and practice are conceived not as autonomous, but as entwined in fields of knowledge and power that prioritize specific types of embodiment, recognition and conduct. Thus, composers, performers and audiences are conceptualized as agents. Their personal choices and actions reflect the field of power/knowledge relationships in which all individuals are embedded. These relationships have to do with class, gender, race, generation, occupation and status. Since these forces precede the individual, and tilt choice and action hither or thither, there is a sense in which personal intentions are 'pre-selected'. However, the interpretation and action of composers, performers and audiences are not *determined*. Agency approaches always insist upon reorganizing the facts of the power of individuals and groups to interpret their position in relation to the context in which they are located and to act upon it. This implies two subsidiary propositions that are important in the analysis of pop.

Firstly, musicians and audiences make lucid musical 'statements' relating to class, generation, ethnicity, gender and other contours of knowledge and power. The post-9/11 music of Coldplay could not have been made without the attack on the Twin Towers, but that it has been made so winningly reflects unique talents and other personal characteristics.

Secondly, musicians and audiences follow some preferred trajectories of behaviour that are either arbitrary or 'pre-selected' by virtue of class, race, gender and status stimuli. For example, to continue with Coldplay, the impact of a song like 'Speed of Sound' (2005) derives from its permutation of words, noises and rhythms that is distinctive from other permutations in the sonic system. A song or a sound is a matter of not merely the creativity of the composer, the skill of the performer, the reflexive power of audiences or broader questions of history, class, gender, race and status. It also reflects a permutation of sonic elements in the sonic chain. This difference makes the song or sound stand out as worthy of attention.

The line of reasoning which postulates the 'arbitrary' quality of pop music is followed most consistently by textualism; the line connecting thought, choice, interpretation and action in popular music factors is most energetically pursued by subculturalism, relationism and transcendentalism.

The agency approach dismisses nominating a determining structure behind human conduct as gratuitous. Instead it focuses upon subjective and group consciousness, the politics of choice and the dynamics of social bargaining and negotiation. This procedure does not discount that a set of causal relationships between practice and underlying forces of motivation exist that condition behaviour. At the same time, it prefers to address the changing equilibrium of power between force and practice rather than isolate and dismantle the mechanics of so-called 'sub-structural' motors of influence that determine choice.

What does it mean to 'address the changing equilibrium between force and practice'? If one adopts the view that musicians and audiences make lucid transpersonal statements, the question is: how do these types of conduct reflect the field of power/knowledge in which individuals are located? Conversely, if one maintains that choice and action are pre-selected, it follows that the choices and actions of individuals and groups do not amount to very much. It would be inexact to maintain that choices and actions are *determined*. On the other hand, the argument that responses to music are conditioned by arbitrary differences in the sonic chain requires more conditional notions of action, choice and interpretation. For, although the notion is only fully realized under textualism, the premise of this version of the agency approach is that choice and action are, in the final analysis, arbitrary.

The meta-theorists informing this position are disparate and various. They include Roland Barthes, Michel Foucault, Jacques Derrida, Jacques Lacan and Fredric Jameson. What holds them together as a category is the principle that action and meaning must be considered not simply with respect to the biographies and motivations of actors. This is because actors, biographies and motivations are themselves regarded to be *discourses* that position individuals and condition trajectories of behaviour. A discourse may be defined as a field of knowledge and practice that renders some forms of belief and action 'natural' or 'normal' and therefore subjectively and collectively compelling. The other side of this is that some other types of belief and action are automatically excluded by reason of their difference.

So much for the general features and analytic distinctions of the agency approach. We must now come to the topic of the main applications of this approach in the analysis of popular music: subculturalism, relationism, transcendentalism and textualism.

Subculturalism

In the study of popular music this perspective is associated most strongly with the work of Willis (1978), Hebdige (1979), Bennett (2001) and Jackson (2004). Its roots go back far deeper via sociology to the study of illegal drug use in jazz subcultures (Becker 1963), youth culture, masculinity and aggression (Cohen 1972); via criminology to deviance and delinquent gang cultures (Cohen 1955; Cloward and Ohlin 1961); and via cultural studies to questions of difference and the politics of resistance (Hall and Jefferson 1976; McRobbie 1980, 1991).

Formally speaking, subculturalism may be defined as an approach to explore social and cultural relations as the articulation of common rules of group practice, and values that depart from, or are in outright antagonism with, the dominant order. Its main identifying characteristics in popular music are dress, vernacular, use of stimulants and attachment to particular social ideals and cultural values. To express a liking for Kasabian, Jay-Z, The Notorious B.I.G. or The Felice Brothers is to make more than a statement concerning musical taste. It is also to express a preference for a distinctive set of subcultural values, social practices (including dress and recreation) and political ideals.

Although individual choices are generally respected, in subcultures social and psychological adhesion to the characteristics of the group is privileged over the idea of personal autonomy. Group identification is expressed behaviourally in a certain way of going about the world and adopting recognizable attitudes to culture, power and authority. Concretely, this may be hard to pin down. This is because so much that glues subcultures together is implicit, assumed or in some other way indirectly communicated. Simon Reynolds (1998) hits the mark in coining the phrase 'vibe tribe' to describe the essence of subcultural formation. It is a matter of feeling that one has come 'home' or that one 'belongs' to the 'vibe' of the group.

In the analysis of popular music, subculturalism has been extremely influential. Analytically, it bifurcated into two distinct phases. In the first phase, spanning roughly the 1970s to the 1990s, the focus was upon the relationship between national music genres and indigenous social solidarity. The role of music in recruiting and integrating groups was pivotal (Finnegan 1989; Bennett 1997; Malbon 1999).

Since the late 1990s, with the rise of academic and popular interest in world music, the focus has shifted to the examination of the various relationships between music subcultures and globalization (Mitchell 1996; Condry 2006).

Let us explore the bifurcation in greater detail.

Recruitment, Integration and Transformation

Initially, the investigation of subcultural formation concentrates upon questions of recruitment, integration and transformation. Relevant factors of analysis are gender, class, race, education and the politics of incorporation and resistance. In this vein, Phil Cohen (1972: 23) famously contends that youth subcultures are responses to the disintegration of working-class communities precipitated by urban renewal and increased geographical and social mobility. For Cohen, subcultures are fundamentally exercises in rebuilding community. The framework of analysis here is explicitly, and unapologetically, British working-class youth culture. Yet in principle, the processes described may be applied in other cases of subcultural formation.

Cohen's (1972) work is paralleled by Willis's (1978) ethnographic study of youth culture, music and the politics of resistance. Willis's main concern with popular music is the question of how it relates to the grain of everyday subcultural life. As he explains in an interview with Roberta Sassatelli and Marco Santoro:

> I wanted to see how music was experienced in common social practices. So, without any formal training, it just seemed to me a good idea to play music to the people and ask them to discuss it, and spend time with them and their music. . . . I didn't play personally. The technique was to go to the boys who were in a bike club in Birmingham called the 'Double Zero' and ask them what music they like. (Sassatelli and Santoro 2009: 269)

For Willis, pop is an essential resource in subcultural recruitment, integration and transformation. His work casts subcultures firmly as forms of resistance and non-conformity to the dominant culture (as is also the case with his Birmingham School alumnus Larry Grossberg). However, as with Cohen, Willis's focus is upon British youth data. Despite the prominence of American pop music in the biker and hippie subcultures that he examines, the question of globalization is not addressed.

Ruth Finnegan's (1989) study of local music in an English provincial town also claims strong functions of social integration in music subcultures. But it does not highlight the dimensions of challenge and resistance in subcultural formation. Instead, it analyses subcultures as taste formations which archive social traditions and musical expressions and establish cultural perimeters of inclusion and exclusion. Drawing on Howard Becker's (1974, 1976) work on the collaborative nature of creative labour in the arts, she explores seven musical worlds: classical, brass band, folk, musical theatre, country, jazz and rock.

Her analysis of local rock groups identifies three types of band: young, inexperienced bands often formed by people still at school; post-school bands who are seeking to establish themselves on the performance and dance hall circuit; and seasoned bands with a secure position in regional pubs and clubs. She therefore departs from the conventional wisdom in the study of pop and rock subcultures in (a) rejecting the presumption that performers and audiences are exclusively young people – her findings indicate a much wider generational range and the active participation of family networks in music subcultures; and (b) questioning the connection between music subculture and resistance and dissidence – her research discovered a strong link between musical subcultures and the continuity or regeneration of community life. Finnegan analyses music subcultures as a key component of integration, providing communities with a powerful sense of place and belonging.

Moving on, her approach belongs to the tradition of cultural analysis, which, in words coined by Raymond Williams (1961, 1977), treats 'culture as ordinary' and as part of 'a whole way of life'. Her territory is not the world of rock stars with Lear jets, country mansions, town houses and trans-continental drug dealers. It is part of the ordinary world in which music is produced, exchanged and consumed as an element of being in the world together and interpreting place, position and past. Elsewhere, Finnegan (1997) compellingly presents pop music as one of the narrative mechanisms through which personal and collective experiences are 'actively enstoried'.

The idea that popular music is a form of 'enstorying', of encoding personal and collective life experience, connects up with the proposition that some music performers are entry points into the cultural biography of a time and place and the related notion that some popular songs provide a 'window' into a specific 'structure of feeling' that is summative of a discernible geography, history and culture (Friedlander 2006). I will return to take up these points in more detail in the conclusion to the book.

Turning to research in the USA, Deena Weinstein's (2000) study demonstrates detailed consistencies between the form of the music, subcultural values, representations of embodiment and disassociation from the dominant culture. She argues that individuals are recruited to heavy metal subcultures by anxieties about a world gone wrong, time out of joint, the irrelevance of organized politics and other intimations of a dominant culture in terminal decline. Heavy metal subculture carves out space for producing meaning and agency that does not so much reconcile tensions with the dominant culture as dramatically accent them through dress, jewellery, hairstyle and other aspects of embodiment.

There are echoes here of the Chicago School tradition to the study of music subcultures pioneered by Howard Becker (1963) in his famous study of jazz musicians. Becker argued that jazz musicians are tightly integrated subcultures based upon a basic consensus over values of community, spontaneity and self-expression, and a perception of isolation from both the commercial world of pop and the larger society. The latter is symbolized by the term 'square', indicating thoughtless conformity to the values of commercialism and consumerism. The 'antagonism' (Becker 1963: 102) between bona fide jazz musicians and their audience and the larger society is reinforced by the related use of drugs. By this means the values of 'straight', 'square' society are further ritually subject to strategies of demystification and denigration. Many Anglo-American studies provide additional details of pop and recruitment, integration and transformation in subcultures (Bennett 1980, 1997; Malbon 1999).

In postwar Western society, youth subculturalism was expressed in various tribal forms that were closely connected to generational divisions. Teddy boys, mods, punks, new romantics, grebos, junglists and other youth groups articulated signs of social inclusion (and, by implication, exclusion) visually, through fashion, make-up, haircuts and jewellery; orally, through subcultural catchphrases, buzzwords and wider issues of vernacular; and politically, through recognizable values about social, economic and cultural inequality. Thus, the look of the Teddy boys consisted of Edwardian drape jackets, sculpted quiffs and crepe-soled brothel creepers and their politics followed traditional working-class goals of redistributive justice. New romantics favoured frilly blouses, heavy make-up, retro glam rock/ science fiction motifs, the *laissez-faire* state and global causes like environmentalism and alleviating Third World hunger. Grebos shaved their heads at the sides and left it long at the top, wore loose, stripy jumpers with baggy jeans or big shorts and were antagonistic to organized politics, especially party machines. The junglist look consisted of camouflage, Moschino jeans and Caterpillar boots and their political values favoured hedonism and libertarianism.

Visual and oral markers of youth subculturalism have receded in the last fifteen years. Of course, youth subcultures continue to exist, but visual and oral markers are less pronounced. The main reason for this is the transformation in the supply routes of popular music. The internet and the iPod have replaced the radio and the club as the prime sources of access. The mobile, private nature of internet consumption militates against the incubation of strong ties of collectivity and solidarity which are the prerequisites to delineate social inclusion and exclusion. It encourages forms of flexible consumption. For consumers are able to download files from many genres, from soul, post-punk, heavy metal, rap, jungle and electronica, without committing to any one of them. The iShuffle function on the iPod is a metaphor for how popular music is widely accumulated and experienced through downloading, streaming and ripping.

Additionally, access to music is now part of multi-media platforms of consumption. Youth groups no longer focus upon one genre of music to the exclusion of everything else. Rather, as part of the process of de-differentiation, they download music files from overlapping genres and combine music consumption with multi-tasking forms of entertainment such as television, DVD, games, mobile phones and print culture. The result is the dilution of metropolitan tribal looks, since access and consumption are often mobile and private rather than public and concentrated in specific social and physical settings.

Arguably, the link between music and subculturalism is stronger in developing and emerging countries, where supply routes are smaller and weaker. Music defines generational forms of social inclusion because economic divisions and the political hierarchy are better defined. For example, Steen's (1996) study examines Chinese rock culture after the 1978 reforms, the rise of affluence in metropolitan centres and the spread of the cassette recorder. According to Steen, the consequence of these developments was that broad subcultures in Chinese youth started to contrast party affiliations with a counterculture based, first, in notions of freedom, diversity and self-expression and, later, in cosmopolitanism and consumerism. For example, the Chinese rock star Cui Jai is an important countercultural figure in the Chinese rock scene. His music protests against social conformity and cultural obedience. This contrasts with 'Gangtai' pop from Taiwan and Hong Kong and *tongsu* music from mainland China, which are embedded in the ideology of the Communist Party.

More recently, the counterculture has been challenged by new subcultures adhering to values of liberty, the market and cosmopolitanism. Nineties pop stars like Faye Wang and Zheng Jun celebrate globalization and cosmopolitanism and fetishize the personal over the political. In doing so they contribute to the commodification of Chinese rock culture and the delayering of politics from questions of ultimate political values to the psychology of the emotions and lifestyle architecture.

Steen's (1996) study reveals how pop music in China is used to code and represent subcultural lifestyle values and political preferences. Music operates as a basis of subcultural recruitment, integration and transformation and has additional capacity to challenge official national codes and representations. Steen relates these forms of subcultural formation to the rise of affluence in China and the permeation of globalization into mainstream styles of Chinese life. But despite being concerned with the opening up of Chinese life to Western influences, there is not much in Steen's study about how travelling subcultures interact. In particular, the question of the reformulation of local traditions through involvement with global influences is not adequately addressed.

In the context of pop on the African continent, Veit Erlmann's (1996) ethnomusicological study of the a cappella music known as *isicathamiya* in South Africa is widely recognized as a major contribution to clarifying the relationship between music, power and subcultural practice. Popularized by Ladysmith Black Mambazo and Paul Simon, the *isicathamiya* tradition of so-called 'night music' is pivotal in the social integration of the Zulu migrant labourer subculture who are the mainstay of its choirs and performers. The music resists the class and racial forces in South Africa that combine to categorize these labourers as mere 'units of production'. Importantly, it creates and reproduces a symbolic 'homeland' of the Zulu rural tradition and cultural identity against the discursive and political conventions of the neo-colonial enclave. Erlmann powerfully shows how the performance tradition risks being undermined by the commercialization of the night-music genre. The inevitable result of commercialization, he argues, is commodification. This abstracts the music from its cultural and subcultural roots and transforms it into sheer entertainment value for international, cosmopolitan audiences that have no direct engagement with the social, economic and cultural conditions and contradictions that produce the *isicathamiya* genre.

Ethnographic studies of music subcultures are often extremely rich in providing details of cultural codes, types of representation and forms of exchange. However, a major defect is that the findings on subculture tend to cancel each other out. This makes it difficult to trace continuities between the forms of musical subculture and to postulate common functions. To put it simply, subcultural studies that use ethnography excel at producing detail, but are less satisfactory in demonstrating or hypothesizing patterns of conduct. Therefore the traffic between research findings and theory tends to be slow and sparse.

Williams: Dominant, Emergent and Residual Subcultures

By way of offering a correction, it may be helpful to revive Raymond Williams's (1977) distinction between dominant, residual and emergent cultures and offer it as a framework for analysing the formation and functions of music subcultures. Williams's typology has unaccountably fallen out of favour in recent years. This is a pity because it offers an efficient way of mapping subcultural formations and coherently discriminating between functions that is still relevant today. What is his case?

Williams (1977: 121–7) maintains that societies consist of dominant, emergent and residual (sub)cultures. The *dominant culture* may loosely be described as the values, institutions and practices characteristic of the class or other social group who occupy a position of advantage and privilege over other social and cultural strata. That is, these values, institutions and practices are *hegemonic* in the sense of constituting the social, cultural and political context of association, positioning and practice.

By the term *residual (sub)culture*, Williams means experiences, meanings, values and practices that were formed in the past but continue as an active element in the present. These experiences, meanings, values and practices persist despite being alternative or dissonant with regard to the dominant culture. Thus, hippie subculture is predominantly residual with its appeal to non-commercialism, non-aggression and peaceful co-existence. Some of the rhetoric and practices of this culture have been appropriated by the dominant culture, in the same way that Frank (1998) describes the appropriation of the counterculture by what I call 'neat capitalist corporations'.[1] Yet hippie culture and the musical traditions and forms that it supports offer a 'social imaginary' which finally points to the transcendence of the commercial dominant culture (Taylor 2004).

The same might be said of punk subculture. For Andy Bennett's (2001: 68) money, British punk 'had all but disappeared' by the end of the 1970s. Yet punk subculture persists in the UK. Furthermore, as Bennett himself shows, it has migrated to other cultures in Western and Eastern Europe and North America. Economic insecurity and political oppression provide rich ground for the transmission of punk characteristics. They remain actively residual, reworking and redefining oppositional values in relation to new economic and social challenges.

Punk subculture is clearly a causal influence on important variations in musical subcultures. The most notable is grunge. In the 1980s the fuzzy, distorted guitar sound of grunge developed as the soundtrack of the so-called 'Generation X', disconnected from the mindless consumerism and imperial revisionism of the Reagan–Thatcher years and the exhaustion of the punk tradition. Its main figurehead, Kurt Cobain, leader of Nirvana, was the archetypal embodiment of alienation from 'normal appearances' and 'involvement obligations'. For alienated youth among Generation X, grunge was an 'involvement shield', fending off capitulation to what was regarded as the essentially degraded and pointless merry-go-round of consumer culture, but without a concrete interest in constructing an alternative form of society (Goffman 1967).

The division of grunge from punk shows how residual subcultures provide a 'parenting' function for emergent subcultures. By the term 'emergent', Williams (1977: 123) means 'new meanings and values, new practices [and] new relationships'. These subcultures constitute a genuine alternative to dominant culture. As such, they are rare. A common difficulty of analysis is that they are confused either with variations of residual culture that endeavour to reformulate relationships with dominant culture, or a new phase in the evolution of the latter. A clear example, memorably captured by Adorno (1973, 2009) in music subcultures, is the emergence of musicians and audiences organized around atonal composition in the years immediately prior to the First World War.

Genuine examples in the history of pop music are harder to come by. The engagement of this music with popular consciousness implies co-dependence with the dominant culture. That is, it criticizes, distorts and demystifies the dominant culture without exactly transcending it. Popular music has provided many examples of this. For example, *Trout Mask Replica* (1969), released by Captain Beefheart and His Magic Band, mixes blues, jazz, folk and avant-garde forms. It is certainly distinct from the dominant mainstream and in many ways critical and dismissive of it. However, it is not genuinely oppositional in the sense of providing an alternative type of culture and society that might prosper. One can say the same of other experimental pop albums such as, for example, *Cheap Thrills* by Frank Zappa (1968), *Discreet Music* by Brian Eno (1975) and *Litanies of Satan* (1988) by Diamada Galás.

So much for the main features of Williams's typology. If one examines musical subcultures it ought, in principle, to be possible to categorize them as dominant, residual or emergent forms. By extension, the analysis of exchange and cross-pollination between the three types should follow suit.

With one proviso, Williams's original typology deserves to be dusted down by students of popular music and explored again. The proviso in question is that his division of (sub)cultures into three categories is peculiarly disembodied. It is as if in struggling to come to terms with the work of the mature Marx and the tradition of Western Marxism that was largely informed by it, he short-circuited an engagement with the writings of the young Marx. The latter are more attuned to questions of the sensuality of practice and the conscious role that men and women play in making their own history. To this end, I propose a supplement that focuses not upon the categories of thought or belonging, but on the categories of conscious action. In terms of subculturalism, the distinctions that I wish to make relate to what I call recruitment, integration and practice.

One way of framing the issues of recruitment, integration and practice is to investigate subcultural formation in terms of a tripartite division of roles between avatars, apprentices and agnostics. Discourse positions actors as, in my terms, *avatars, apprentices* and *agnostics* with respect to questions of taste and knowledge. What do I mean by these terms?

Avatars provide the 'directional clues' and 'keying' components that transform a genre of music into a popular new wave. They consist of artists, critics, rebels and youth leaders. The buzz about a new sound or a new look can extend group identification and intensify media attention. In the 1970s avatars praised the immediacy and honesty of punk against the overblown pretensions of prog rock and jazz–rock fusion. Johnny Rotten, Siouxsie Sioux and Joe Strummer became spokespersons for a generation, valued for their direct outlook and no-nonsense vocabulary. The 'No Wave' movement in New York's Lower East Side relished the bravado of punk and scorned the half-baked complacency of prog rock and jazz–rock fusion forms, drawing on idioms and motifs from minimalism and performance art. No Wave was not about construction or transcendence. Instead it relished the irrevocable decay of transformative action and projects designed to improve social conditions. As Reynolds (2006: 140) puts it, 'No Wave music irresistibly invites metaphors of dismemberment, desecration and "defiling rock's corpse"' – without, however, being interested in proposing an alternative. It created a new edge to the punk reaction that attracted performers like Lydia Lunch, Teenage Jesus and the Jerks, Bush Tetras, DNA and Mars.

Apprentices emulate the directional clues and keying components provided by avatars. They embrace these cues as material to engineer the transition from lifestyles organized around 'normal appearances' to emergent cultures of resistance and opposition (Goffman 1971). As such, they carry the characteristics identified in the literature on fans and fandom: that is (a) strong emotional intensity or 'affect' with the persona (rather than the person) embodying musical and lifestyle texts; (b) recognition of shared narratives of belonging that are represented in dress, values and musical taste; and (c) willingness to distribute resources in exploiting and developing trajectories of affect over a sustained period of time (Jenkins 1992; Hills 2002).

Although there are obviously close parallels between subcultures and fans, Cornel Sandvoss (2005: 9) warns against treating the terms as synonymous. Subcultures are structured around beliefs, values and lifestyle. While these elements are often mobilized in fan cultures, they are subsidiary to star culture. Marilyn Manson's fans are goths and Manson exploits and develops goth beliefs, values and lifestyle in his stage act and music. Yet Manson is the foundation of the fan base. It is his public pronouncements and his on-stage presence and off-stage behaviour that act as the magnet for fans. Apprentices may follow the example of avatars without ever progressing or aspiring to the status of dominant leaders. As Willis's (1978) study of bikers and hippies and Weinstein's (2000) work on heavy metal subculture richly demonstrates, in musical subcultures, apprentices are typically content to learn and practise the lifestyle trade as marks of distinction and difference from both dominant cultures and other subcultures.

Agnostics are either oblivious, or indifferent, to new wave considerations. They may be indifferent to music subculture or they may be so totally immersed in their own music subcultures that they are impervious to the new wave. The claims of new wave avatars and apprentices to push music out to a new edge leave them cold.

In musical culture, and pop culture in general, intimations of what is 'happening' in the phenomenology of musical taste, youth subculture and networks of composers, performers and audiences are extremely important in setting agendas of musical innovation and social action. The buzz about a new sound or a new look or, more generally, a combination of the two can generate sufficient momentum to produce subcultural formation.

Subculturalism and the Turn Towards Globalization

Lately, the primary trend in the subculturalist tradition in the study of pop music is to steer away from local studies of subcultural formation to examine the interaction between the local and the global.

Hebdige anticipated this in the 1970s. In an important article, he (1976) broke with the nationalist tradition exemplified by Phil Cohen (1972) by proposing that youth subculture is primarily related to global commodity fetishization. That is, highly desired commodities such as motor scooters, designer sunglasses, Italian suits or cool, hip music – all of which, either directly or tacitly, privilege consumption over production – are the basis of recruitment, integration and transformation.

From this viewpoint, subcultures are enclaves of taste that challenge standard obedience to the work ethic, respectable values and other types of social conformity. Instead of casting subcultures as essentially nostalgic projects designed to reformulate collective values violated by economic and social change, Hebdige (1976) analyses them as reactions to the enlargement of global consumer culture. On this logic, advanced capitalism produces commodities. Some of them trigger new environmental and social risks. Others provide a sense of stability and security in an ocean of change. All constitute bases for recruitment, integration and transformation that are symbolized and enhanced by music.

More recently, the proliferation of academic and popular interest in world music has focused attention in subculturalism upon the complex social, cultural and economic forces that precipitate cultural transmission, redefine genres and produce hybrid musical forms. For example, Mitchell (1996: 150) argues that the forms of rap music that emerged in Italy in the 1980s had strong roots in local traditions. They sprang from the *centri sociali* (social centres) created by left-wing militants and dissident youth in the 1970s. But the catalyst for them is, of course, the American contribution of rap to the global market. Naples, Turin, Sardinia, Calabria and Puglia are major localities for rap. Italian rappers redefined the 1970s militant agenda and extended it to address *fin-de-siècle*/new century preoccupations with the corruption of Italian officialdom, unemployment, impoverishment, Mafia brutality, racism, immiseration and media manipulation. Thus, Frankie HI-NRG's 'Fight da Faida' urges 'national consciousness' resistance against Mafia blood feuds. Other groups, like South Posse, use dialect to protest about the racial abuse of Southern Italians by Northern Italians and the exclusion of immigrants of African origin. Mitchell shows how Italian rappers customize the American genre of rap by tailoring it to local conditions and practices.

Ian Condry's (2006) detailed analysis of the cultural diffusion of hip hop in Japan follows a similar path. He examines the actual sites of hip hop in Japan: *genba* (settings of musical happening). In doing so he reveals the processes of cultural appropriation and reformulation through which Japanese hip hop artists relate to the American, black urban form. For Condry, Japanese hip hop artists use music and performance art to parallel African-American forms of cultural and political engagement with the dominant culture. Marginalized and neglected cultural demographies, such as the Japanese population of Korean descent, engage frontally with Japanese histories of ethnocentricity and cultural exclusion. The ethos of collective labour against Japanese traditions of isolation and exclusion is fundamental in explaining the popularity of hip hop in Japan. *Genba*, a term that possesses inimitable connotations of place and identity in Japanese language, are crucial axes of cultural transmission and regeneration because they involve the direct confrontation between the hip hop artist and the performer. *Genba* are theorized as an interface in which the global directly confronts the local. Condry (2006: 94) refers to this process as '*genba* globalization because it highlights the ways the global, here meaning everything one can draw on (not just "foreign" ideas), is refracted through performative locations and thereby put back into the world'. He shows how music subcultures travel and are overhauled via engagement with issues of class, race, gender and status in cultural transmission and assimilation. Japanese improvisation of Afro-American hip hop themes has produced a new subcultural form that enables meaningful involvement with Japanese questions of cultural hierarchy, social and economic inclusion and exclusion.

Today, the main action in the subculturalist tradition in the study of pop revolves around issues of subcultural synthesis. The most powerful metaphor is supplied by the example of world music that appears to mesh subcultural forms into a new cultural musical value that is greater than the sum of its parts. In the history of pop there are many candidates for the title of progenitor of world music. For example, John Coltrane's late style of jazz improvisation drew on references from Africa and Asia and fused them with local US traditions. Similarly, Chris Blackwell, who founded Island Records, initially limited himself to introducing Western audiences to Jamaican ska. The breakthrough record in the UK was 'My Boy Lollipop' (1964) by Millie Small, arranged by the Jamaican guitarist Ernest Ranglin. By the 1970s, through the diversification of the label with progressive British bands like Traffic, Jethro Tull, Free, King Crimson and Emerson, Lake and Palmer, Island was a staging post in which Western and post-colonial forms of music could meet and develop.

The classic example is Bob Marley and the Wailers, who released *Catch a Fire* (1973) and *Natty Dread* (1974) for the label. Blackwell made the crucial intervention in popularizing Marley's sound by insisting on the inclusion of Western-style guitar solos to expand the reggae format. *Catch a Fire* and *Natty Dread* achieved relatively modest sales. But Blackwell's fusion approach paid dividends with *Bob Marley and The Wailers Live!*, recorded at The Lyceum, London, in July 1975 and released in December that year. The album was a huge success, consolidating and enlarging Marley's fan base in Europe and opening up the North American market, to say nothing of acting as a calling card for the roster of reggae bands that Island managed: Toots and the Maytals, Black Uhuru, Aswad and Steel Pulse.

The trend in subculturalism, then, has been to move away from regional or national studies of recruitment, integration and transformation to the level of global diffusion and synthesis. The rise of world music has expanded the perspective of travelling musical subcultures and deepened our understanding of how music transfers data relating to cross-cultural politics, diet, fashion, ethnicity and sexualities. Subculturalism has some claim to be classified as the first sociological application of the agency approach to the analysis of pop. However, in the last two decades it has been supplemented by powerful new perspectives.

Arguably, subculturalism has a claim to be identified as the leading expression of the agency approach in the study of pop music and pop culture. The sheer range of studies, particularly those based in detailed ethnographic methods and data, is exceptional.

Yet there are serious difficulties with the subculturalist position. The attention to detail and concrete practice often goes hand in glove with an under-developed theoretical position. Questions of power tend to be glibly brokered with unparticularized references to the logic of capitalist political economy (Cohen 1972; Hebdige 1979) or uncritical, quasi-celebratory accounts of hybridity and globalization (Condry 2006). The space for a systematic analysis of subcultural practice and corporate manipulation, state regulation, media authority and the causal chains behind generational 'structures of feeling' remains vacant. So does the precise relationship between subcultures and deeper structural categories like class, gender, ethnicity and race.

In addition, subculturalism tends to discount questions of value in favour of a sort of blanket relativism. The right for subcultures to be different, and to interpret themselves and the world in which they are concretely situated in distinctive ways, is vigorously defended. But the question of whether the productions of punk, post-punk, grunge, house, techno and other subcultural formations possess deeper cultural value is side-lined. The result is an expansive form of analysis. It permits a thousand flowers to bloom and presumes not to judge the worth of this or that system of cultural production. Thus, Condry's (2006) excellent social anthropology of hip hop music in Japan is largely descriptive. It imparts hardly anything about the cultural or aesthetic merit of the music, while the political effect is glossed by the argument that international hip hop brings people closer together. The question is: in what selective ways are they brought together? The active process of subcultural integration and resistance is not a matter of a cultural corridor of international exchange. Rather it is a question of how global forces of inequality, manipulation and social ordering promote and reproduce the rules of the game by which all subcultural groups live. To understand these forces requires an analysis of the location and interaction of subcultures with universal social and economic agents relating to accumulation, ideology, knowledge and power.

One result of this is that subculturalism has practically nothing to say about social and economic transformation or transcendence. Although it is profoundly political, for example, in insisting on the right of subcultures to have their 'voices', it has been unable to generate a politics that will contribute to an easing of the structural divisions and inequalities that cause subcultures to form and resist. So many of the slogans of music subculture, such as the hippie mantra 'feed your head', or the rave injunction to 'fight for the right to party', smack of the inclination to either retreat from society, or co-exist as sacrificial units that promote social disapproval without changing the rules of the game that reproduce division, fraction and inequality.

This is not to say that music subcultures are politically insignificant. Tom Frank (1998) and Jim McGuigan (2009) clearly demonstrate that the hippie counterculture of the 1960s and 1970s left an indelible mark on Western civilization in respect of culture, politics and business. However, their decisive point is that the mind-expanding effect of the counterculture was primarily cultural and was assimilated by dominant economic and political interests. It did not lead to a social revolution that fundamentally transformed the pyramid of political power or the distribution of wealth. Indeed, the messages to listen to the people, take care of your head and body and respect social difference were successfully colonized by entrepreneurs and used to revive capitalism by producing 'cool' or 'neat' forms of it.

Subculturalism, then, only takes us so far in understanding pop music and pop culture. It is enormously abundant in detail about the fabric and texture of music subcultures and the conditional ways in which they interact with the trans-subcultural world. Willis (2000: 28) ventures that examining subcultures as sensuous forms of life reveals general ideological meanings since they enable us to compare the sensual fullness of subcultural forms with the poverty and meanness of wider capitalist society and its demands for subordination. As for the subculturalist tradition, taking the next step, which is to propose a social, political and economic strategy of transformation that would ensure equality, justice and the end of want, persists as an unwritten promise rather than a concete realization.

Relationism

Within the study of pop music, relationism is a nascent approach. Properly speaking, it is still confined to one full-length study, namely Sarah Thornton's (1995) investigation of UK club cultures. The reason for assigning it prominence here stems from the extraordinary, largely posthumous (at least in the Anglo-American sphere), acclamation of Pierre Bourdieu as a seminal theorist of modern culture and the penetrating relevance of his thought to culture for the study of popular music. Thornton's approach makes liberal use of Bourdieu's ideas and arguments, but, as we shall see, by no means exhausts the potential of his contribution.

Now, Bourdieu never wrote at length about pop. Yet his account of the field of cultural production (Bourdieu 1993) abounds in transferable principles that apply readily to the subject of pop music and pop culture. Although it is part of the agency perspective that portrays individuals as knowledgeable, active agents, it does so by imposing a realist stamp upon research and debate.

Realism holds that an objective, material world exists independently of, yet accessible to, consciousness. Our perspectives and behaviours are not arbitrary matters. We cannot act just as we please, nor are our thoughts and perspectives the product of chance. Rather, thought and action are products of the objective world. The mistakes we make have objective causes. The more we understand them accurately, the greater is our power to act productively upon the world.

What Bourdieu (1993: 30) proposes of the science of the literary field transfers easily to the analysis of pop:

The science of the literary field is a form of *analysis situs* which establishes that each position – e.g. the one which corresponds to a genre such as the novel or, within this, to a sub-category such as the 'society novel' or the 'popular' novel – is subjectively defined by the system of distinctive properties by which it can be situated relative to other positions; that every position, even the dominant one, depends for its very existence, and for the determinations it imposes on its occupants, on the other positions constituting the field; and that the structure of the field, i.e. of the space positions, is nothing other than the structure of the distribution of the capital of specific properties that govern success in the field and the winning of external or specific profits (such as literary prestige) which are at stake in the field.

Cultural production, then is understood as a field of force and a field of struggle.

In Bourdieu's sociology, the term 'field' possesses a technical rather than a metaphorical meaning. It refers to a structured space that conditions the behaviour of individuals. By describing cultural production as a field of force, Bourdieu is seeking to convey the notion that action is structurally positioned. That is, it bears the imprint of class, gender, race, nation, religion, occupation and other social divisions. Conversely, by making the differentiation between fields of force and *struggle*, he is directing attention to the role of subjective and group consciousness in propagating action. This is important because relationism rejects both the proposition that action is structurally determined (structuralism) and the proposition that it is simply a matter of personal creativity and motivation (agency). Instead, it strives to combine the insight that subjective and group action is structurally conditioned with the recognition that social actors are knowledgeable, capable, competent and reflexive agents situated in contexts of cultural scarcity.

For relationism, society consists of a plurality of relatively autonomous fields in which individuals are situated, and through which they engage in transactions. So there is the economic field, the political field, the field of the arts, the field of pop music, and so on. Similarly, within the field of pop there are sub-fields based around genre and subculture: rhythm and blues, soul, progressive, punk, post-punk, folk rock, grunge, techno, hip hop, rap, and so on. Each field is structured by distinct conditions of resource allocation, institutional frameworks, aesthetic codes and systems of representation and accompanying protocols of behaviour.

Agency is therefore presented not as a matter of freedom, but as a matter of situated action. What this means is that relationism proceeds as if all individuals have the capacity for conscious action; but consciousness and action are comprehended as positioned in relation to coherent fields of economic, social, cultural and political difference and inequality. It is this social positioning that applies a governing influence upon thought and action. But this positioning is also understood as the resource from which subjective and group agents deliberately launch innovation.

Thus, with respect to pop music, composition, performance and consumption are understood to be, above all, matters of social positioning. The question is: how are individuals and groups positioned? Relationism presents social positioning to be a subject of access to cultural and other forms of capital. Bourdieu and Passeron (1990: 30) define cultural capital as the cultural goods transmitted by families. The family provides the individual with the principles that generate and organize perception, a sense of belonging and the tools of social practice.

Bourdieu (1990: 53) uses the term *habitus* to refer to these principles and practices. Although the term clearly suggests 'habits' of thought and behaviour, it is polyvalent. In Bourdieu's (1984, 1990, 1993) work the main meanings of *habitus* are:

(a) the generative mental and linguistic framework that conditions thought and agency;
(b) the 'feel for the game' or 'practical sense' that enable individuals to negotiate with, and impact upon, social life;
(c) the preferences that individuals make for the whole range of cultural goods and practices; and
(d) the 'second sense' that individuals possess to go about living in, and acting upon, the world.

Habitus is the precondition for agency since it equips individuals with the know-how, sense of body and cultural orientation to do this or that. The concept is distinct from rational choice models of human behaviour, for integral to it is the premise that partial, partisan and irrational cultures are transmitted to individuals as well as rational ones.

While the family is pivotal in *habitus*, it is in no sense singular. The nature and quality of cultural goods that each family transmits are a product of the objective world and the actions of the family as an agent upon that world. The primary social components of the modern objective world are distinctions of class, race, ethnicity, nation and status. The family is permeated by these distinctions. They are all components of *habitus*. From the standpoint of relationism, how could anything other be the case? According to this perspective, singularity – and, by extension, creativity – is not understood as a unique, non-recurring phenomenon. Rather, it is socially formed in the sense that our capacity to understand and communicate its meaning derives from language and shared understanding. As such, it is integral to *habitus*. Creative action is the intersection of *habitus* with field. When a 50 Cent or a Chris Martin enters the field, respectively, of rap or post-9/11, he brings with him the *habitus* in which he is positioned. At its best, the engagement of *habitus* with field produces new values that transform the meaning of both *habitus* and field.

Thornton and Club Capital

Earlier I stated that the principal full-length study of Bourdieu's approach in the study of pop culture and pop music is Thornton's (1995) investigation of dance and club culture. What does she say? After Bourdieu, she portrays dance culture as, first and foremost, a field of cultural capital. Actually, her term is 'subcultural capital'. By this, she means the resources that young people exploit and develop in order to acquire distinction in the field of club culture (Thornton 1995: 185). In terms of the subcultural hierarchy outlined in the previous section, young people seek to use music, fashion, drugs and language to achieve the status of avatars and apprentices. The status struggle in the field of dance and club culture fastens upon being recognized as cool or hip (or having what Bourdieu calls 'distinction'). Upon the successful social acknowledgement of this perception, rewards follow.

Now, being perceived as cool or hip presupposes considerable social and cultural awareness. In the terminology applied to describe the hierarchy of subcultural formation, the individual must be conversant with the rules and expectations of the field and, in addition, produce tags of competence, credibility and relevance that not only broker acceptance, but also bestow the cachet of an avatar. By being astute in the accumulation and transaction of subcultural capital, individuals can employ markers of age, gender, sexuality and ethnicity to neutralize factors of class, income and occupation (Thornton 1995: 105). For Thornton, the *habitus* of subcultural capital is fanzines, the music media and generational cultures. Today we might add Facebook, MySpace, Last.fm, Twitter and YouTube.

However, it does not suffice to develop social practices that are cool and hip; they must be recognized as such. Thornton's study clearly conveys the point that distinction is not merely asserted, it must also be *recognized* and *practised*. For example, through entry quotas, clubs impose standards of social discrimination that govern subcultural recruitment and integration. This is consistent with the main principle of relationism, which is that cultural production is not simply a matter of action on the part of the apparent producer, namely, in the field of pop, the composer, the musician and the subcultural avatar. The questions of who authorizes the apparent producer, and what gives the latter the authority to claim individuality, creativity or leadership in the field, are also decisive (Bourdieu 1993: 76).

After the 1960s, the close connection between distinction, audiences and music sales dramatically boosted the power of distribution and marketing divisions of record corporations. From the perspective of relationism, music is, in part, a means of conveying distinction. It follows that the geography of distinction is a major preoccupation in the record business since profit and loss accounts ultimately depend upon it. Accurately measuring trends and anticipating changes in the market have become life-and-death issues. Because of this, the power of marketing and distribution divisions which supply market data about what product types work with an audience has become more important than the gut feeling or hunches of A&R men or record producers. Keith Negus (1999: 174) argues that there are two main reasons for this.

Firstly, distribution and marketing divisions are key corporate 'repositories of knowledge' about artistic trends and listening habits. Market research about what kind of music genres and musicians are popularly associated with distinction influence corporate decisions relating to contract policy and production strategy.

Secondly, these divisions play a vital part in monitoring sales. This is the basis for developing rewards and sanctions governing the number of recordings produced and released by music corporations.

Negus (1999) is far from being a disciple of Bourdieu. Nonetheless, he provides an insightful understanding of the potential value that a relationist approach can bring to the analysis of pop music. He submits (Negus 1999: 20) that the chief contributions of relationism are as follows:

1   *Defining musical interest as related to habitus and field.* Bourdieu's approach is holistic. It approaches musical taste preferences as expressions of wider fields of force. It encourages us to view music as part of 'a whole way of life'. This carries important implications not only for how music is produced and exchanged by musicians, but also for how it is distributed and marketed by record corporations.

2   *Combatting an individualistic-economistic view of musical production.* Music is the
     outcome of meaningful practices that are interpreted and comprehended in a
     variety of ways and given meaning in many different social situations. Just as
     the output of the musician derives from the intersection of *habitus* with field,
     the production of the record company is not driven primarily by an economic/
     organizational logic, but by the intersection of the corporation with market
     culture.

Negus (1999: 20) concludes, à la Bourdieu: 'Culture, thought of more broadly as
a way of life and as the actions through which people create meaningful worlds
in which to live, needs to be understood as the constitutive context within and
out of which the sounds, words and images of popular music are made and given
meaning.'

So much for the potential of relationism in the analysis of pop. What of the
strengths and weaknesses of the approach?

Relationism describes things very well. It challenges the charismatic ideology
in pop music which privileges the composer and the star as decisive sources of
creative value. The *habitus* of composers, performers and audiences is given its due
for being unique.

But what matters in the communication of culture is the intersection of *habitus*
with the field of production. The field of production is understood to be a field of
force and struggle in which artists and audiences are socially positioned to face
a series of available options in the practice of social action. The dynamics of the
field are concerned with the social struggles of agents intent upon accumulating
cultural capital. A pop song or pop genre that captures the structure of feeling
characteristic of a particular time and place generates both economic resources and
cultural power.

For example, Nirvana's 'Smells Like Teen Spirit' (1991) quickly became a grunge
anthem and a calling card for Generation X: that is, the generation raised in the
context of the end of the Cold War, the revival of neo-liberalism and the expansion
of the computer in work and recreation settings. The popular success of the song
created a horizon for emulation. The shift of economic and cultural resources to
grunge conditioned the available options open to pop by setting the bar against
which other musical productions were measured.

Relationsism is anti-reductionist in two ways. Firstly, it rejects the 'great man'
theory of pop, which explains creativity in terms of the prowess of the individual.
Secondly, it refuses to analyse practice in pop music culture as the reflection of
the interaction between *habitus* and field. As the term implies, relationism involves
examining agency and practice in the context of interlocking circuits of production.

The main criticism of relationism is that it has not overcome the dichotomy
of control and resistance from which it aspired to exit. The concept of 'field'
was designed to generate a more flexible approach to cultural production. In
particular, it aimed to avoid the homogenizing tendencies of subculturalism: that
is, the proposition that subcultures are monolithic vibe tribes bound by common
standards of dress, language, taste and uniform types of practice. Thus, Thornton's
(1995) study of dance and club culture honed the concept of subcultural capital
to convey variation and suppleness in music taste cultures and fasten upon the

central significance of embodiment and performance. However, her work has been criticized for failing adequately to relate taste cultures to wider forms of popular culture. Thornton's analysis of clubbers is attacked for presenting them as cultural monads who only become fulfilled in club settings. It is as if she leaves the rest of their lives as a blank page and merely assumes alienation therein (Carrabine and Longhurst 1999: 128).

Similarly, Dan Laughey (2006: 41) argues that underlying Thornton's emphasis upon embodiment and performance is an older mindset which sentimentally portrays club cultures as fronts of resistance. As such it is vulnerable to the charge that it ultimately *revises* subculturalism rather than reworks it into a genuinely new paradigm. The concepts of *habitus*, field and subcultural capital are reminiscent of class/status location, class/status boundaries and cultural inequality. Relationism is therefore viewed as guilty of the old fault of pouring new wine into old bottles.

Transcendentalism

From Robert Johnson to Jimi Hendrix , Hank Williams to Lucinda Williams, The Doors to Led Zeppelin, Frank Zappa to Elbow, Marvin Gaye to Jay-Z, pop music articulates various intimations of transcendence. The term has two separate meanings that correspond to the religious and secular outlooks.

In organized religion, transcendentalism refers to the existence of creative realities located at the edge of sense experience. Thus, superhuman forces, be they thought of in terms of a deity, the gods or some other cosmic power, are credited with possessing active influence upon the affairs of humanity and nature (Strawson 1966). Transcendentalism is described here as a version of the agency approach because it involves the proposition that individuals and groups consciously use music to expand consciousness. This expanded state may inhere in everything we are and all that we do, but music is acknowledged to be the key that unlocks the door.

The secular meaning of the term has been explored in political philosophy from Locke's theory of natural rights, through Marx's theory of communism, to Hardt and Negri's (2000) commentary on the necessary steps to achieve the emancipation of the 'multitude'. Simply put, what is common to these writers is a vision of a society of plenty that acknowledges distributive justice, the legitimacy of difference, social inclusion and the death of religion and superstition. The salient implications that follow from this are threefold.

Firstly, human form and experience are understood to be limited. From the religious standpoint, the limitations follow from absolute, ineffable forces that exert ultimate influence upon the world. Secular thought holds a very different conception of limitation, having to do with the form of society and, in particular, the relations of production, which are held to act as shackles upon the full realization of human potential.

Secondly, both the religious and secular perspectives are founded in the proposition that humans have a presentiment of a greater or higher universal existence that lies beyond the fringes of current conditions. From a religious standpoint, we can touch the feet of God or converse with cosmic forces through disciplined holy actions or forms of rational behaviour. The secular tradition views religion as superstition and the product of social control. Yet it possesses a strong commitment to go beyond existing social conditions by acting decisively to break the social, economic and political binds that truss human experience.

Thirdly, both the religious and secular perspectives acknowledge the value of ceremonial or ritual actions in operationalizing and extending presentiments of greater or higher forms of existence. In religion, sacred contemplation, devotion, prayer and collective worship perform this function. In the secular tradition, collective agitation, organization and resistance are pivotal.

The philosophical influence underpinning transcendentalism is, of course, Hegel. According to Hegel (1949, 1977), culture is a key instrument in achieving the fulfilment and unity of the human spirit. In order to achieve this unity, the spirit must dissolve the hurdles between itself and the object of its contemplation. For our purposes, pop is, first, an object of contemplation and, second, a cultural means of dissolving the obstacles between the human spirit and the external world. Through it, the spirit attains fulfilment and unity. In Hegel's view it is unacceptable to suppose that perfect ultimate unity and fulfilment are possible. This is because evolution is based in the idea of the perpetual negation of the previous stage of attainment.

A Hegelian reading of pop music, then, would see the various historical genres of hippie, progressive, reggae, punk, post-punk, riot-grrrl, grunge, nu-metal, rap, hip hop and bhangra as the unfolding of the absolute human spirit. The negation of each genre is implicit in the contradictions of the previous stage and the human spirit's unquenchable yearning for complete unity.

There is a deep connection between music and religious and secular forms of transcendence (Gay 1996: 24–5). The exponents of pop music are frequently regarded as possessing Christ-like, sacrificial qualities. As early as the 1860s, Cosima Wagner was comparing music to secular religion. 'Our art', she declared in a letter to King Ludwig II, 'is religion, its bearers are martyrs' (quoted in Gutman 1968: 252). The early deaths of Buddy Holly, Elvis Presley, Sam Cooke, John Lennon, Jimi Hendrix, Jim Morrison, Janis Joplin, Marvin Gaye, Ian Curtis, Kurt Cobain and Michael Jackson appear to fulfil the association of a sacrificial cult organized around popular music that challenges conventions and breaks boundaries.

The relationship between music and religion is central in most tribal societies. According to Mircea Eliade (1964: 175, 179), music is employed as a 'magical instrument' that supports the undertaking of ecstatic journeys and ensures their success. Anthropologists have documented the relationships of drums, bells, singing and dancing to the shamanic trance. Music is held to raise group awareness of boundaries (liminality), the passage of transitions from youth to maturity and life to death, the migration to the spirit world and ceremonies of belonging and exclusion. In tribal ritual and ceremonial practice, music transports the individual and the group from ordinary consciousness to states of ecstasy and sublime experience.

The German ethnologist Holger Kalweit (2001) describes the central relationship between music and transcendence in his observation of six stages in the shamanic séance performed for the purpose of healing at a Tibetan refugee camp. In the first stage, the lhapa, or 'god-man', burns incense and commences to sing softly. Gradually, a drum and bell are used for accompaniment. As the beat ascends to a crescendo, the lhapa begins to enter a trance state.

In the second stage he dons an apron, a lotus-shaped drape is placed over his head and a red cloth binds his forehead. As the trance quickens, and the self-abandonment of the oracle approaches, he emits a soft 'melodic' whistling. The sound signifies the presence and gradual possession of the spirits.

The third stage of complete possession is marked by the lhapa 'losing himself in waves of sound' and blessing the crowd (through sprinkling water and throwing rice over them). The drum-beats accelerate and intensify and the lhapa dances rhythmically, casting piercing glances back and forth as he communicates with the spirits.

The fourth stage is marked by the lhapa asking a spirit to answer questions put to him by the crowd. The answers are accompanied with more drumming and dancing. Whistling is used to signify the arrival or departure of a lha, another spiritual being.

The fifth stage consists of healing. Again to the accompaniment of drums and bells, played at a different rhythm and pitch, a cloth is laid over the painful spot on the body of the supplicant. A drum is laid over the cloth and the lhapa sucks out the sickness. In time he rises slowly, and expectorates a string of black fluid before cleansing and refreshing his mouth with water.

The final stage of the séance involves the renewal of separation from the presence of the spirit world. The lhapa kneels, again accompanied by 'vigorous' drum-beats and chants, to be led back from the spirit world. The departure of the lha is signalled by soft whistling and the séance closes with 'utter silence'.

In Kalweit's (2001: 181–3) words, the trance and presence of living spirits are symbolized in various ways, most notably by the 'drum rhythm', 'the hellish din', 'the high voice of the oracle', the 'sound of the bell' and 'the unbridled movements' of the lhapa. The Tibetan healing séance uses musical methods of sensory overload, refined over millennia, to create a 'contagious' 'wild symphony' that 'fragments the ego structure' and produces a 'state of sympathetic flow, dissolution, emptying out, pure being'.

Anthropologists have explored analogous cases of the privileged relationship between music, shamanism, trance and 'pure being' among tribes in sub-Sahara (Wilson 1985), Western North America (Park 1938), Siberia (Dioszegi 1968) and South-West Africa (Marshall 1962). The African musicologist W. Komla Amoaku (1985: 34–5), in a study of the Ewe of Ghana, refers to the power of music to produce 'spiritual upliftment', 'transcendental imaginations of a 'spirit world' and a route into 'the world beyond'. In the literature, the link between music and transcendence is understood to be universal (Sylvan 2002).

For example, Gurevich (1972: 61) demonstrates that music is a device for promoting transcendence in medieval Christian religion. To the medieval mind, it reveals the harmonic unity between humanity and the universe. Music is understood to transport humanity to the heavenly spheres. Here the orderliness of the world, and discord and strife, are perceived as coming from the mouth of God. Music helps to achieve the joyful acceptance of God, and the sorrowful falling short of his example. Attali (1977) makes a similar point in his advocacy of the thesis that music produces a collective sense of order that militates against primordial psychological fears of impending annihilation by the vengeance of God, the indifference of nature or human warfare.

The secular tradition also identifies a strong connection between music and transcendence. Max Weber (1922: 157–8) notes that music and dance exert an 'intoxicating effect' that disarm inhibitions. He argues that they have been employed with other stimulants such as alcohol, tobacco and drugs to produce 'acute toxic states' that induce euphoria and ecstasy.

Charisma and Pop

In the classical sociological discussion, Weber (1922: 2) notes:

> Charisma may be either of two types. Where this appellation is fully merited, charisma is a gift that inheres in an object or person by virtue of natural endowment. Such primary charisma cannot be acquired by any other means. But charisma of the other type may be produced artificially in an object or person through some extraordinary means.

Thus, charisma is either an unmediated quality, in that the person who possesses it simply commands authority over others; or it is a mediated quality that is produced artificially by specific types of governance.

Most commentators agree that the charismatic form of authority is most commonly found in traditional society (Hamilton 2001; Zuckerman 2003). This is because modern societies possess a number of social institutions, such as the political system, the education sector and the mass media, with the capacity to expose the hiatus between the assertion and verification of charisma. Yet, charismatic forms survive into contemporary society.

Burns (1978) developed an influential theory of charismatic leadership. He argues that charismatic leaders provide forceful role models, based upon transparent values, strong vision and confident powers of communication. Among followers, when it is successful, charismatic leadership promotes obedience, emotional involvement, affection and strong trust responses. Burns concludes that charisma is still a meaningful force in contemporary society.

Other commentators argue that it is a misuse of the term to apply it to the business sphere. The original meaning of charisma identifies it as a dynamic and transformational force in the whole of society. For its part, the charisma of business leaders is generally more limited to a reaction against routinization, emphasizing the organizational advantages of decisiveness, glamour and energetic action. But this is quite different from Weber's concept, which identifies charisma as a total revolutionary force.

In this manner, Bryan Wilson (1975: 124) holds that the strongest survival of charismatic qualities can be found in leisure-time, recreational activity, in the mass appeal of popular entertainers. However, as with the category of charismatic business leaders, this is a 'weak manifestation' that exists 'peripherally' and 'interstitially' in contemporary society:

> The language used of these entertainers echoes – perhaps only in consequence of the debasement of the linguistic coinage by publicity agents – the language of charisma. They are *idols*, their performances are *magic*, their qualities are *fantastic*, and *fabulous*. . . . The manifestations of individual

ecstasy and group frenzy at their performances perhaps outdo those at the
reception of messianic claimants in the past. But such figures enjoy neither
political significance nor enduring social regard. They make no specific
claims for themselves: they are simply the recipients of extraordinary social
acclaim, and the stimulators of extraordinary psychological responses.
(Wilson 1975: 124, emphasis in original)

Thus, Wilson concludes that the charisma of popular entertainers is weak and
segmented compared with precedents in traditional society. It is largely a mediated
form that relies upon the management skills of pop impresarios. Such charisma is
packaged and publicized and very different from the real thing.

The press regularly uses the appellation 'charisma' to describe modern pop
performers. Jimi Hendrix, Mick Jagger, Robert Plant, Bob Marley, Sting, Nick
Cave, Neil Young, Tom Waits, Bono, Prince, Beyoncé, Shakira, Christina Aguilera,
Madonna, 50 Cent and Ice-T have all been so described. What is the evidence that
these performers are truly charismatic? To begin with, the extraordinary qualities
that they possess are limited. While magical powers are often attributed to them,
they are compartmentalized from the rest of life. It is one thing for Bono, Madonna
or Shakira to exert a magical effect on the stage. But discomfort and reaction
follow strongly when the same stars affect to transfer this magical effect to the
sphere of politics. Cooper (2008) demonstrates that celebrity diplomats such as
Bono, Michael Jackson and Sting have engendered questions about sincerity and
the misuse of power. Paul McCartney's attempt in 2009 to launch 'Meat-Free
Mondays' for the advanced world prompted similar reactions, to say nothing of
outright hostility from the meat farming lobby.

Another difference is that the authority of these stars is not primarily linked to
organized religions or political institutions. It is true that the relationship between
some pop stars and religion is well publicized. Madonna's faith in Kabbalah is
a case in point. However, unlike traditional charismatic figures, pop stars are
essentially secular agents playing to audiences that are, on the whole, secular.
Pop songs may act as allegories of the better society and be compatible with some
forms of quasi-mystical experience. However, they are not, as such, sacramental,
nor do composers and performers consistently operate with a division between
a theocracy and the laity. To be sure, when pop stars have claimed religious
sensibilities, such as Michael Jackson, George Harrison, Bob Dylan or Yusuf Islam,
they have provoked scepticism, ridicule and incredulity.

Another difference is that traditional charismatic figures were primarily
spiritual. Their dynamic, revolutionary force resided in the extraordinary qualities
inherent in or claimed for their personalities and their associated vision of
alternative, higher forms of being and society. In contrast, pop stardom correlates
strongly with materialism. Even where they have criticized materialism, as is
the case with the music and lives of George Harrison and Michael Jackson,
their personal wealth was not abandoned or significantly shared out with the
disadvantaged. Bono's role in care-giving and charity is so ubiquitous that Cooper
(2008) refers to the 'Bonoization of celebrity diplomacy'. Notwithstanding this,
Cooper (2008: 120) goes on to comment that, in contrast with other celebrity
diplomats, notably Angelina Jolie, Bono is 'not a generous donor' to the causes

that he supports. Bono's primary role is to network and channel resources from wealthy backers such as Bill Gates and George Soros.

In sum, the balance of evidence suggests that celebrity charisma possesses conspicuous limits when it is transferred from the vector of entertainment and applied to wider society. Pop stars who turn to celebrity diplomacy may use emotional cues and performative tactics derived from the world of the shaman. But their authority is strictly limited. Just as Wilson (1975) submits, the charisma of the pop star operates within tight boundaries, and is concentrated in the realm of entertainment. To refer to the charisma of pop stars as a dynamic or revolutionary force is therefore a misuse of the term.

At the same time, the states of fervour, intoxication and transport achieved by some types of pop music can be culturally significant. While it may be rash to see them as a total revolutionary force, they can have tangible spiritual effects. For example, Robin Sylvan's (2002) research into the fan base for the San Francisco acid rock group The Grateful Dead discovered strong associations of enchantment and delivery from the cares of the world and 'billowy' bliss with the music. The music enables fans to lose themselves, to gain a sense of expanded consciousness and make the transition into 'something other'. It creates a limited sense of universal oneness.

The society of 'peace and love', popularized by hippies in the 1960s, anticipated many of these themes. Brotherhood, sharing, non-violence, peaceful hedonism and other anti-materialist sentiments were ubiquitous features of the subculture. 'Our House' (1970) by Crosby, Stills and Nash, 'All You Need Is Love' (1967) by The Beatles and 'San Francisco (Be Sure to Wear Flowers in Your Hair)' (1967) by Scott McKenzie became hippie anthems. The music eschewed aggressive power riffs. The lyrics focused upon going beyond the ego and materialism to explore a community founded upon peace, love and understanding. Hippie subculture placed great faith in the value of interpersonal simplicity. Experimentation with hallucinogenic drugs and the selected forays into Eastern religion imbued hippie lifestyle with an 'eclectic orientalism, representing a return to contemplation and mystic experience' (Hall 1968: 8). Hippie subculture privileged empathy and experience over action and engagement. The music celebrated unity, solidarity and opposition. Todd Gitlin (1987: 201–4) characterizes the music of the counterculture as dividing into two genres:

(1) *Fantasy individualism*: that is, a form of music that allows the individual to act out illusions of autonomy and creativity. The music concentrated upon cultivating *inner space*. The purpose of the music of fantasy individualism is to urge the individual to *space out*.

Gitlin cites Bob Dylan's 'Mr Tambourine Man' (1965) as a leading example. The wave-like chord progressions back up lyrics that speak of 'Taking a trip/Upon your magic swirling ship; and 'Take me disappearing/Through the smoke rings of my mind'. It is a song that enjoins the listener to take a voyage into inner space, to navigate hidden psychic coastlines and submerged emotional waterways that have been blocked off by the repressive organization of capitalist accumulation.

Later, Dylan added to the palette of his repertoire by developing songs of social protest and social realism. 'Mr Tambourine Man' was sufficiently influential to inspire emulation, of which the most successful exemplars were, arguably, the Byrds, James Taylor and Crosby, Stills and Nash.

(2) *Communard utopianism*, that is, a music genre that concentrates upon unity, social inclusion and ethical progress. Hippie communards proselytized a 'one world' vision of life in which the periphery is recognized, embraced and incorporated. The question of incorporation into what was left fuzzy and unparticularized. Prior to the task of generating a strategy of progressive transformation is the business of opening yourself up to free love and the spirit of positive change. For Gitlin, a typical example of this genre is 'Let's Get Together' by Jefferson Airplane (1966), with its invocation to 'smile on your brother' and 'love one another right now'.

Communard utopianism was buttressed by a strong belief in fate and the liberal use of mystical wisdom. The *I Ching* was a revered accessory of subcultural lifestyle. It provided a glimpse into the inalienable forces of fate. Communal gatherings praising togetherness and peace were also popular, such as the 'Human Be-In' (1967) in San Francisco and the climax of the hippie age, the so-called 'Festival of Life' held at Woodstock, New York State (1969).

For a while, the positive atmosphere of hippie subculture kept the fissures between ego and collectivity, materialism and anti-materialism at bay. In Gitlin's (1987: 206) words: 'The tension between the individualist ethos of "Mr Tambourine Man" and the communality of "Let's Get Together" was, for the time being, submerged in a great surge of animal joy. The emerging counterculture longed for both, for the fusion of the two.'

The year of Woodstock, 1969, was also the year of Altamont, the event, above all others, that signalled the end of the so-called 'Age of Aquarius'. This was a West Coast 'Free Festival of Life', heralded by The Rolling Stones as the finale of their successful tour of North America, in which Jagger persistently flirted with the incarnation of the devil in his stage act. Altamont was an abject catastrophe. The concert was policed, on a semi-official basis, by Hell's Angels. The Stones arrived late on stage. The three hundred thousand-strong crowd, besotted by alcohol and pumped up by amphetamines and LSD, were bored, restless, glazed and unruly. The Angels were charged with protecting the stage and had been rewarded with free beer throughout the day. Some of them broke rank and became aggressively undisciplined. Marty Balin, a member of one of the support acts, Jefferson Airplane, was head-punched and knocked unconscious. But this was not why Altamont became notorious in the annals of rock festivals.

Meredith Hunter, a black man, high on amphetamines, offended the Angels by trying to get too close to the stage. As Jagger sang 'Under My Thumb', Hunter drew a revolver from his pocket. The Angels restrained him but in the ensuing fracas he was knifed and died.

At Altamont, the hippie dream disintegrated. It was not just a matter of the murder of Hunter. Altamont was not about an overwhelming, authentic connection between performers and an audience. Rather, it was about the audience being herded like cattle with inadequate food, drink, sanitation or medical services, and a headline act that was so cosseted and pampered with the trappings of fame that they were disassociated from the discomfort of their fans, and unable to execute authority over their praetorian guard.

Altamont was the antithesis of transcendence. It was absurd to talk about peace, love and understanding in a setting where Hell's Angels threatened the crowd with baseball bats and pool cues and the audience carried guns in their pockets. As the rock journalist Greil Marcus reminisced: 'It was the worst day I'd ever been through. Not just in a direct, personal sense of being physically threatened and seeing awful things over and over again, but seeing everything I had devoted myself to as a writer and editor turn to garbage' (quoted in DeRogitas 2000: 61).

Hippie culture changed many aspects of postwar society. It both reflected and reinforced the values of the permissive society, and unwittingly sowed the seeds for the neo-liberal revolt of the 1980s and 1990s. It gave capitalism a human face, demanding the right of the consumer to be heard and the producer to provide relevant products that make a difference (Frank 1998; McGuigan 2009). This was so momentous that some commentators use terms like 'cool capitalism', 'the new capitalism' and 'neat capitalism' to signal the emergence of a new type of capitalist formation in the 1960s (Rojek 2007; Sennett 2007; McGuigan 2009). Fantasy individualism and communard utopianism carried a certain elasticity that rendered them adaptable to rapidly changing conditions. Notwithstanding this flexibility and the impulse to collectivism that it supported, the result was the production of new cleavages, based initially around the ownership and control of cultural capital, and later upon the crystallization of economic divisions.

The urge to transcend economic, cultural and social divisions and reach higher states of consciousness is common in youth subcultures. Because youth subcultures precede the disciplines of paid labour, career, family and home ownership, they are often fiercely anti-materialist. For example, rave culture, which peaked in the UK in the so-called 'second summer of love' (1988/9), was organized around propulsive DJing and a party ethic. Rave drew on three metropolitan musical influences: Detroit techno, Chicago house and New York garage. All three were forms of industrial music privileging rhythm and driving bass/drum arrangements over harmony and melody. The musical origins stretch further back to the 1970s with the European 'post-human' synth and drum music pioneered by European artists like Kraftwerk, Can and Gary Numan.

Rave was based in turbo-charged, electronically generated 'dance music', like 'house', 'electronica', 'jungle' and 'techno'. Ideologically speaking, the origins of rave lay in an amalgamation of psychedelia (the second summer of love, counterculture, drug use), punk (do it yourself, the brutalist noise aesthetic) and disco (dance, party) (Reynolds 1998: 520). The subculture made prolific use of drugs like LSD and Ecstasy (MDMA). In a parallel with hippie culture, MDMA was associated with expanding consciousness and an underground sensibility.

Initially, rave eschewed politics in favour of mere escapism, spontaneity, celebration of embodiment and social inclusion. Raves offered a 'glorious communal experience' and the 'illusion of exhilarating unity' without any necessary religious connotation (Garratt 1998: 258). The use of MDMA, and the media-reported risks that are said to surround it, revived the relationship between popular music and sacrificial cults. However, in a move that signalled a profound change in the relationship between the artist and the consumer, the sacrificial cult was now focused on the audience. The audience was now literally dying for the music.[2]

In the beginning, rave regarded itself as part of an anti-capitalist moment that saw through the illusions of the work ethic. As such, it defined itself against mainstream corporate values and possessive individualism. Reynolds (1998: 520) gets it right when he describes rave as a 'post-socialist culture'. Various types of entrepreneurial activity were pivotal, such as organizing warehouse or 'chill-out' parties, promoting events, running small labels, DJing and selling CDs. In terms of cultural capital rave favoured flexible accumulation – changing party settings, seizing abandoned space and redefining it as a dance club, bootlegging, creating a downloadable DJ set, and so on. Gradually, from fighting for the issue of 'the right to party', the culture became interested in wider questions of power and control. This never solidified into a coherent political platform or genuine organized politics. On the other hand, it magnified the spirit of resistance against forms of capitalist censorship and punishment that were castigated as arbitrary and dispensable.

Rave was part of a youth culture ethos, reaching back to the first days of jive and rock and roll, which appreciated and relished the observation that pop music can get you out of your head and create connections with strangers that are so potent that an inexorable sense of euphoria and solidarity ensues. Anyone who attends a successful pop concert or clubbing night knows this. If you hear 'No Future' by The Sex Pistols, Television's 'Venus De Milo' or Dr Dre's 'Nuthin' But a "G" Thang', you either immediately connect or react to, respectively, punk, post-punk and hip hop subculture. The music is a gateway into the lifestyle and suggests a bigger, richer personal and collective form of existence, a 'concrete unity', to repeat Lévi-Strauss's term. The particulars of the whole situation, and the bigger, richer picture, are unspecified. Yet their effect may be life-changing. It might not lead to religion, but it does permanently expose much that is common in everyday life as listless, gnomic and in need of an emulsifying brush of some sort of sacred quality.

Sylvan (2002: 215) brings all of this together when he writes of popular music and the state of transcendence:

> The musical experience is a unique mode of being-in-the-world in which the dualities of subject–object, body–mind, and spiritual–material are transcended in a unified field. Music allows people to become part of the unified field in which the spiritual dimension is directly expressed as a powerful state that is integrated with all the other levels.

What can be said in response to this? The capacity of music to transport us from routine and the cares of the world to engender positive feelings relating to precepts of a greater whole and unity is so richly documented that it is not in serious doubt. The critical issue turns on the nature of 'revelation'.

In their heyday, rave DJs and acid rock bands like The Grateful Dead and Jefferson Airplane were widely held to transport audiences into contact with absolute, ineffable forces that might be called God, Buddha, spirits, the divine, or what have you. The music is presented as, to borrow a term from Husserl's phenomenology, effecting a 'bracketing-out' of experience, levering listeners from the material level into some sort of cosmic fountainhead. The claims that The Grateful Dead, Jefferson Airplane or rave has the power to extract audiences from this world to other-worldly, transhuman realms may appear to be fantastical to us. But the intensity and persistence of these claims with devotees should not be taken lightly. Transparently, this music carries spiritual qualities for audiences. Yet the proposition that this music 'brackets out' consciousness from material experience and relates being to the divine is objectionable, on at least three counts.

To begin with, the first-person experience of 'bracketing' raises the difficult question of why not all people acknowledge the divine when they come into contact with rave music or the music of The Grateful Dead, Jefferson Airplane and other transcendental bands. If the divine is universally obscured from ordinary consciousness by veils shielding perception, why is it that only some people experience contact with the divine through transcendental genres?

Secondly, if it is accepted that divine experience is bracketed out of the realm of material consciousness, upon what basis is it plausible to regard transcendental music as providing access to this excluded realm? Moyn (2005), drawing on Levinas's concept of 'overflowing', argues that the notion of a radical 'bigger thing' permeates all experience. To submit that transcendental music is the expression of the 'overflowing' of experience is one thing. To propose that transcendental music provides direct contact with the divine is altogether more controversial and problematic.

Thirdly, if it is viable to analyse music as text, how can it be held that the effect of transcendental music is the result of contact with the divine rather than the mere organization of notes, silences and words? If the limits of experience are demarcated by texts, as Ludwig Wittgenstein and others have proclaimed, what is the basis for holding that transcendental genres go beyond these boundaries? Another way of looking at it is that they are the articulations of textually defined desires and yearnings to 'go beyond'.

For the transcendentalist, the plea for evidence is an issue of faith. One either believes in the experience that the music seems to be creating or one doesn't. Turning this around, the anti-transcendentalist school regards this belief precisely as the problem. The late 1990s Eurotrance style associated with Paul Van Dyk, Ferry Corsten, Tiesto, Energy 52 and Three Drives On a Vinyl aimed to create overwhelming feelings of euphoria and what might be termed 'the blissed unity' of the dancefloor. Ecstasy, which had suffered from associations of unreliability, was enthusiastically re-adopted as the dance drug of choice (Reynolds 1998: 439). The strong collective feelings of transcendence that are undoubtedly associated with Eurotrance are consonant with a belief in consciousness raising.

If natural reason is to be supported, this physical, mental and spiritual transport is not necessarily a matter of religious or spiritual agency. More prosaically, on biological and psychological grounds, the euphoria and empathy produced by Eurotrance might be said to be the result of the chemical action of Ecstasy, the pulsating beat of the music and the practice of ingesting the drug in groups. Similarly, from the perspective of social psychology, it might be the result of avatars, especially DJs, inducing clubbers to have overwhelming 'oceanic' feelings of transport and togetherness. There can be no doubt that DJs played a shamanic role in rave culture. As Reynolds (1998: 441) puts it, in respect of the British Eurotrance scene:

> Because E generates a surfeit of love and will-to-belief, a lot of energy ends up focused on the DJ. This syndrome of Ecstasy-induced worship elevated the first wave-of-rave DJ godstars like Sasha and Oakenfeld, and now it created a new pantheon of crowd pleasers like Tall Paul, Judge Jules and Paul Van Dyk. . . . Although Van Dyk himself rejected the linkage of his popularity to the Mitsubishi upsurge and claimed to have never tried Ecstasy, the dewy-eyed melodic refrains and twinkling textures like his glorious remix of Binary Finary's '1998' fit the MDMA sensation like a glove.

Marx (1964) famously describes religion as 'the opiate of the masses' in the 'Introduction' to his *A Contribution to the Critique of Hegel's Philosophy of Right*. He regards it as a component of ideology used to control and stupefy the people. Gramsci (1971) follows this tradition by maintaining that religion is a component of hegemony: that is, the system of compliance designed to achieve 'voluntary consent' by drawing the horizon of agency and practice within a given social formation. Hegemony does not proscribe debate and resistance. Rather it predisposes debate and resistance to follow tracks that comply with the persistence of the formation. From this vantage point, religious transcendentalism is nothing but capitulation to the *status quo*. It concentrates resources upon entering the higher or greater order of things. Pete Seeger, Paul Robeson, Bob Dylan, Phil Ochs, John Lennon, Crosby, Stills and Nash, Neil Young, Victor Jara, Silvio Rodriguez, Bruce Springsteen, Melba Moore and Devendra Banhart are town-criers of protests against political intrigue, demagoguery or the mere arbitrary nature of the current organization of everyday life. This genre of pop music elicits sensations of belonging, euphoria and transcendence. It is a continuation of Charles Taylor's (2004) idea of the social imaginary. Here, there is an intoxicating mixture of complaint, hope and aspiration.

The politics of transcendence in pop music has regular recourse to clichés like 'All You Need Is Love', 'We Are All Together' or 'Gotta Have a Friend in Jesus' (because we are all spirits in the sky). The motifs of 'coming together' or entering the universal kingdom of heaven thus conjured up are immediately attractive. However, for most people, on a second look, they do have a hollow ring. We cannot escape transcendentalism. If we are of a religious persuasion, we have faith in an afterlife and a supernatural purpose. If we are post-religious, and have risen above mere naked self-interest, we transfer this emotional energy upon a political plain and put our trust in various forms of progressive politics. Either way, the journey that precedes the destination becomes self-perpetuating. The tragedy of transcendentalism is that it tempts the birds from the trees, but condemns them to a state of eternal flight. A believer goes there with faith. But what of the remainder, who do not possess even the comfort of a belief in flight?

Textualism

Textualism is an approach that investigates pop music and pop culture as a sign system. While it has been extensively modified, the work of Saussure (1974) is of foundational importance in the textual approach. Saussure famously maintains that the linguistic sign is arbitrary. Thus there is no necessary connection between the word 'dog' and the animal quadruped. Saussure argues that language is a system of *signifiers* (words) linked in an arbitrary system of relationships to *signifieds* (concepts). The meaning of each sign derives from its relationship to other signs in the sign system. Hence, the analysis of signs has the power to reveal latent meanings that have an operational capacity upon cultural conduct.

Further, Saussure also distinguishes between *langue* (system of language) and *parole* (utterances). This opens the way to investigate meaning in terms of not only the meaning of words in the structure of the sign system, but also the inflection of meaning through the use of language in social practice. Saussure's method promised to establish a pure science of signs capable of decoding meaning and revealing the latent sense in communication.

The early work of Roland Barthes (1991, 1993, 1997) achieved prominence by adopting this method to examine commonplace cultural objects and practices in order to reveal their latent meanings. If Saussure's method promised a pure science of signs, Barthes sought to apply it in the analysis of pop culture. His work is not exactly in the Marxist tradition. Nevertheless, his use of the term *mythology* to describe the effect of popular cultural objects and practice upon the consciousness of the masses clearly suggests the systematic distortion of meaning and mass manipulation. This term is central in his work at this time. Inferentially it implies a commitment to overcoming ideology and achieving liberation.

Barthes's (1990: 295) famous distinction between the *pheno-song* and the *geno-song* parallels the distinction made by Saussure between *langue* and *parole*. The *geno-song* refers to the structural system that differentiates between the voice and inscription that make communication, representation and expression possible. For its part, the *pheno-song* refers to the idiolect and style of the composer and performer, that 'something' that a musician like Edith Piaf, Leonard Cohen or Bono brings to a refrain or entire song. With this somewhat conventional distinction, Barthes seems to be maintaining faith with semiotics as a pure science of signs: that is, a science capable of decoding the influence of class, ideology, racial supremacy, gender authority and national prejudice.

However, semiotic analysis never combined easily into models of class politics. An interest in the fertility of the sign, an acknowledgement that signs stubbornly refuse to be confined to fixed meanings, pushed against a union between semiotics and Marxism. This tension was reflected in Barthes's own writings. After he published *The Pleasure of the Text* (1975), the accent on manipulation and ideology recedes and is replaced with a polysemic reading of signs. Polysemy means that each sign potentially possesses an infinity of meanings (since it reflects the paradigmatic permutations of meaning temporarily excluded by a given utterance or inscription). Referring directly to music, albeit classical music, Barthes (1985: 245, 60) observed that modern listening 'no longer quite resembles . . . *listening to indices and listening to signs*. . . . What is listened to here and there . . . is not the advent of a signified, object of recognition or of a deciphering, but the very dispersion, the *shimmering* of signifiers' (emphasis in the original). This metaphor of *shimmering* is what concretely left its mark on the textualist approach to pop culture and pop music. For instead of being restricted to the task of decoding meaning by examining the relationships between *langue* and *parole*, analysis now moved on to consider the style and settings in which these relationships are articulated and how articulations are multiply signified and multiply interpreted. Inevitably, this raises separate questions of power and knowledge.

For students of pop culture and pop music, all of this was pulled together and developed most cogently by Dick Hebdige. His book *Subculture* (1979) is arguably the most influential textualist analysis of pop music and pop culture. It provided a semiotic approach to the study of pop culture and pop music which recognized social divisions and relations of power that engaged directly with the reggae and punk revolutions of the day. The book developed a semiotic analysis of style that enables readers to understand polysemy and the mobility of signifiers in relation to music, media, fashion and the vernacular of youth subcultures. Hebdige is not afraid to borrow concepts and methods from different perspectives to buttress his analysis. For example, in addressing the question of the use of piercing and the safety pin in punk fashion, he applies Lévi-Strauss's structuralist concept of *bricolage*. This refers to the mixture of different codes of culture and systems of representation that articulate a group logic in order to elucidate the world. Thus, the punk appropriation of the safety pin from the domestic setting and its relocation in the politics of youth culture were designed to redefine an object associated with the virtues of the household and re-label it as a sign of cultural confrontation. The effect was culturally unsettling. It symbolized misplaced arrangements and disorder that gelled with the punk outlook on political questions of unemployment, the family, the welfare state and bourgeois hypocrisy.

The method of *bricolage* was also evident in punk music. It drew upon elements of 'narcissism', 'nihilism' and 'gender confusion' from glam rock and mixed them with the minimalist aesthetic of American punk (The Ramones' 'Pinhead' and Crime's 'I Stupid'); the 'cult of the street' and sacrificial cults (self-laceration and piercing); Northern soul with its working-class ethos and 'acrobatic dancing'; reggae with its 'exotic and dangerous aura of forbidden identity', 'its conscience, its dread and its cool'. The effect was confrontational and unsettling. In the words of Hebdige (1979: 25), 'all these elements constantly threatened to separate and return to their original resources': the 'shimmering' of signifiers, to repeat Barthes.

Hebdige's work was securely located in the context of Britain in the 1970s. Significantly, the book has never been updated, suggesting perhaps the author's belief that it is a document of its time. It preceded the rise of globalization and the interest in world music and hybrid cultural forms that have dominated subsequent decades. Paradoxically, a later book by Hebdige, *Cut 'n' Mix* (1987), anticipated some of these developments in popular music and popular culture in the context of Caribbean youth culture, identity and lifestyle. But it was written before the significance of globalization was fully appreciated in the social sciences. It therefore does not quite give due to the extraordinary mixture of styles, acknowledgement of concealed ancestry and combination of contrasting musical genres represented by the world music tendency.

Other textualist approaches to popular music have been more adventurous. For example, Fung and Curtin (2002) examine the appeal and impact of the Chinese pop diva Faye Wong. Cinepoly, a Hong Kong subsidiary of a global multinational, constructed Wong's image as the embodiment of cosmopolitan modernity and

traditional Chinese femininity. This involved the calculated mixing of signs
to generate a positive response from the audience. For example, she adopted
the Cantonese pronunciation of her name, Wong Ching-Man, and an English
pseudonym, Shirley. Her large almond-shape eyes and tall stature were exploited
in publicity shots and promo videos to signify a female type that had critically
departed from traditional Chinese gender conventions. The erotic imagery that was
part of this construction was counterbalanced by the message in interviews and
song lyrics, such as 'Fragile Woman' (1992), that erotic fulfilment could only be
found in conventional, heterosexual marriage.

In 1991, Wong broke with these marketing devices and related image
constraints by taking a six-month vacation in New York to study music. She came
back with cover versions of songs by Björk, The Cranberries and The Cocteau
Twins that were unknown to Chinese audiences. Her public pronouncements
became more assertive and individual. She proclaimed that she is stubborn and
that her parents can't control her. This more international, spikey image translated
into commercial success. She became a heroine to teenage girls seeking 'lifestyle
alternatives' and fantasizing about gender relations 'outside the conventions of the
Chinese recording industry' (Fung and Curtin 2002: 274).

Pepsi-Cola exploited this new image by using Wong in a 1999 advertising
campaign. The ad focuses on Wong in an empty old school in Bejing looking at a
photo of herself as a young pupil dressed in a Mao-style uniform. This brings the
old classroom back to life and a teacher summons Wong to play the piano. From
the first chord, the screen is saturated in colour and Wong appears as an adult
rock star, with dreadlocks and a flowing dress, dancing in computer-animated
surf. She dances joyously and spontaneously, conveying a clear sense of release
and emancipation. Fung and Curtin argue that Faye Wong embodies and reflects
contradictory signs in Chinese sexual politics. A song like 'Chess' (1994) operates

> in the context of patriarchal Chinese societies. Rather than challenge
> patriarchy, the song is surprisingly resigned to a traditional play of power
> in domestic affairs. Yet when interpreted against Faye's star persona, an
> intertextual reading might suggest that modern women separate their
> domestic and professional roles. At the same time that a Chinese woman
> may resign herself to traditional love relations, she nevertheless finds
> possibilities for achieving control over certain aspects of her working life,
> suggesting a slippage between the public and private realms of experience.
> (Fung and Curtin 2002: 282)

Madonna's career in the Anglophone world supplies a relevant parallel. Her songs
and videos mix signs of experimental female sexuality and rebellion with idealized
typifications of daughterhood and maternity. Madonna recognizes herself to be
the perfect collection of female imperfections. Her song and video work convey
not one woman, but all women. As her career developed, she was criticized for
shuffling the pack of female roles and mood swings, from devoted mother to S&M
dominatrix, while remaining steadfastly faithful to the orthodox capitalist goal of
maximizing market share (Kaplan 1993; Tetzlaff 1993; Castles 1997). The point
that the image of Madonna is not truly polysemic, since the person it represents
remains quite ruthlessly attached to the profit motive, offers food for thought,

especially with respect to the commercial imperatives of the pop music business and the role of coding and representation in, so to speak, 'dissolving' reality (Aronowitz 1994).

The accent that textualism places upon coding and representation privileges an understanding of social reality as socially constructed. In this regard, the music video, which became an essential component of selling songs in the 1980s, especially through the influence of MTV, offers an entire field of study. Music videos do not simply represent songs, they entice preferred readings of narrative structure and social reality. Thus, the U2 video of 'One' (1991) condenses a stream of images relating to racial prejudice, disability, unemployment, disempowerment and poverty with a subtle set of connotations having to do with the overpowering might of stadium activism. Similarly, the promo for the Eels song 'Novocaine for the Soul' (1996), which features the band in gravity-defying weightlessness, combines denotations of the bio-chemical effect of the drug with images of quirkiness, estrangement from the dominant order and the misfit sensibility of alienation from consumer culture.

Drawing on Stuart Hall's (1980) path-breaking discussion of encoding and decoding, Cora Kaplan (1987) argues that music promos are styled to appropriate fragments from popular culture and mix them with selected presentations of contemporary culture in order to produce preferred readings which privilege this or that consideration. To enter the pop promo world is to enter a multi-textured space of embedded meanings that serve to confer distinction upon the *cognoscenti*. For example, the promo for Madonna's 'Material Girl' (1985) is a pastiche of the movie *Gentlemen Prefer Blondes* starring Marilyn Monroe and Jane Russell. For Kaplan the pop promo for MTV was littered with knowing references to other songs, films, TV shows and pop culture trivia.

Kaplan identifies five dominant types of encoding in pop promos:

1 *Romantic.* These feature a strong narrative, a standard dichotomy between loss and reunion and portray strong authority figures (usually parents).
2 *Socially conscious.* These consist of varied narrative structures, motifs of a struggle for independence and the problems of love, and present authority figures as objects of criticism.
3 *Nihilist.* These are against narrative structure and convey meaning through opposing or clashing images. Sadism, masochism and homoeroticism are often strong motifs. Authority is presented as problematic and the value of resistance through nihilism, anarchy and violence is positively stressed.
4 *Classical.* These consist of strong narrative content with logical plot lines typically organized around the male gaze and orthodox boy-meets-girl scenarios.
5 *Postmodern.* These promos operate through pastiche, polysemy and post-identity. Irony and humour are used to destabilize orthodox readings of agency, structure and social reality. Postmodern promos have no coherent political position. Rather, they operate with a perspective of popular music and popular culture and are multi-layered and multi-textured.

Kaplan's discussion shows how the pop promotional video provides a separate layer of meaning to music and lyrics that carries the potential to intensify impact upon consumers.

From Discursive to Multi-Discursive Modes

Before MTV, pop songs were understood as a conversation between the performer and the audience. Direct and uncluttered, communication was fetishized as the supreme expression of artistic temperament. Speaking from the heart, or the soul, was considered to be the height of authenticity. By the same token, the wise-cracking, show-biz, corny values of Hollywood that the movies of Frank Sinatra's Rat Pack and Elvis Presley exemplified were regarded as discredited and *passé*. In the 1960s and 1970s, singer-songwriters like Bob Dylan, Joan Baez, Joni Mitchell, Buffy St Marie, James Taylor, Cat Stevens, Graham Nash and Jackson Browne presented themselves as holding the same political preoccupations and speaking the same language as their audience. This was an application and extension of the 'communard utopianism' described so well by Gitlin (1987). Nowhere was unity expressed more cogently than in the cosmetics, hairstyles and dress worn by composers/performers. Light coiffure, dressing down, jean jackets, T-shirts, smocks, dungarees and Levi's were the order of the day. Pop stars dressed in the same uniform as the people who bought their records.

With the rise of glam rock and, later, MTV, the production, exchange and consumption of pop music started to move away from a discursive to a *multi-discursive* mode (Goodwin 1991, 1993). The distinctions between avatars, apprentices and agnostics that developed spontaneously in subcultural traditions were deliberately accentuated. Anyone who was at school in the early 1970s could be in no doubt that David Bowie was an avatar of glam rock, which signified a break from communard utopianism into pompadour electicism. David Byrne, Kurt Cobain, Chris Martin, Jay-Z occupy the same avatar status for, respectively, post-punk, grunge, post-9/11 and rap. These avatars and the network of apprenticies and agnostics that surrounded them cried out for a multi-discursive approach to analysis. For the avatars were in no sense single or even confined sign systems. Bowie's glam rock signified the cultures of rouge, glitter, bisexuality, materialism, science fiction, post-hippie exhaustion, trans-nationalism and many other aspects of what we now call lifestyle architecture.

In the field of pop music, the multi-discursive approach is currently ascendant. It is a form of textual performance (and analysis) that directly treats music and performance as a complex unity of layers, textures and patterns. It is pop music for the web generation in which the recipients (the audience) are as much in on the act encoding and decoding as the producers. Meaning is conveyed along many fronts. However, a basic distinction can be made between horizontal and vertical multi-discursive presentation and analysis.

Horizontal multi-discursivity refers to the production and exchange of pop music texts. It relates to the productive side of the geno/pheno-song. When Barthes (1985) refers to the 'pheno-song' as the idiolect or style of the performer, he does not differentiate the pertinent interconnected discursive fields. The distinct fields that comprise the space of pop music include the aesthetics and politics of embodiment, fashion, choreography, role/status bending and religion. Each field has conventions, precepts and rules of its own and intersects with other fields in distinctive ways that require additional decoding. Moreover, these fields involve the participation of multiple cultural intermediaries: DJs, producers, fellow musicians, specialists in hair, skin, grooming and callisthenics. Together the fields condition the reception of the sign.

Reception here is not understood to be an end point. As we saw in chapter 2 (pp. 71–5), Adorno (2009) portrayed audiences as plastic and passive. They are positioned to be so by the logic of consumption and civic participation created by capitalism. Against this, textual analysis promotes an approach that recognizes the audience as an active agent (Fiske 1992). By extension it has contributed to understanding the production of the sign as an intertextual undertaking. Producers of signs seek to place horizontal boundaries around them. This is one reason why the use of recordings in broadcasts and the image of the performer are copyrighted. But once a sign is out there it cannot be kept on a leash. It is inflected, caricatured, raided and in other ways *used* and *revised*, through the process of exchange and consumption.

The concept of vertical multi-discursivity is designed to encompass this aspect of the sign. It refers to the fields involved with the exchange and consumption of pop music. Examples include news and interview items, reviews, gossip columns, authorized and unauthorized biographies, internet blogging sites, word of mouth, the media rumour mill and fan newsletters.

Since the production, exchange and consumption of music are intensively media-saturated it follows that multi-discursivity assumes variation *within* discourses. To be concrete, the presentation of the latest single by a given artist on a Top 40 show will involve a different field of discourse to the presentation of the same song on a radio review show. This variation points to something of the complexity of analysis that this field requires.

Textual analysis is based upon the proposition that music and performance are socially constructed. Everything is understood to be synthesized, coded and *performed*. There is no sense of an underlying essence or binding reality. The pleasure of the promo resides in completing the clues in the sign puzzle, much as Lévi-Strauss's structuralist account of music suggests.

Intertextuality is the term generally used to refer to the permeation of meanings and the convergence of sign systems in a given text. As Kaplan maintains, it is often most penetrating when it draws upon self-referential images extracted from pop culture. Hence, in pop music multi-discursive performance draws on elements from the history of film, music and commodity culture and fuses them with elements from politics, society and culture that convey common recognition between performers and recipients. Here, the unity is quite unlike the conversational togetherness that characterized much of the most influential pop music of the 1960s and early 1970s. Now, unity is associated with competence in being *au fait* with the cultural references embedded in the music, knowing the pop trivia and understanding the cultural dynamics in the presentation of style. It requires performers and audiences to be silos of pop culture, accumulating data that may be reconfigured or may be left latent. The Smiths and Morrissey have been extraordinarily successful in working this seam of common association around intellectually and culturally misplaced white, working-class youth, combined with a kitchen-sink realism that owed much to television broadcasts from Granada and the BBC in the 1960s.

The Multi-Discursive Avatar: Michael Jackson

However, the performer *par excellence* who fuelled and symbolized the transition from discursive to multi-discursive performance was the late Michael Jackson. In his solo career, Jackson raised dance and lifestyle architecture to unprecedented trademark heights. While the 'Moon Walk' has origins in dance steps from Cab Callaway's stage act in the 1930s, the work of the tap dancer Bill Bailey in the 1950s and James Brown's gigs during the 1960s and 1970s, it was Jackson's performance during a TV special, *Motown 25: Yesterday, Today, Forever* (1983), which transformed it into an MTV sensation and a genre-busting event. The impact of Jackson's 'Moon Walk' dance led directly to the emergence of today's boy/girl bands, in which dance is as prominent as music in generating audience appeal. It made complex, choreographed dancing the prerequisite of a particular type of successful popular music. Nor was this all.

Prior to Jackson, the music video was secondary to the song. Looking back at the first promo films used by mainstream acts for singles like 'Hello/Goodbye' or 'Strawberry Fields Forever' (both 1967) by The Beatles, they appear to be like clumsy home movies. The same is true of their full-length BBC TV film *The Magical Mystery Tour* (1967). Although some sequences depicting the songs made reference to psychedelia, the bulk of the film looked like an amateur road movie.

Not much more can be said of the forays of top-billing 1960s acts into the world of cinema film. The Beatles' *Let It Be* (1970), grandly billed in contemporary adverts as 'an intimate bioscopic experience', or the sequences focusing on The Rolling Stones in Godard's *Sympathy for the Devil* (1968), are essentially footage of rehearsals and the recording process.

The contrast between these movies and Michael Jackson's music video for 'Thriller' (1983) is akin to the difference between amateur videos and the Hollywood mainstream of today. Jackson's 'Thriller' footage is more properly described as a miniature movie than a promo video. Directed and co-scripted by the successful Hollywood film-maker John Landis, the movie deploys the slick production values of a mainstream Hollywood horror flick. The choreography and make-up are complex and world-class. The movie does not simply support the song, it opens a new, mutually reinforcing dimension or layer to the music. Pop culture references to Hammer horror films and 1950s independent movies like Ed Wood's *Plan 9 from Outer Space* (1959) were sealed with a voice-over by the horror film legend Vincent Price. Today it is impossible to listen to the record without remembering the film.

Throughout Jackson's career, his image became a sort of laboratory of multi-discursive interventions and effects. His stage sets, costumes, hairstyles and dance moves became ever more slick and stylized. The releases of the music videos for 'Bad' (1987), 'Smooth Criminal' (1987), 'Earth Song' (1995) and 'You Rock My World' (2001) were organized like film premières. These innovations became an industry standard. Multi-discursive technologies of performance constructed around sound, vision, dance and drama were widely emulated, with arguably Madonna and Prince providing the greatest rivals to Jackson.

By definition, multi-discursivity operates on a multitude of levels. The musical performance is not judged simply by the arrangement and performance of the song, but by visual accompaniments and stage effects, costume, make-up and dance. It is perhaps no accident that as the pathways of Jackson as a popular musical spectacle multiplied, so too did rumours about his private life and the lifestyle architecture built around it. The multiple public faces of Jackson – the singer, the dancer, the pop culture fanatic, Peter Pan, the black prince who entranced a court of Euro-American entertainment dominated by white power, the humanitarian – were paralleled by plural private faces – the crank, the spendthrift, the New Age devotee, the abused child, the child molester. The press reported that he slept in a hyperbaric oxygen chamber to prevent ageing. His best friend was said to be Bubbles, a chimpanzee that he purchased from a laboratory. He was alleged to have attempted to buy the skeleton of Joseph Merrick, the Elephant Man.

The most damaging press reports about Jackson's private life centred on his sexuality. He was accused of child sexual abuse by 13-year-old Jordan Chandler in 1993. He was reputed to have eventually reached an out-of-court settlement with the boy's family for $22 million. In 2003 he was charged with seven counts of child sexual abuse. The two-year investigation went to court. In 2005 he was acquitted on all counts. It is during this time that he allegedly became addicted to pethidine (Demerol).

Following Jackson's acquittal, his finances became subject to intense public scrutiny. The media reported that he was hovering on the brink of bankruptcy. The fifty concerts that he committed to performing at the London O_2 centre in 2009 were widely interpreted as the last ditch to clear his creditors and avoid financial ruin. In the event, on 25 June 2009, he died from a mistaken administration of a sleeping drug.

A textualist approach to Michael Jackson requires many levels of textual differentiation at both the horizontal and vertical levels. Richard Dyer (1986, 1998), in an influential textualist contribution to celebrity studies, argued that the star is the crossroads of many pathways of social construction and ideology. Jackson broke through the race barrier to become a major star embraced by both black and white audiences. Yet the whitening of his skin, which he claimed was the result of a medical condition, also coincided with material success. Whatever the cause, the skin whitening raised contradictions and tensions about his position as an emblem of black upward mobility. These were supplemented by ambiguities relating to his sexuality, judgement and maturity. By the end, the media treated him as a pariah and a sort of impending autopsy. His public life was like extended open-heart surgery, and his retreat to Neverland was mired in media-fuelled suspicion and intrigue. At the mercy of advisers who shaped his investment portfolio, scheduled his concert tour commitments and determined his regime of painkillers and sleeping potions (one of which killed him), Jackson, as a person, seems to have disappeared a full decade and a half before he physically died.

The decentring of his music seems to have gone hand in hand with a psychological decentring whereby his ability to judge reality diminished. He progressively handed himself over to a squadron of advisers and helpers who managed his financial affairs, appraised his friends, monitored publicity reactions, determined his diet and ultimately regulated his pattern of sleeping and emotional equilibrium. All of this is quite consistent with the central tenets of textualism, which maintain that the effect of popular music is the result of complex contrived codes and representations that dissolve the notion of privileged reality. But it is no way to live, as indicated by Jackson's tragic death, and the long publicity decline that preceded it.

Textualism and *The X Factor*

A counter-example to the textual position that entertainment and impact are nothing but the contrivance of codes is apparently supplied by the rise of reality/talent TV and, in particular, its role in the social construction of pop music stardom. Through phone voting, shows like *Pop Idol, The X Factor*, the *Got Talent* franchise, *American Idol* and *Popstars* appear to give unprecedented, unmediated power to the audience to create stars based upon popular perceptions of talent. In the UK, Will Young, Leona Lewis, Paul Potts and Susan Boyle and, in the USA, Kelly Clarkson, Carrie Underwood and Jennifer Hudson were discovered on these shows. They have gone on to achieve considerable chart success. This appears to vindicate the proposition that people have the power to override the politics of media coding and make real decisions about real people doing real things. TV appears to be the portal to the discovery of musical talent, providing a veritable consumer democracy in an increasingly prominent branch of the music industry.

Su Holmes (2004) offers a striking critique of this logic. She points out that a number of problems quickly percolate once the question of the relationship between reality/talent TV and stardom is posed. From the outset, the process of finding a star on *Pop Idol* and *The X Factor* is highly synthesized. The 'discovery' of the star is a product of many interventions, in which the audience is far from necessarily dominant. As Holmes (2004: 153–4) demonstrates, the reality/talent TV format involves four stages:

1 *Regional auditions.* Unknown performers are encouraged to apply to try out for the show and are pre-selected before appearing on the show.
2 *Professional auditions.* Potential contestants perform on the show to a panel of experts who articulate their judgements and decide if the performers will get through to the next round.
3 *Audience jury judgements.* Viewers influence the outcome of the show by voting for their favourite performers.
4 *Finale.* This stage consists of the ten finalists performing and the registration of phone votes that determine the winner soon after the performance broadcast ends.

For Holmes, it is naïve to regard this format as open consumer democracy. Instead, she contends it represents the epitome of manufactured pop. As early as stage 2, the unknowns have received impression management advice, voice coaching and grooming tips from experts employed by the producers of the show. The programme works upon the principle of staged authenticity.[3] Despite the mooted 'power to the people' principle of the phone voting system, the show is based upon the conventional inequality between producer and recipient that characterizes traditional media presentations of pop music and pop culture. The audience participate in encoding practice, but they do so from a calculated semiotic construct. As Holmes (2004: 168) puts it: 'In choosing the winning idol, the audience is given the power to decide which set of semiotic meanings is launched most visibly into the sphere of popular culture, but they do not get to shape their discursive construction.' What Holmes is driving at is that the power of audiences is constrained by the capitalist context in which shows like *The X Factor*, *Pop Idol* and *Britain's Got Talent* operate and which they exemplify. It is all very well to insist on the polysemy of meaning, but the buck stops when the ratings of a talent show decline or the record sales of a reality pop idol plunge.

This points to a major defect in the textualist approach. For Nick Couldry (2000: 67–90), the focus upon encoding and decoding in textual analysis is crucial in elucidating the role of social construction in popular music. But to dwell upon it gets analysis off on the wrong foot. We all now know that texts are encoded and that audiences practise decoding. The real question is how encoded meanings are *naturalized* in popular culture. The process of naturalization involves the manipulation of codes and representations, but it also raises the question of who the material power brokers are in production, exchange and consumption. In the case of the *Got Talent* and *X Factor* franchises, the key power broker is the production company Syco, owned by the pop impresario Simon Cowell. The *Pop Idol* franchise is owned by Cowell's sometime associate and business rival Simon Fuller. The reality/talent TV format leaves little to chance in the appropriation of revenue, despite putting the choice of the winner in the hands of the TV audience.

In the 1980s and 1990s, Madonna's practice of multi-discursivity was associated with changes in image that were so frequent that no-one could guess what she would do next or pin down her essential self. This was widely taken to mean the arrival of the polysemic pop star, a recording agent whose codes and representations are infinite. Why this fails as a convincing mode of analysis is that it ignores the problem of the material forces behind manoeuvring the audience to accept this or that image of the pop star. The late John Castles (2008: 10) makes the decisive point in relation to an analysis of Madonna's popularity as a polysemic star of the 1980s and 1990s:

> Madonna's frequent changes of image raise the possibility that her 'real' self is, as she asserts, hidden and different from all of them. But by the same token, her image changes are understood to be manipulations, that is, deliberate acts on her part. She is never entirely withdrawn from her mask-like visage because it is she who selects and lives the masks, she who 'reinvents' herself.

The point can be extended from the role that an individual plays in 'selecting' the image that he or she wishes to present to the world, to the more subtle (because less subjectively realized) role of cultural and social influences. For example, no serious study of the impact of Coldplay in twenty-first-century popular music and popular culture can analyse the texts of their songs in isolation from post-9/11 issues relating to risk and globalization, and changes in accessing popular music relating to illegal downloading and streaming and the challenges that these technological issues present to the music industry. These issues may be understood as the texts which Coldplay use to interpret artistically for a wider audience. But they are also the seismic changes in material culture that enable a band with Coldplay's repertoire.

In the light of the role of history and socio-economic institutions in coding and representating popular music and much else besides, Couldry (2000: 70) asks: in what sense does it remain useful to talk about 'texts'? There are several aspects to this point, which may be differentiated with respect to cultural production, textual naturalization and textual decoding.

To take the issue of cultural production first, unquestionably Coldplay's 'Viva La Vida' (2008) is the product of Chris Martin and his band. The difficulty is that the music and its impact upon popular culture are so complex and have so many intersecting axes covering public relations staff and advertisers that, from a methodological standpoint, it is naïve to treat it as independent or self-referential. It is one thing to recognize that texts (songs) are encoded. But this raises an altogether more difficult set of questions relating to how the song's subjects of love, social criticism, political dissent or what have you, are accepted as 'credible'.

We saw in our account of relationism that *habitus* is associated with generative structures that predispose individuals and groups to react positively, negatively or neutrally to codes and representations (Bourdieu 1990, 1993). What made Nirvana's song 'Smells Like Teen Spirit' (1991) instantly, and well-nigh universally, accepted as the authentic 'voice' of Generation X? Is it really just a matter of the power of the music and lyrics? Or must we delve to bring a wider range of factors into our viewfinder, having to do with the 'structures of feeling' among youth groups raised under the neo-con revolution of the 1980s and 1990s, wider consciousness of environmental degradation, the de-industrialization of the Western economy, the rise of speculative investment and profiteering on the global stock market and more traditional concepts like 'generation', 'class' and 'race'?

Finally, with respect to the question of textual decoding, if it is right to submit that texts are coded by a multitude of interpenetrating social, cultural and economic forces, it follows that our capacity to decode texts is influenced by various locational factors. To return to Richard Middleton's (2002) neo-structuralist distinctions of popular music, the *generative* and *syntagmatic* levels of the social construction of popular music presuppose a *paradigmatic* level in which the immense array of alternative readings of a musical utterance or inscription are, so to speak, 'organized out'. The question is: what situates us within a location so that we can 'organize out' this or that choice paradigm and privilege another which supports generative taste cultures and syntagmatic chains of reason and desire that we suppose to be 'normal' or 'natural'? Textual analysis has a tendency to get stuck at the levels of encoding and decoding, so that the question of the naturalization of meaning, with all of its profound implications for elucidating the apparatus of ideology and resource distribution, is suspended in abeyance. As such, the application of the approach to the study of popular music and popular culture has serious limitations.

Part III

The Mode of Production

The examination of the chief perspectives in the field of popular music has fulfilled the first important task of this study. Now we must proceed to more practical matters. The various theoretical perspectives on popular music and popular culture discussed in the last part did not arise out of thin air. More properly, they may be described as efforts to grapple with the complex feedback loops between pop music and cultural practice. Tacitly, this discussion entails consideration of questions relating to the history and social institutions engaged in the organization and dissemination of pop: that is, the mode of production.

By the term 'mode of production', I mean the complete ensemble of productive forces and relations of production involved in the production, exchange and consumption of popular music. The *productive forces* refer to the economic, technological and cultural capital involved in generating popular music: that is, the instruments, technical means of broadcasting and recording, spatial settings, networks of representation and labour power applied in the production and exchange of pop.

The term 'labour power' refers to the musicianship, lyrical proficiency and business acumen of composers and performers in generating pop music. At the crux of any worthwhile approach to pop and pop culture is an emphasis upon human creativity. The expenditure of creative labour power can refer to many different things. As an example, we might consider where a musician creates a new character in a song. The invention of Ziggy Stardust by David Bowie in 1972 is a case in point. Ziggy represented much more than an arbitrarily selected bisexual glam rock star. He was built to be an icon of generational change from the communard utopianism of the 1960s to the *bricoleur* style of the 1970s in which no underlying reality or truth is respected. He embodied gay, materialist connotations in popular culture that, on the whole, hippie culture repressed. Elements of Ziggy's character were clearly transcribed from everyday experience. They also included a version of fantasy individualism projected through glamour and camp rhetoric. At its most accomplished, the use of creative labour power in constructing characters in songs and musical genres gives the construct a life of its own. This clearly happened with Ziggy. The character became an archetype that formed the cultural biography of an entire generation.

Similarly, creative labour power may be put to the task of musical genre-busting. Bob Dylan's introduction of the electric guitar at the Newport Folk Festival in 1965 outraged the traditional folk audience. At a subsequent concert performed in the Manchester Free Trade Hall (1966) he was famously called 'Judas' by a member of the audience.

Creative labour power is, of course, pivotal in reframing typification, transcription, harmony, convention, semantics, syntax and genre. However, it is a mistake to restrict it to the artist, since the production of music is a collaborative process. It thrives upon making connections and establishing relations. The question of creative labour power therefore requires the use of a wide-angle lens.

The *relations of production* refer to the form of human relationships engaged in the production, exchange and consumption of popular music: that is, music corporations, managers, the star system, audiences, technology and the media apparatus. These may be referred to as the *allocative mechanisms* of pop music, since they participate centrally in the distribution of economic, social and cultural resources.[1]

The mode of production is the result of human practice. As such, it requires the adoption of an historical perspective, since human practice changes over time. Through human agency the conditions in which practice occurs also change, often in unanticipated and unexpected ways.

The question of roots therefore kick-starts the discussion in this part of the book. The narrative of pop is dominated by a history of stars and musical genres. Without wishing to exclude or belittle this, there is also the question of the industrial planning of pop. The postwar history of Western popular music is a story of the industrialization of the form: that is, a commercial assessment of the costs of supply and the rewards of relating to demand.

This basic equation has concentrated power in the hands of the multinational music corporations. These have been subject to progressive rationalization via the agglomeration of business units. At the time of writing, the pop music business is dominated by four global corporations: the Universal Music Group (UMG), the Warner Music Group (WMG), Sony-BMG and EMI. These four units support a variety of specialist niche labels. Common to all of them is the diversification of aggregation from the production of recorded music to video, merchandising, tour operation, advertising and direct digital retailing. To adopt the terminology of relationism, these four global units supply the *habitus* in the field of pop music through which production, exchange and consumption devolve. Over the years they have proved to be extraordinarily adroit in neutralizing the challenge from indie labels. The latter will always be a feature of the music business. Genre-busting music, like punk and rap, generally emerges at the periphery of the field: that is, in settings and subcultures situated beyond the industrial business framework of the 'Big Four'. Indies have competitive advantage in responding to genre-busting music because they are small units, carrying low overheads. However, these business strengths turn into weaknesses when new genres become ascendant, since the costs of production and distribution eventually out-pace revenue streams. When this juncture is reached, the tendency is for global multinationals to absorb indies, generally retaining the brand, but subjecting the business to corporate business discipline.

Music corporations are situated at the intersection between music producers and audiences. Various business models have emerged to confer competitive advantage in handling this traffic. Until the digital revolution, the balance of power was unequivocally in the hands of the major, global record companies. They exercised seigneurial might over artistic contracts, the production of music, the control of master tapes, the regulation of retail distribution chains and the management of audience perceptions through advertising, marketing and special promotions. Digital technology has turned this around in various ways. Laptop recording systems have reduced production costs and freed musicians from reliance upon record companies for studio space and production time. Similarly, the emergence of new digital platforms like MySpace, Facebook, Google, Twitter and YouTube has diminished the power traditionally enjoyed by A&R (Artists and Repertoire) units in scouting for talent by making new music universally accessible on the web for free. The web is also an unprecedented resource for the exchange of music files and unauthorized downloading of intellectual property. The challenge of P2P platforms has annihilated the revenue streams produced by the postwar industrial planning model constructed and managed by the music business cartel. The economics of the field have been thoroughly turned over and a new business framework has not emerged. The major labels have been slow to respond to the new challenges presented by technology, artist autonomy and new forms of flexible accumulation among audiences.

This section of the book therefore focuses upon a field of relations between corporations, technological suppliers, media hubs, managers, artists and audiences that is in profound transition. The mode of production is struggling to find new stable models of aggregation. In doing so, it is moving from a traditional focus upon recorded music to a bespoke model in which the extraction of value in recorded music is tailored to other channels of popular culture, notably television, advertising and fashion.

The crisis extends into the music media. The traditional model of terrestrial channels and print weeklies and monthlies has been weakened by cable, unauthorized downloading, blog sites and social network communities. Online access to music reviews, news and tour information has lowered the premium of print culture, and the availability of music videos for free on YouTube and Last.fm has weakened the power of MTV to set the agenda.

In examining the mode of production it will quickly be apparent that the old assumptions that governed the industrial planning model have been nullified by online technology and the culture of sharing. We are in the midst of a massive process of de-differentiation. The music business first responded to the transformation with a reactionary policy of asserting DRM (digital rights management). But it has discovered that there are no means to effectively enforce the provisions of legislation. So the DRM strategy has been supplemented by CRM (customer relationship management) strategies. In effect, the major record labels have learned from unauthorized P2P exchange and social network sites. They have experimented with 'buddy' models of online sales organized around the creation of web communities designed to promote brand loyalty. In short, and to reiterate, the mode of production is in a moment of profound transition.

5

Roots

A common misconception is that popular music began with rock and roll, and, by extension, rock and roll was born with Elvis Presley. The facts are well documented and well known. Presley's first Sun recording session occurred in July 1954 with Scotty Moore on guitar, Bill Black on bass and Johnny Bernero on drums. This session harvested his first hit: 'That's All Right (Mama)'. The song was not an Elvis original. It was written by the black Tupelo bluesman Arthur 'Big Boy' Crudup. From its origins, rock and roll carried traces from earlier musical forms, of which blues, folk and country are arguably the most significant. While now secure in the rock and roll pantheon, 'That's All Right (Mama)' was little more than a regional cult success in its day. It reached number 1 in the Memphis country charts. As a promotion exercise, Presley appeared on Nashville's showcase music radio show *The Grand Ole Opry* (where he was advised, on air, to go back to the day job: truck-driving).

'Heartbreak Hotel' was Presley's breakthrough. It entered all three *Billboard* charts in March 1956. Eighteen months is a long time in popular music. In July 1954, Elvis was a hick hopeful, somewhat schooled in Negro spirituals and country music, but erratically so, lacking a professional manager, earning a living as a truck driver, nurturing a confused sense of personal identity and appropriate recording material, and nervously trying out his rockabilly style with Sun Records. A year and a half later, his five Sun releases achieved sufficient chart success to attract the interest of a dedicated – although, as the passage of time proved, ultimately unscrupulous – manager, 'Colonel' Tom Parker, and a new record label, RCA.[1] In January 1956 his first RCA recording session in Nashville yielded 'Heartbreak Hotel', with Chet Atkins playing on rhythm guitar, Scotty Moore on guitar, Bill Black on bass, D.J. Fontana on drums and Floyd Cramer on piano. Three months later it was number 1 for eight weeks in the pop chart, and for seventeen weeks in the country chart, and number 3 in the R&B chart.

Presley became the premier figure in rock and roll, a pin-up idol for teen girls, a pop idol for young men and a *cause célèbre* for the national and global press, in which conservative critics, like the columnist Jack O'Brian in the *New York Journal American*, thundered that Presley's dance style was akin to the 'suggestive animation

. . . of an aborigine mating dance' (Friedlander 2006: 46). It is easy to see why Elvis seemed to be the well-spring of an entire new era of youth music.

However, there are at least three things at odds with the view that Presley invented rock and roll, and these have to do with what we might term historical myopia, sociological blinkers and cultural deafness.

Historical Myopia

Presley and rock were not a rupture or break with the history of popular music, but a continuation of deep-rooted trends. As we have already noted, pop music is the backbeat of urban-industrial life. For its inspiration it draws upon the city and the workplace, concrete-cement, the automobile, consumer culture, achieved status, mobility, worker–boss conflict, the marriage market, town hall red-tape and many other urban-industrial stimuli. These roots go back for at least a century and a half. Skiffle, jazz and R&B have obviously been huge influences; as have the pre-electronic genres of folk, blues, bluegrass and country (Clarke 1995; Friedlander 2006).

Pop's strength is that it recognizes no inhibition in drawing from different genres and inscribes them in its own image. Sampling does this by electronically appropriating chunks of R&B, punk, post-punk and country and relocating them in a rap motif. David Bowie's career included long periods of experimentation with pop collage and conscious stylistic revisions of older musical genres. This was typically based around characters invented and played by Bowie such as Ziggy Stardust, Aladdin Sane, Halloween Jack and the Thin White Duke. Station To Station (1976) originally incensed European fans because the Thin White Duke character appeared to abandon the sexual ambiguity and media archness of Ziggy Stardust for a blatant lift of the arriviste, hetero-style of the black soul singer James Brown. Bowie later claimed that the passionate R&B style was built on ice, as the Thin White Duke character was a cocaine-fuelled persona, imprisoned in Los Angeles Celebrity-World.

So borrowing from different genres, collage, sampling and pastiche are integral to pop. Unlike classical musicians, most pop musicians have no formal training. They relate to pop music and pop culture with the same 'cut and paste' attitude as ordinary consumers. Indeed, the 'ordinary' nature of pop music is one the main reasons for its vast and enduring appeal.

In the industrial era of pop music, cut and paste practices were pioneered in the blues of the plantation states in the American South and the British music hall/variety tradition (1850–1960) and American vaudeville (1860–1930). The legendary Delta blues player Robert Johnson (1911–38), who has a strong claim to be the first blues mega-star, drew on the style of Charlie Patton, William Brown and Eddie 'Son' House. There are parallels with the European troubadour tradition here, in cross-fertilizations from different repertoires, singing and playing styles (Briffault 1965). Working in a largely aural tradition, Johnson adopted a pragmatic approach to source materials, borrowing and adapting from others, as the mood took him, and while generous in acknowledging that his music stood on the shoulders of others, he was by no means scrupulous in paying his debts.

Similar cut and paste patterns prevailed in the development of popular music in the British music hall and American vaudeville traditions. British music halls developed out of drinking and entertainment cultures in eighteenth- and nineteenth-century pubs and taverns. They provided a venue for professional variety acts that performed comedy, magic and a mixture of sentimental, jig, polka, folk and patriotic numbers. Often the music offered up-to-the-minute commentaries on topical events such as famous love affairs, scandals, corruption in high places, international conflict, infamous murders, epic trials, and the like. This solidified the connection between pop music and demotic forms of resistance and protest.

The music hall bill was constructed around a system of top-drawer acts that were encouraged by impresarios to devise signature numbers. Music hall stars included Marie Lloyd, Vesta Tilley, Alfred Vance, Gus Elen, Harry Lauder, Florrie Forde and Harry Champion, from around 1900; and later George Formby, Gracie Fields, Max Miller and Flanagan and Allen. These acts often developed stage anthems that became standards in popular culture.

Just as Paul McCartney is known today for 'Yesterday', 'Hey Jude' and 'Let It Be', Harry Champion was celebrated for 'Any Old Iron' and I'm 'Henery the Eighth I Am', Mony Cash for 'I Live in Trafalgar Square' and Marie Lloyd for 'My Old Man Said Follow the Van' and 'Oh Mr Porter' (Russell 1997; Faulk 2004).

Vaudeville grew out of minstrel shows, Yiddish theatre and medicine shows. It focused on distinctive forms of American life, with a strong accent on emerging urban-industrial settings that mixed elements of slave culture, émigré experience, jugglers, comedians and magicians with Wild West exotica. Vaudeville exploited the fractious and diverse tradition of popular dramatic entertainment and showmanship. But its influence on American nineteenth- and early twentieth-century culture was the result of nation-wide industrial planning applied to the entertainment sector. Vaudeville impresarios B.F. Keith and Edward Albee established a chain of theatres in the major urban-industrial towns and controlled a regimented programme of headline and novelty acts. Forgotten stars of the vaudeville era, such as Julian Eltinge, Leonara Dare, The Hanlons, The Wilson Brothers, Baby Rose Marie and Tony Pastor, became major regional figures, mainly on the Eastern seaboard, where the population concentration was greatest.

Later, twentieth-century legends such as W.C. Fields, Buster Keaton, The Marx Brothers, Jack Benny, Bob Hope and Judy Garland were born and nurtured in vaudeville. However, they went on to prosper in radio and film. The cinema, and especially the talkies, signalled the death knell for American vaudeville (Gilbert 1963; Stein 1983; Gottschild 2002).

Long before Presley, radio, the gramophone and eventually television and cinema made national and global pop idols out of Bing Crosby, Hoagy Carmichael, Rudy Vallée and Frank Sinatra. In the 1940s, Sinatra, with whom Presley recorded an infamous TV special after his discharge from the army in 1960, was also accused by the media of corrupting youth by displays of overt sexuality (Rojek 2004).[2] A view that dates the birth of rock to Presley therefore falls foul of the charge of historical myopia.

Sociological Blinkers

The public furore around Presley in the mid-1950s reflected social and economic factors that preceded him and were beyond his control. They provided the indispensable context for his apparent overnight success. The austerity of the war years interrupted the interwar affluence of youth culture, evinced by the moral panics against cash-rich young people in the Flapper and Swing eras.

During the war, Sinatra provided a celebrity substitute for young servicemen fighting overseas. The adulation that he received from besotted female fans was widely condemned as morbid and, along with allegations of his sympathies with Red politics, contributed to the interlude of unpopularity that he endured until the release of his career comeback movie, *From Here to Eternity* (1953).

By the mid-1950s, full employment boosted the disposable income of young people and dramatically raised the profile of youth culture (Muggleton 2005; Fowler 2007). Presley's notoriety articulated the fears of the media and older generations that youth culture was running wild. These anxieties centred on questions of sexual licence, free spending and politics.

Sam Phillips, the owner of Sun Records, famously observed that he would become a billionaire overnight if he could find a white singer with the 'Negro sound' and 'Negro feel' (Friedlander 2006: 16, 44). Elvis, who grew up in Tupelo, Mississippi, in the midst of black gospel revival meetings and local bluesmen like Arthur 'Big Boy' Crudup, was the answer to Phillips's prayers. In being so, he unwittingly both reflected the growing attention given to black music in white popular culture and aggravated conservative critics who feared the decline of white American power.

Presley and rock symbolized a loosening of social controls in postwar culture. Emotional and sexual considerations were permitted to be more direct and forceful articulations. But it is far-fetched to maintain that Presley was responsible for this loosening. Rock and roll was part of a much deeper social process of social informalization (Wouters 2007).

This process involves deep changes stretching back for over one hundred and twenty years. It has to do with lengthening the chains of interdependence between people, which precipitated greater tolerance of difference, and concentrating powers of legitimate policing and punishment in the hands of the state. The result of these changes was partially to unbind the tight social controls constructed in earlier stages of the development of urban-industrial society to elicit passive obedience and regimented order in the masses. Standards of restraint did not vanish. Rather, older convictions about the necessity of hierarchy and inflexible principles of social interaction were reconfigured. In concrete terms, the taboo against free expression was diminished, the plight of the excluded and the underdog was awarded greater acknowledgement and measures were taken to ameliorate inequality by expanding access to education and health care.

Sociologically speaking, the rock and roll moment was part of a well-entrenched informalization process which widened the radius of leniency and tolerance in social relationships. The publicity that it achieved in the 1950s reflected the establishment of nation-wide television networks throughout the West.

Because of this, it is incorrect to view it as a cultural or musical *revolution*. The loosening of rigid cultural hierarchies and the extension of free speech had been underway for much longer. Cas Wouters (2007) identifies the 1890s and 1920s as two significant tidal waves in the process. The first articulated the *fin-de-siècle* contradictions of patriarchy and Empire, whereas the second was a social and psychological reaction to the mass destruction and futility of the First World War, when, in the words of the cliché, 'lions were led by donkeys'. Pop music often articulated and crystallized this complex process of social reconfiguration because it deals with manners, power and emotion in direct, often poetic, ways. For example, a song like Bob Dylan's 'Blowin' in the Wind' (1963) seemed to encapsulate progressive anxieties fastening upon authoritarianism, the Cold War and the repression of civil rights.

Wouters (2007) contends that the 1960s and 1970s, with the reaction against Viet Nam, the further unravelling of Empire, the rise of civil and consumer rights and feminism, was another tidal wave in the loosening of chains of social hierarchy and rigidity.

Thus the rock and roll moment of the mid-1950s followed well-worn steps in the history of pop. As we shall see presently, however, there are reasons why a different view, having to do with the pre-eminence of creativity and rebellion in the history of pop, claims ascendancy.

Cultural Deafness

The public typically understands the history of pop music to be a succession of 'big things'. The conventional wisdom is that rock and roll led to psychedelia, progressive music, glam rock, punk, post-punk, grunge, rap, hip hop, electronica, techno, house, microhouse, and so on. This genre-based model naturally privileges the artist as the author of musical breakthroughs. Elvis Presley, Chuck Berry, Bob Dylan, The Beatles, The Rolling Stones, The Who, The Doors, Genesis, ELP, Pink Floyd, Yes, David Bowie, The Sex Pistols, The Clash, Grandmaster Flash, 50 Cent, Jay-Z, Björk, The Chemical Brothers, Moby and DJ stars like Jason Jollins, Carl Cox, ATB, Erik Morillo, Roger Sanchez, Jonathan Peters, Sander van Doorn, Paul Oakenfold and Anthony Pappa have each been presented as the originators of the new sound of the day that is championed as the 'big thing' in pop.

What is amiss with this popular rendition of the history of pop music is that it is deaf to the cultural participation of managers, corporations, the media, stylists and PR personnel. This backroom network surrounds and supports artists and plays a vital role in finessing the image of the star, communicating music effectively, wealth creation and orchestrating media representation of the act as a cultural phenomenon.

By the same token, a number of studies have insisted on the pivotal importance of the audience in pop music (Kaplan 1993; Sandvoss 2005; Jenkins 2006). There are many aspects to this literature. John Castles (2008), drawing on the writing of Morin (1960) on celebrity and Dufrenne (1973) on the phenomenology of consciousness, makes a most intriguing case. He argues that the pop star is a vehicle of projection through which fans compensate for their deficiencies by identifying with the image of the star. Castles makes the important observation that a crucial element in pop is that as well as worshipping the star, the audience responds to itself as a spectacle, and, further, that this response is part of a circuit of recognition that musical performers ignite and, so to speak, legitimate. It is not that the performer would be nothing without the audience, still less that the audience is only meaningful when the performer is added. It is rather that the circuit of production and consumption in pop requires the audience and the performer to be active agents in observing the ritual.

The position taken here is that the dominant, folklore approach privileges creative or 'rebellious' artists in pop music history. Thus, the story of pop is measured by the metric of artistic impact of legendary stars. Elvis Presley, Bob Dylan, The Beatles, Jim Morrison, Jimi Hendrix, The Rolling Stones, Brian Wilson, Bruce Springsteen, Marvin Gaye, James Brown, Michael Jackson, and so on, are examples of performers who are said to have changed the face of pop. The key objection to this 'great man' history of pop is that it neglects that behind every legend there is not only an audience but also a record industry. An approach that articulates only the power of creativity and rebellion in pop music nearly always indicates that the pendulum has swung too far: that is, in favour of the creativity of the artist and away from the industrial machinations of the recording industry. The reasons for this distortion have to do with the mechanics of production, distribution and consumption in the exchange of pop.

Pop and Industrial Planning

Keir Keightley (2004: 375–6) gets it right in submitting that the study of pop music is marred by what he calls 'boomer historiography', which operates with 'unrecognized continuities' in the pop music business. The 'big thing' in pop pursues an industrial logic designed to manufacture consumer demand. In the postwar years, three principles have underpinned the industrial logic of the pop business:

(1) *Market segmentation.* Market segmentation along age and generational divisions has been widely examined in the analysis of pop (Chapple and Garofolo 1975; Denisoff and Romanowksi 1991). By the early 1950s, vinyl releases had diverged into two distinctive markets: the singles market, which aimed at young people, and the more adult-orientated album market.

By the 1960s, record companies were marketing singles as ephemeral commodities. The higher margin associated with album sales engendered a business strategy pushing recording artists to concentrate on album production. This was legitimated aesthetically by connoting the album with 'mood music' or a 'personal statement', similar in artistic impact to poetry and literature (Frith 1996).

The weight of balance in the industry was shifting towards the album. Artistic considerations are often presented as driving the rise of the album. In fact commercial considerations had more to do with it. True, album investment and production-led teams eclipsed the immediacy of the single. However, the higher price and longer shelf life of albums meant that the pie of revenue created with them was potentially far greater than was the case with the singles market.

(2) *The rise of the album as the dominant vinyl commodity.* Between 1932 and 1948 the exclusive phonograph format was the 78 rpm record. By today's standards the 78 format was extremely limited. It allowed for a recording of only one song on each side of the disc. In 1948 Columbia introduced the 33⅓ rpm format, and RCA quickly supplemented this in 1949 by introducing the 45 rpm format. The technologies that eventually supported the album and the single commodity form were thus born. Changes in consumption patterns were relatively sluggish, however, indicating a degree of market inertia on the demand side. As late as 1953, sales of 78 recordings in the US outpaced those of 33⅓s and singles combined ($89.7 million against $83 million). In 1952–3, LPs represented only 19% of the combined sound recordings market. Nevertheless, within eight years, by 1960, album sales had quadrupled, amounting to 80% of all sound recordings sales. In the UK 17 million albums were sold in 1962; by 1972, sales were up to 84.5 million (Elborough 2008: 267). The rise of the album coincided with the decline of the single. In 1975 singles were reported to account for no more than 8% of the record market (Keightley 2004: 378–9).

(3) *The growth of the back-catalogue as the industry anchor.* The record industry quickly realized that albums have a longer back-catalogue life than singles. The single is built around intense, expensive marketing of a commodity that is designed to burst into the market and then be replaced by something new. In contrast, the album is a more durable commodity that has a greater claim to capture the spirit and tones of the time and make a sustained artistic statement because it is based in 10–12 cuts rather a single recording (Straw 1990). In the 1970s, the industry standard held that albums last ten times longer in the charts than singles (Keightley 2004: 383). Technological innovation is co-opted into this marketing philosophy. The move from vinyl to CDs in the 1980s was promoted by the record corporations as producing a cleaner, more authentic, scratch-free sound. It was indisputably successful. By 2008, vinyl sales amounted to hardly 1% of the market (Elborough 2008: 392). Similarly in 2009, the entire Beatles back-catalogue was re-released in digitally re-mastered stereo versions. Purportedly, re-mastering captures the authenticity and integrity of the analogue recordings and eliminates extraneous sound glitches to offer listeners 'the real thing'. In September 2009, Nielsen SoundScan reported that The Beatles re-releases held nine of the top ten slots on *Billboard*'s catalogue chart, with first week sales of 626,000 units.

The business strategy plainly capitalizes on the search for distinction (Bourdieu 1984) and a focus on the adult market with higher disposable incomes. By the early 1990s, album back-catalogue sales were estimated to account for up to 40% of all record sales (Garofolo 1997: 457).

For a long time, these principles were the unchallenged foundation of the pop business. The technological move from vinyl to CD format was accomplished within this framework. The aggregated dividends that accrued from the transfer of the back-catalogue have not been computed. Obviously, they were substantial.

The digital revolution has been like a thunderbolt to this mode of organization. Access to music has been vastly expanded. Illegal downloading has made the concept of point-of-sale costs irrelevant for millions of consumers. We shall come to the business crisis in the music industry in the next chapter. At the present juncture, it will suffice to observe that the digital revolution poses a fundamental rethink on the business model of production, exchange and consumption. Recording artists and music corporations are still experimenting with solutions to the digital revolution.

Institutional Autonomy and the 'Rock Window'

Before closing this chapter on the history of pop music, one further task remains. Friedlander (2006: 4–13) pays tribute to the capacity of pop songs to frame a political stance and/or historical moment. This extends the point made at the start of the book that some pop stars can be read as providing a cultural biography of the times. What Friedlander is saying is that some pop songs provide a window on a particular time and place. Protest songs like Midnight Oil's 'Beds Are Burning' (1988), which protested against the Australian government's exploitation of Aboriginal land rights in the Outback, or Pearl Jam's 'World Wide Suicide' (2006), which launched a broadside against the George W. Bush administration and the Iraq war, are musical broadsides fired against the dominant political authorities.

They stand in a long line including Billie Holiday's 'Strange Fruit' (1939), Malvina Renolds's 'Little Boxes' (1962), Phil Ochs's 'I Ain't Marching Anymore' (1965), Bob Dylan's 'Maggie's Farm' (1965), James Brown's 'Say It Loud, I'm Black and I'm Proud' (1968) and Marvin Gaye's 'What's Going On' (1971). Not all protest songs have an immediate or intended effect. Sometimes there is a delayed reaction in which the original meaning of the song is redefined. For example, as Friedlander (2006: 7) notes, Otis Redding released 'Respect' in 1965. It charted at number 37. Two years later, Aretha Franklin released a cover version that was rapidly recognized as a plea for racial equality and women's rights. It went to number 1.

The commercial and cultural success of protest songs runs counter to Adorno's (2009) thesis that popular music is about mass compliance. It suggests that music can indeed offer a space for social criticism and utopianism. Jason Toynbee (2000: 27–9) submits that some forms of popular music have what he calls 'institutional autonomy'. That is, they are produced in settings that are not fully commodified and therefore resistant to industrial planning. They underline the significance of non-economic bonds of solidarity in music communities: that is, non-pecuniary pathways of attraction based around subcultural inclusion, the love of rhythm, dance and performance. Toynbee presents this argument as a corrective to the structuralist view that privileges the importance of economic value and industrial planning in music making.

Miege (1989: 30) makes a separate argument that supports this point. Positions of distinction in the pop music industry are scarce. There is only one Eric Clapton or Christina Aguilera. The capitalization of the industry requires a high labour supply because demand is unpredictable. Few A&R personnel predicted the punk revolution in the 1970s or the market appeal of grunge in the 1980s. Because of this, the pop music industry tends to generate an over-supply of labour. This consists of musicians who can be drafted into recording contracts at short notice.

This over-supply is consistent with a culture of free gigs or fringe performances. In these settings, labourers develop compositional and performance skills that enhance their market power and trail their value to record company executives.

Many of these points are captured by Friedlander, albeit in a somewhat different tradition of pop music analysis. He devised a five-point metric, which he calls 'the rock window' (Friedlander 2006: 4–13). By this he means dimensions of articulation that enable analysts to compare and contrast pop music. The five points are: (a) the music, (b) the lyrics, (c) artist history, (d) societal context and (e) stance (cultural and political).

Friedlander presents these as a method of reading and comparing popular music. Hence, in trying to analyse the production, exchange and consumption of a rap classic like 'Dead Presidents' by Jay-Z (1996), or a rock anthem like 'Jesus of Suburbia' by Green Day (2004), these five dimensions need to be separated and the interrelations between them pinpointed. But the rock window schema also reiterates the folly of regarding music as (a) the simple product of abstract forces of social manipulation, such as the culture industry or industrial planning programmes; and (b) the spontaneous emotive expression of an individual or ensemble that is devoid of history or politics. Artist history, societal context and cultural-political stance are fundamental in pop music. But through creative labour songs can be composed and arranged that crystallize 'the structure of feeling' (Williams 1961, 1980) of a cultural moment or setting and operate as a 'window' on generational values and characteristics (Friedlander 2006).

6

Corporations and Independents

Between them, the four major musical corporations in the world today – Universal Music (UMG, owned by Vivendi), Warner Music Group (WMG), Sony-BMG Music Entertainment and EMI (owned by Terra Firma) – control over 85% of global record sales. In terms of market share, UMG is the top player with 31.6% in 2006. After UMG, Sony-BMG has a share of 27.4%, WMG has 18.1% and EMI 10.2% (Gallo 2007).

Acquisitions and mergers mean that nearly all of the labels that we think of as independent are actually owned and controlled by the 'Big Four' (see Table 6.1).

Since the online revolution, music corporations have struggled to get to grips with the new challenge of weightless consumption. They have developed a variety of methods to combat what they define to be a threat, rather than an opportunity, for their business. These include litigation against unauthorized servers; the development of dedicated subscription download platforms or the accumulation of others via corporate takeover (for example, in 2001 Vivendi/Universal purchased MP3.com for $372 million); the introduction of lockbox technologies designed to block or frustrate unauthorized downloading; substantial investment in public

Table 6.1 Record labels wholly owned by the 'Big Four'

UMG	WMG	Sony-BMG	EMI
A&M	Asylum	Arista	Angel
Decca	Atlantic	Bluebird	Bluenote
Geffen	East/West	Burgundy	Capitol
Island Def Jam	Elektra	Columbia	CMG
Lost Highway	Rhino	Epic	Manhattan
Machete	Roadrunner	J Records	Mute
Mercury	WEA	Provident	Parlophone
Motown	WMG-Nashville	RCA	Televisa
UMG-Nashville		Silvertone	Virgin
Verve		Zomba	

education programmes; advertising in the music media; and extending the machinery of rights control and regulation.

However, these measures have hardly staunched the haemorrhage of revenue caused by piracy, illegal private downloading and the growth of peer-to-peer (P2P) file exchange sites. Criminalizing these sites has proved to be far trickier than the music business anticipated. In part, this is the result of the exponential growth in access to the technology and the capacity of illegal platforms to satisfy demand. Over 500 million users have downloaded software programs that permit file-sharing, with over 60 million based in the USA alone. Similarly, the capacity of unauthorized platforms dwarfs that of authorized servers. For example, at its height Kazaa's P2P archives traded on average ten million files online per day, compared with the entire licensed archive available on iTunes of 700,000 tracks.

Kazaa is only one of a swarm of P2P platforms, including Gnutella, Rapidshare and Soulseek. P2P servers and unauthorized downloaders have been targeted by the Recording Industry Association of America (RIAA), which represents 90% of music companies, and various industry government coalitions in Europe, Asia and Latin America. Until recently, the mantra they have followed is to make life more difficult and dangerous for offenders. As part of digital rights management (DRM) strategies, they have launched a crackdown on illegal music downloading based upon three fronts:

1 *Litigation against servers.* So far, the successful case against Napster (2001) is the prize victory in the campaign of the music business against unauthorized servers. More recent campaigns against Gnutella and Kazaa have achieved further restraint in unauthorized trade. But litigation is costly, protracted and the legal results are uncertain and inconclusive.

2 *Litigation against individuals.* A zero-tolerance strategy against unauthorized downloaders has labelled offenders as guilty of theft and led to the imposition of fines by the courts. In 2005 the International Federation of the Phonographic Industry (IFPI) initiated 2,100 legal cases against individuals in five countries in Europe, Asia and Latin America. The majority of offenders were young men between 20 and 30. The average fine levied was $3,000.

3 *Sanctions against high offender groups.* In 2007 the RIAA targeted twenty-five US universities as institutions in which the worst offenders are enrolled. It sent 15,000 complaints, three times a year, to university authorities. The action follows a US Senate resolution, sponsored by Senator Lamar Alexander, calling upon universities to eliminate illicit file-sharing across campus networks.

The three-pronged approach has not exactly eliminated illegal downloading. Each front of activity carrys PR costs. Litigation against servers risks turning the outlawed brands into pop culture heroes, celebrated for waging a David and Goliath struggle against the entrenched interests of multinational music corporations. Targeting individual offenders risks creating martyrs and victims who attract public sympathy rather than censure. The focus on university campuses carries with it the charge of reinforcing stereotypes about offenders (unauthorized exchange is not confined to the under-25 age group) and creating scapegoats.

Nor is there reliable evidence that the combination of sanctions and litigation is reducing unauthorized exchange. On the contrary, the crackdown on P2P servers has precipitated migration to safer forms of unauthorized exchange. Access via proxy servers, encryption, ripping from the internet and radio are becoming more popular because they are undetectable. Given the immense problems of access and capacity, DRM initiatives are like flies in the whirlwind. The numbers who trade in illegal downloads per day far exceeds the capacities of detection or the abilities of the courts to process law suits.

In general, criminalization strategies have failed to appreciate that open digital access is a revolution in the technology of production, exchange and consumption of intellectual property and that it is connected to a generational lifestyle change in how consumers view entitlement and fair exchange. Three out of every four teenagers in the USA believe that the capacity to share music files should be made legal (Kusek and Leonhard 2005: 43, 89–90, 101). Research commissioned by the British Rights Management (BRM) group found that 95% of the people surveyed engaged in some form of unauthorized downloading. An offender rate of 88% was reported for 14–17 year olds and 92% for 18–24 year olds. Among the 25-plus age group, unauthorized downloading was found to apply to over 80% (Allen 2008).

Most leading commentators conclude that the thinking of authorized suppliers and umbrella organizations like the RIAA which represent their interests is outmoded (Kusek and Leonhard 2005; Burkart and McCourt 2006; David 2010). They have obstinately pursued a business model that has been rendered obsolete by web technology and generational cultural changes in lifestyle architecture and the perception of fair dealing in consumer transactions.

The latest figures on worldwide CD/vinyl and digital sales make stark reading for record company executives (see Table 6.2). Throughout the world, CD and vinyl sales are in precipitous decline. In 2007–8 the CD/vinyl market in the USA shrank by nearly one third; in Europe and Latin America the drop was in the region of 10–12%. Globally, in 2007–8, digital/vinyl sales were 15.4% down.

Independent music distribution networks and retail chains have also been traumatized. Pinnacle Entertainment, the UK leading indie distributor, and Amato Distribution, which represented 100 indie labels, collapsed in 2008. A year later, the major retail chains Zavvi and Woolworths went under.

As 'physical' record sales have declined, there has been some compensation in the form of the growth of authorized online sales and performance rights income. Digital sales encompass online downloads from stores like iTunes, Rhapsody, Music-Match, BuyMusic, Wippit, OD2, Sony Connect, Wal-Mart Music Downloads and the new Napster, and also sales from mobile channels, ad-supported services, mono/polyphonic ringtone incomes and bundled subscriptions.

Table 6.2 Sales of recorded music, 2007–8 (% change)

	Physical	Digital	Performance rights	Total
Europe	−11.3	+36.1	+11.3	−6.3
USA	−31.2	+16.5	+133.3	−18.6
Asia	−4.9	+26.1	+14.6	+1.0
Latin America	−10.3	+46.6	+16.7	−4.7
Global	−15.4	+24.1	+16.2	−8.3

Source: International Federation of the Phonographic Industry.

Performance rights refer to income derived from third-party licences for the use of sound recordings in music videos in broadcasting (radio/TV), public performance (nightclubs, bars, restaurants and hotels) and specialized internet use.

However, these enlarged revenue streams are insufficient to cover the gap. The orthodox industrial business model of the postwar years is in meltdown. As we have seen (pp. 126–8), Keightley (2004) outlined the general features of this postwar model. It is now time to go into the details of this approach more closely in order to assess why the music business has been slow and inadequate in adapting to the challenges of the online revolution.

The Industrial Business Model

In business terms, the Big Four are the latest iteration of a postwar oligopoly that, through mergers and acquisitions, has sought to defend market share and directly control the supply and distribution of recorded music. On the production side, they have sought to achieve a closed market in the production of recorded music by financing and developing artists, monopolizing the production process and exerting sole or joint copyright over recordings.

The postwar orthodoxy was founded on the basis of locating an artist (usually through the A&R branch of operations) and negotiating an advance. Typically, royalties (7–12% for a new artist and 15% plus for an established artist) were not awarded until the advance was earned back through sales. Contracts were based on the principle of exclusivity, so that in agreeing to rights for their first record release, artists were generally bound to the treadmill of multi-year record contracts that specified a non-negotiable number of annual releases. Thus, in effect, the artist bears the cost of recording and marketing the product in the first instance and commits to a multi-year contract to boot. Typically, the contract term spanned seven years.

On the distribution side, the Big Four either created or entered partnerships with global publishing firms, A&R departments, record clubs and retail stores. Their size conferred competitive advantage in marketing and promoting records. This extended into reported cases of price-fixing. Between 1991 and 2001 the major record corporations are said to have inflated the price of a CD by 12.53% (Burkart and McCourt 2006: 32). Thus, the major record companies are alleged to operate as a cartel, using their privileged position in supply and distribution chains to engage in anti-competitive practices.

The music business has a long history of bribing radio DJs to plug records. 'Payola' refers to the use of financial bribery, kickbacks, call girls, drugs and other inducements to give air-time or print columns in the music media to promote artists or recordings. The term is best known to refer to the so-called 'Payola' scandal of 1960 in which the DJ and music promoter Alan Freed was found guilty of accepting bribes to plug records. The case led to Congress passing a statute making Payola a misdemeanour, punishable by a maximum fine of $10,000 and/or a year in prison. To date, no-one has served time on Payola charges.

Yet, far from proving that the industry has learned from its mistakes, and despite the Senate inquiry (1986) into the so-called 'New Payola' scandals, Dannen (1991) contends that Payola remains institutionalized in the music business. He documents a long history, involving both major and independent labels, of making undisclosed payments and offering other inducements to media personnel to plug artists and records. The consolidation of radio stations in the USA during the 1980s and 1990s streamlined the process through which 'independent promoters', acting for record labels, can bribe radio bosses to influence broadcast schedules to showcase a designated playlist.

Since the late 1950s the major corporations have rationalized competition through mergers and acquisitions. Their business was based in managing low production costs and achieving high rates of return at point of sale. The concentration of power in fewer hands gave the major corporations considerable heft with retail and rights agencies. Until the rise of web trading, distribution was rooted in the high street music store. The market share of the major corporations gave them power to negotiate favourable rates of retail discount and to defray the costs of retailing to the independent service sector. The online revolution in production, access, exchange and consumption has turned the orthodox business model upon its head.

As we have already seen (p. 36), initially, record corporation executives responded to the challenge of unauthorized downloading with a mixture of dismissal, denial and legal repression. Even after the decline in 'hard' CD sales and the relatively feeble performance of legitimate platforms of digital sale, the response of the industry has been slow and uneven. Although it remains in a state of flux, two dominant business strategies have emerged and crystallized. Customer relationship management (CRM) initiatives operate through corporate sponsored subscription networks and social network communities to build brand loyalty and educate users in authorized exchange. Digital rights management (DRM) strategies are designed to be punitive and to punish offenders with fines and blacklisting. This is a classic carrot and stick response to the management of risk.

CRM is the carrot end of the equation. It uses web technology to build brand loyalty and accumulate personal data about customers. Access is directed through a subscription portal. Subscription may be free or it may be fee-based. Either way, transactions require the subscriber to supply personal data to the supplier which are organized into personal dossiers and categories of class, gender, race and age that can be used to prompt choices ('recommendations' for purchase) or traded to corporate divisions or external interests.

A case study of successful CRM in the music business is Last.fm. It is a music recommendation system based upon Audioscrobbler technology. This technology creates dossiers of personal musical taste by tracking and encrypting subscriber choice of listening. The dossier base is used to construct an internet 'community'. Registered subscribers have access to Last.fm forums, send and receive messages, list events, make recommendations and add to the Last.fm client music playlist (currently 3.5 million individual tracks available in over 200 countries). An artist page section allows musicians to post recordings and track hits. Official music videos from YouTube are also available online. Customer data are based upon music choice, but Last.fm exploits this data stream to construct wider consumer profiles of income divisions, buying habits, lifestyle values and cultural preferences that can be used for the purposes of promotion or traded to external interests. In sum, the site uses entertainment facilities to produce a massive global resource of free, self-enrolled, self-refreshing market research data. In 2007 the company was purchased by CBS Interactive for £140 million ($280 million).

CRM initiatives are favoured by the major music corporations as a strategy to re-colonize the internet. They work on a 'Big Buddy' principle. That is, the web platform is positioned as a virtual friend, facilitating musical choice by providing playback facilities, recommendations and chart lists and encouraging subscribers to become members of a web community that offers additional opportunities for establishing relationships and participation. The Big Buddy principle makes a highly public virtue out of appearing to be enabling, non-discriminatory, non-judgemental and non-disciplinary.

The industry's second response to the challenge of unauthorized downloading is DRM. We have explored the main features of this response above. This is the 'stick' side of the equation. DRM initiatives use a combination of encryption technology, policing and legislation to regulate copyright infringement. Encryption technologies aim to confine access to authorized users through lockout or watermark algorithms.

Evidence from an anti-piracy crackdown in Sweden and South Korea suggests that legislation and policing do have an effect. Anti-piracy laws passed in 2009 resulted in an 18% rise in sales in both markets (IFPI 2010). In the long run attitudes to unauthorized downloading may not have changed in Sweden and South Korea. But the year-on-year evidence currently suggests that high publicity about sanctions can produce short-run changes in behaviour.

However, the legislation has prompted a counter-response from pressure groups like the Open Rights Group, who question whether harsh measures are the right solution to the problem. Instead, they advocate the restructuring of distribution services in the direction of more legal, relevant online music sources such as Spotify. There is reason to suppose that music corporations are becoming more persuaded by this line of argument.

The switch of the Big Four from a blanket policy of DRM protection to licensed online CRM-based access is already well underway. WMG, Universal, Sony-BMG and EMI have all made part of their catalogue available online, often in partnership with dedicated online distributors like iTunes and Amazon. This is a tacit acknowledgement that inflexible, punitive DRM strategies are counter-productive.

This is not to say that the DRM camp in the music business has given up the ghost. Music subscription services such as Realnetwork's (RNWK) Rhapsody and ad-supported services like Ruckus continue to use DRM technology to ensure that access stops when the subscription stops. However, this represents only a tiny sector of the market. In general, the Big Four have concluded that DRM punished the innocent more than the guilty and scaled back activities in favour of boosting CRM-based subscription models.

Doves in the Big Four and the RIAA argue that hawks are quite unrealistic in believing in a 'big fix' technology to neutralize the information technology of unauthorized exchange. A crucial item in the case of the doves is what has come to be known as the SDMI fiasco. In 1998 the music industry, acting in partnership with security technology companies, sought to introduce a DRM industry standard through the so-called 'Secure Digital Music Initiative' (SDMI). The aim was to develop an infallible encryption protection technology to preserve copyright. In

2000 a watermark-based encryption system was unveiled and declared to be an industry breakthrough. An open letter was written to hackers and cryptologists inviting them to break the code and gain access to the music. In the event, a team led by Ed Felten, a Professor of Computer Science at Princeton University, broke the code within three weeks. Felten's plans to publicize the neutralization of the watermark at the Information Hiding Workshop in Pittsburgh in 2001 were blocked by a legal injunction issued by the RIAA and the Verance Corporation (a sound technology company).

The expansion of internet trade since 2001 has resulted in the development of more sophisticated systems of encryption, such as Sony's Connect service for ATRAC-encoded digital music files, Microsoft's WMA system and Apple iTunes AAC-encoded system. However, no infallible system of digital data protection has emerged. Indeed, some commentators now reject the entire project of finding one as pie in the sky. For, logically, there is no plausible way of preventing a data protection system from being cloned and disabled by determined unauthorized users (Kusek and Leonhard 2005; David 2010).

The determination of the hawks to make unauthorized exchange difficult and dangerous does not merely turn on the allegation of theft. The question of unacknowledged Research and Development costs and associated risk management issues in the music business is also moot.

It is easy for critics to impugn the Big Four and the RIAA as fat cats who have flagrantly mistaken the commercial opportunities of online exchange. But this is to gratuitously ignore the high levels of risk in the music business. According to Vogel (1998), only one record in ten releases breaks even. In 1999, eighty-eight records, out of nearly three thousand releases, accounted for 25% of sales (Mann 2000). Less than 10% of artists recoup their royalty advances. Only 250 album releases sell more than 10,000 copies a year and fewer than thirty achieve platinum status (one million sales).

The prominence assigned in the music press to rich and famous musicians distorts public understanding of industry standards. The American Federation of Musicians union reports that of 273,000 musicians working in the USA, only 15% have steady gigs. The average annual income of members is only $30,000 (Kusek and Leonhard 2005: 108).

Music is therefore a high-risk business in which record corporations seldom make a return on investment. Of course, when an investment pays off it can result in substantial, renewable revenue. But for every Michael Jackson, Coldplay, Beyoncé, Britney Spears or Jay- Z who is discovered, there are thousands of releases that are rapidly discounted, remaindered or pulped.

However, in return for bearing this risk, the Big Four have traditionally issued record contracts that turn musicians into not much more than indentured creative labourers. Allegations of unfair record contracts and injustice are rife. For example, in 2002, Courtney Love filed a lawsuit against Vivendi Universal for a recording contract that she argued was punitive. It is estimated that 99.9% of audits expose record companies for underpaying their artists (Strauss 2002).

In reviewing the industrial planning model of the postwar music business, Patrick Burkart and Tom McCourt (2006: 35–6) contend that the major corporations have a history of 'collusive behaviour'. More specifically, the music business is held to have consistently subjected artists to prejudicial record contracts, regulated distribution networks through bribery, plugging and price-fixing and rigidly enforced the provisions of copyright.

The music oligopoly initially responded to the challenge of unauthorized internet downloading by litigation against unauthorized suppliers and downloaders, developing lockout or blocking technologies, 'educating' the public, building their own subscription platforms and, since the 1980s, diversifying revenue streams. In addition to record sales, the major corporations now pursue a strategy of bespoke interlocking revenue accumulation encompassing advertising revenue, movie tie-ins, streaming, ringtones and tour bookings (Garafolo 1999).

The business has moved slowly and painfully, from defining the web as a threat, to exploring legal ways of exploiting and developing copyright revenue from online exchange. However, it would be a grave error to regard this as a live-and-let-live philosophy. The CRM/DRM carrot and stick strategies, developed by the Big Four and the RIAA, are not attempts to make free music available or give power to the people. On the contrary, they are strategies to regulate music business on the net, obliterate the competition and maximize market share.

The Independents

In the 1950s Sun Records played a notable role in popularizing rock and roll and country and western. Sun had Elvis Presley, Johnny Cash, Carl Perkins, Jerry Lee Lewis and Roy Orbison on the books. Chess, Atlantic, Stax and Motown were crucial in popularizing black music. Some artists also got into the act. Frank Sinatra founded Reprise Records in 1961 with a brief to guarantee creative freedom and a fair rate of return to artists. Reprise artists were allowed to retain publishing rights. Sinatra co-opted fellow Rat Pack members Dean Martin and Sammy Davis Jr to the label, as well as Bing Crosby and Rosemary Clooney. The label also represented the early recordings of Jimi Hendrix and The Kinks. Sinatra sold the label to Warner Brothers in 1963.

Apple Records, created by The Beatles under the aegis of EMI in 1968, championed the same principles of artistic freedom and fair return for artists. First and foremost, the company was designed as a vehicle for Beatles recordings. As such it offered the band more creative control and potentially higher revenue streams. In addition, reflecting the communard utopianism of the day, Apple sought to give a break to struggling musicians and unsigned acts. It ran adverts in the music press encouraging unknowns to mail in demos. Acts were also signed on the basis of recommendation from The Beatles or their circle. Badfinger, James Taylor, Mary Hopkin, Ravi Shankar, John Tavener and Doris Troy were all contracted via these routes.

For fledgeling musicians or established artists dissatisfied with conventional record contracts, the free-form, non-hierarchical managerial principles of Apple were one of the big attractions of the company. It also resulted in financial mayhem. In 1969, Apple introduced stringent cost-control measures that pushed the idealism of the company onto the rocks. Apple continued trading, but its sphere of operations was firmly fixed on the re-packaging, franchising and merchandising of Beatles recordings and film footage.

Other notable indie labels should be mentioned. In the UK the Immediate label, founded in 1965 by The Rolling Stones' manager, Andrew Loog Oldham, represented Fleetwood Mac, The Nice, Small Faces, John Mayall, Savoy Brown and Chris Farlowe; Chrysalis Records, founded in 1969 by Chris Wright and Terry Ellis, represented Blondie, Billy Idol, Rory Gallagher, Pere Ubu, Procol Harum and Sinéad O'Connor; the Charisma label, created by Tony Stratton Smith in 1969, represented Genesis, Van der Graaf Generator, Peter Gabriel and Audience; Chris Blackwell's Island Records, founded in Jamaica in 1959, represented Bob Marley, U2, Traffic, ELP, Free, Fairport Convention and The Cranberries; Dave Robinson and Jake Riviera created the Stiff record label in 1976, with a portfolio of artists including Elvis Costello, Nick Lowe, Richard Hell and The Voidoids, Ian Dury and Madness; Beserkley Records was founded by Matthew King Kaufman along with members of Bay Area band Earthquake in 1973 and represented Jonathan Richman, The Rubinos and Greg Kihn; Interscope was launched in 1990 by Jimmy Iovine and Ted Field and represented Beck, Eazy-E, Foxy Brown and The Sugarcubes; and Death Row Records was founded by Dr Dre and Surge Knight in 1991 and represented 2Pac, Snoop Dog, Jewell and Tha Dogg Pound.

Indie labels purport to offer a more personal, flexible service to artists. The bedrock of the company is usually a charismatic business leader such as Phil and Leonard Chess (Chess), Berry Gordy (Motown) or Tony Wilson (Factory). This creates succession problems when the leader either leaves or dies. It is one reason why indie labels are susceptible to takeovers from the Big Four. Thus, Motown and Island are now subsidiaries of UMG; Atlantic was absorbed by WMG in 1967; Charisma was acquired by Virgin, which was itself purchased by EMI in 1992; and Chess was sold to General Recorded Tape in 1969.

Distribution deals are struck either with the major labels or with independent supply chains. Typically, they fasten upon niche markets. So Charisma aimed at the progressive rock market, Interscope and Death Row Records at rap music and Island at reggae, progressive and folk.

Indie labels can achieve spectacular success in short order. Low overheads provide fluidity and the cachet of being outside the formal music business. This can act as a magnet for new musicians. Additionally, indie labels often feed off a breakthrough in musical genres that the big record labels have under-represented or ignored. Thus, Stiff, Beserkley and Radar broke major punk artists in the 1970s and 1980s and Interscope and Death Row established themselves as labels of choice at the start of the rap and hip hop era.

Corporate renegades from the established music business, hobbyists and fans are often the instigators of indie labels. Because they are out-riders from the official machinery of the music business they are often run, at least at the outset, on a shoe-string. This results in structural problems of capitalization and distribution. The capitalization issue often acts as an impediment to growth, whereas the distribution question generally results in over-dependence upon the major record labels. As capitalization issues bite, indies face disgruntlement from artists who become frustrated with the financial barriers to maximizing sales and turn to the major labels or entertainment cartels for financial support. This is often the first step on the slippery slope to outright accumulation by one of the Big Four.

Challenges to the Big Four

As we saw in the last chapter (pp. 126–8), until recently, record corporations operated with a fairly stable industrial planning business model. The central pillars were settled market segmentation niches (teen, youth, AOR audiences); product organization around the LP; and packaging options based around the back-catalogue.

Prior to the digital revolution there were significant challenges to this model. For example, in the 1980s a high-profile campaign was launched against home taping. The British Phonographic Industry (BPI) launched a copyright infringement crusade based on the slogan 'Home Taping is Killing Music'. However, the campaign faltered because the industry registered an unprecedented boom in the 1980s with the growth and consumer acceptance of the CD format. In general, the basis has relied upon stable demand for albums and exploited the shift from vinyl to CD formats as a cash cow by re-packaging the back-catalogue.

Most media businesses are driven by front-of-catalogue sales (new product). This is why, in the 1960s and early 1970s, record corporations placed a strong accent upon solo performers and bands releasing singles on a regular basis. Later, this translated into the edict that market position requires successful musicians to release an album every year. The CD revolution turned this business model upon its head. Through re-packaging and marketing campaigns that dwelt upon the acoustic superiority of the CD format, the back-catalogue was reinvented. Consumers who had purchased vinyl recordings in the 1960s and 1970s dutifully replaced them with CD copies. In such circumstances the plea from the record business that home taping was killing music fell on deaf ears.

Besides the CD revolution, the most significant thing that happened in the 1980s was the introduction of mobile devices (the Walkman and, later, the iPod and MP3 players). This multiplied the settings in which music was played for personal use. Crucially, it made settings mobile. Creating a selection of mood music from your record collection enhanced the pleasure of the listening experience by personalizing choice in the car, on public transport, while watching TV or reading.

The digital revolution that began in the 1990s constitutes a quite different scale of challenges for the industry. Re-packaging is not an option because online exchange threatens both the traditional supply and distribution routes of the orthodox business model. In order to facilitate comprehension it may help to divide the challenges into supply-side and demand-side risks.

Supply-Side Risks

Supply-side risks may be sub-divided into two categories: studio control and commodity distribution.

Studio Control

The conventional postwar business model involved music corporations leasing studio time to artists. Leasing arrangements often extended to the use of studio space and instruments owned by the record corporations and producers independently contracted by them. Typically, the costs were cross-subsidized against future royalties. Studios were either franchised or owned outright by record companies. For example, the legendary Abbey Road studios in St John's Wood, London, where The Beatles recorded nearly all of their studio output, are owned by EMI. Similarly, the Electric Ladyland Studios in Greenwich Village, New York, have a history of financial links with Warner Brothers.

Studio ownership, franchise deals and cross-subsidization strengthened the hand of record corporations vis-à-vis the musicians contracted to them. In effect, they supplied musicians with the basic tools of the trade, extending from instruments and recording space to specialized staff (including producers and sound engineers).

Digitalization has transformed this arrangement. The introduction of samplers, sequencers and MIDI (musical instrument–digital interface) since the early 1980s has disembedded the musician from the recording studio. Samplers are portable devices that store and re-configure musical data. Sequencers are digital programs that reproduce and replay music. MIDI systems are a formation of computer languages that enable samplers, sequencers and other digital instruments to communicate with one another.

The result of these technical innovations is to release musicians from the technical constraints of recording studios and, by extension, the record corporations that control them. For Brian Eno, in the 1980s, the studio is an instrument that transforms the compositional process:

> You no longer come into the studio with a conception of the finished piece. Instead, you come with actually rather a bare skeleton of a piece, or perhaps with nothing at all. I often start working with no starting point. Once you become familiar with the studio facilities, or even if you're not, actually, you can begin to compose in relation to those facilities. You can begin to think in terms of putting something on, putting something else on, then taking some of the original things off, or taking a mixture of things off, and seeing what you're left with – actually constructing a piece in the studio. (Eno 2004: 129)

Supply-side digitalization has replaced the recording studio with the laptop as the main digital compositional tool. It might be said that the laptop has *become* the studio, providing most of the opportunities for experimentation and serendipity recounted by Eno. This has loosened the reins of corporate control over musicians. If you can gain acceptable acoustic levels of recording in your bedroom or living room, you do not need to get in hock to the major record labels for studio time.

Commodity Distribution

The traditional sales model was based upon a contract in which musicians voluntarily assigned rights to record labels, including a share of copyright, in return for an advance, studio facilities and access to a global marketing and sales team. We will come to look at the question of the recording contract in more detail presently (pp. 157–8). As we have already seen, digitalization has substantially freed the musician from the studio. The same process has dismantled the conventional system of distributing recordings. Musicians are no longer forced to deliver master copies to record executives who then transform the original into commodities and arrange for global marketing, sales and retail distribution. Digitalization makes distribution synonymous with having access to a laptop and an internet connection and eliminates the traditional requirements for sales and distribution by making exchange weightless.

Various mainstream musicians, such as Nine Inch Nails, Brian Eno, Peter Gabriel and Mick Hucknall, have made their recordings available for commercial exchange in the form of digital downloads. To date, the most famous example is Radiohead's *In Rainbows* (2007). Self-released, the album was packaged as a zip file and sold at a price determined by the consumer. Three months after the release of the digital download, a 'discbox' with bonus recordings and enhanced packaging was released. The album achieved a greater financial return for the band than the final album in their former EMI contract, *Hail to the Thief* (2003).

Digital download exchange is growing in sophistication. In 2005, the BPI reported that digital downloads out-performed CD/vinyl sales for the first time. It is reported that 46% of all 12–17 year olds in the UK visit a music website at least once a month. The market potential and cost savings (by cutting out the record label) are obvious. Online downloads are also associated with a non-hierarchical, democratic ethos that contrasts with the traditional music business. This is appealing to musicians and audiences. There are four business models:

1 *Hosting platforms.* MP3 hosting sites, such as Tune Tribe (endorsed by Groove Armada), Total Band and Morpheus. Tune Tribe offers musicians 80% of royalties with bands setting the download price.
2 *Digital labels.* Magnatune, Artist Share and Karma Download offer musicians a percentage on sales and, generally, exclusive copyright. A price-fixing strategy is sometimes determined by consumers.
3 *Dedicated posting sites.* These are based in converting audio files into MP3 format in combination with a file transfer system, such as Queue FTP. Dedicated site postings carry costs in (a) web design, (b) marketing, (c) regular updates of releases and gigs and (d) a payment system through PayPal or WorldPay.
4 *Remixing sites.* Sites like CC Mixter enable legal sampling, mashing and interaction. This is licensed under the non-profit online organization, Creative Commons, which offers flexible copyright arrangements.

Demand-Side Risks

Computer-mediated exchange transforms the organization of consumption from a closed chain to an open system. The closed chain is based upon the producer supplying the retailer with a commodity for exchange in a dedicated setting. So the record label contracts the musician, receives the master copy of the recording, presses copies, markets them and supplies the record store with the commodity.

The open system is compatible with unregistered exchange in the form of illegal downloading, digital piracy and P2P exchange. As Manuel Castells (1996: 356), maintains, the rise of the internet inevitably expands the population of computer hackers and network hobbyists who engage in unauthorized exchange. However, the use of the term 'piracy' cannot be confined to organized gang-based theft and counterfeiting. This is because the digital revolution makes unauthorized, non-commercial downloading or CD burning an option available to anyone who owns a computer (Marshall 2004: 190).

According to the Recording Industry Association of America (RIAA), music piracy results in the loss of $12.5 billion revenue per year and 71,060 job losses in the USA (*www.riaa.com/physicalpiracy.php*). As noted above, the IFPI estimates that, despite increasing digital sales, 95% of all music downloads are illegal: that is, without payment to the artist or the record label. Forty billion files were shared illegally in 2008. The loss to the UK recording industry was estimated to stand at £180 million (*www.ifpi.org*). These figures are supplied by the record industry and, as such, may not be entirely reliable. Even allowing for some exaggeration, they point to a very considerable problem for the industry. To illustrate this, let us briefly consider the question of piracy and policing.

Lee Marshall (2004: 191) distinguishes between six types of piracy:

(a) *counterfeiting*: the unauthorized commercial provision of copyright material through copying;
(b) *pirating*: the unauthorized selection of tracks from legitimately released albums and re-packaging;
(c) *bootlegging*: the unauthorized copying and/or recording of music that has never been officially released;
(d) *tape trading*: the private swapping of tapes of unauthorized material;
(e) *home taping/CD burning*: copying copyright material on CD or analogue tape; and
(f) *file-sharing*: utilizing P2P software, users 'share' music on the internet.

Unauthorized exchange therefore occurs along a number of fronts. This complicates policing and legislation. Illegal supply chains are often organized around international cartels or gang operations. This requires highly resourced and organized global policing responses which, currently, have not been achieved. Moreover, the question of legislation is complicated by the question of fair use. What is fair use to the consumer is often copyright infringement to the record company or artist. The root of the problem here is that once a commodity has been traded it is very difficult to enforce barriers on its exchange. The practices of sampling and scratching in club culture, hip hop and rap reveal how exchange is the basis for using creative labour to change the value of recorded music, while selling a bootleg of a concert by Fleetwood Mac or The Eagles, even if it is well engineered and adds to the creative understanding of the music, is seen as unacceptable.

The end of the closed-chain model of consumption has inevitably generated the proliferation of gangs and international cartels who supply music illegally. In 2009 what was alleged to be the world's biggest music piracy ring, Rabid Neurosis (RNS) in the USA, was busted. RNS used a network of bribed suppliers in CD manufacturing plants, radio stations and retailers to gain access to pre-release material. It was alleged that 25,000 copyrighted titles were pirated during its decade of operation. RNS made Cassandra Wilson's album *Thunderbird* available fully a week before its official release.

The digital revolution creates problems of policing intellectual property that are currently insurmountable. Effectively, private copying is detection-proof. Commercial exchange of copyright material is only marginally more susceptible to policing, for suppliers are effectively deterritorialized and change servers when need be.

The Digital Millennium Copyright Act, 1998, and After

The Digital Millennium Copyright Act (DMCA, 1998) has become notorious because it illustrates the scale of the policing problem. Ostensibly, the Act criminalizes the production and dissemination of intellectual property that is protected by copyright. As Goldstein (2003: 175–85) and Burkart and McCourt (2006: 114–19) demonstrate, there are two major flaws with the DCMA.

Firstly, it fails to adequately discriminate between illegal and fair use. Photocopying and home taping are not exempt, making the category of unauthorized use a minefield of lay and legal interpretation and dispute.

Secondly, the law is unenforceable because, currently, there is no effective encryption system to prohibit illegal downloading. As Goldstein (2003) notes, a couple of months after the DCMA was passed, the Secure Digital Music Initiative (SDMI), which, as we have seen, consists of a combined effort of the RIAA and major record corporations, sought to design encryption technology to preclude unauthorized access and copying. Their solution was *watermarking*: that is, an anti-access technology which is inaudible, but prohibits piracy. However, watermarking has not proved to be impregnable.

The efforts of industry-based organizations like the RIAA and BPI to sue unauthorized downloaders has been counter-productive. Court cases are widely recognized to be the tip of the iceberg. Hence, legal action makes martyrs out of unauthorized downloaders. It locks the music industry into a David and Goliath syndrome which generates bad publicity and, in any case, fails to address the problem. In a nutshell, the problem is that music copyright law has not fully caught up with the options that digital technology produces for both creative artists and consumers.

The present legal situation is well captured by Paul Théberge (2004: 139): 'Where revision in copyright laws have [sic] sought to address the new realities of music practice that stem, in part, from technological innovations in music making, they have been adopted and applied in such an uneven fashion that confusion, inequality, and the stifling of creativity have been the result.'

Counter-intuitively, even if a fail-safe security mechanism were to be invented, it would not necessarily prevent unauthorized exchange. This is because the transference of the watermark to gangs and cartels could never be ruled out. If Universal Music defend the latest album by Sting or 50 Cent with a supposedly fail-safe system of watermarking, there is nothing to prevent music theft by an employee or associate of Universal Music and illegal pressing and distribution.

The present period, then, is one of the creative recasting of the role of musician and comprehensive retooling of the music business model. Musicians have the capacity to record demos to a high professional standard and distribute them for free or at nominal charge at gigs or through a web server. Nor are they any longer at the mercy of a record company to supply video-recording facilities to market their compositions. Musicians now apply a do-it-yourself approach and use MySpace, Facebook, Twitter and YouTube for postings and broadcasts. The Arctic Monkeys, Lily Allen and Little Boots have credited MySpace with building an audience for them. The traditional A&R function relied on a network of recommendations and intensive scouting of amateur music venues. Digitalization has not exhausted this service. Crucially, in conjunction with it, A&R executives spend a much greater proportion of time surfing the web and filtering music postings than clubbing or attending concerts.

As for the record corporations, all of the major labels have struck distribution deals with online providers and created their own channels of digital provision. For example, the Universal Music Group has distribution arrangements with INgrooves. INgrooves distributes all of Universal's mobile products, including ringtones, ringbacks, games, video, streaming and wallpaper as well as UMG's wholly owned record labels, Interscope Geffen A&M, Island Def Jam, Universal Motown Republic Group, Decca, Universal Music Latin Entertainment and Universal Music Group Nashville. UMG also has an internet distribution arrangement with Napster.

Warner Brothers also offers digital sales and has an agreement with Alternative Distribution Alliance (ADA), the number one independent music distributor in the USA according to Nielsen SoundScan data. According to SoundScan, Warner's digital sales increased from 18.10 % (2004) to 22.08 % (2008) (*news.cnet.com/8301-1023_3-10159985-93.html*).

Sony-BMG offers a subscription-based digital sales model. Partnered with UMG and Abu Dhabi Media Company (ADMC), Sony is a major investor in VEVO, a new music, video and entertainment service powered by YouTube. Along with UMG, it is a major investor in MP3 format firms (McPhail 2006: 133).

In 1988 EMI streamed the first album over the internet (*Mezzanine*, Massive Attack) and pioneered the release of the first digital album download (*Hours*, David Bowie). In 2002 it made its new music available digitally at the same time as it is serviced to radio stations. It is partnered with a variety of companies offering digital downloads via subscription, online jukeboxes, video jukeboxes, custom compilations, kiosks, mobile phone rings, master ringtones and digital car stereos. Indie labels have struck similar custom-built deals with online providers of music and video entertainment.

One response to the online challenge that major record corporations have developed is to restructure organizational capacity. Instead of identifying records as a cash cow, they have developed models of bespoke aggregation in which recordings are franchised as ringtones, internet streaming, advertising jingles and computer games. This involves exploiting and developing strategies of synchronization which splice music into TV ads, TV series and films and the game industry. Aerosmith are said to have earned more through royalties of the game Guitar Hero than they have from the past two decades of album sales. Since its launch in late 2005, Guitar Hero has sold 23 million copies. Compare this with sales of the biggest selling album of all time, namely The Eagles' *Their Greatest Hits* (1976), which, to date, has sold 29 million units (Black 2009). An exemplary case of the multinational synchronization model is Vivendi, who own the world's largest music label, Universal.

Corporate Synchronization: The Vivendi Model

The term *synchronization* refers to the consolidation of separate or loosely linked brands or functions into an organized, corporate whole. The process is pursued through two mechanisms. *Conglomeration* refers to the purchase of separate brands to achieve business synergy in different spheres of activity. Typically, this involves sharing good business practice and building product lines through synchronized business strategies. For example, when Sony purchased CBS Records in 1998 and EMI accumulated Virgin Records in 1992, they rationalized product lines instead of competing with one another. In 2007 the parent company merged Virgin Records with Capitol Records to create the Capitol Music Group.

The second process of synergization is when a corporation creates a new distribution channel that enables the various subsidiary brands to 'talk' to one another more freely. This is behind the investment of UMG and Sony-BMG's partnership in VEVO.

In the last twenty years there have been many examples of synchronization in the music business. The scale of the transition and the fronts of activity are contingent upon the financial resources of the corporation. The four major labels have learned from indie labels like Stiff, Cherry Red, Fat Wreck, Rhino and Matador. They have tried to engineer strong, non-hierarchical trust relations between the executive and the artist and diversified into tour promotion, artist management, merchandising and franchising. As we shall see presently, brand diversification within the major music corporations has been used as a strategy to develop links between the entertainment and telecommunications industries. Through this means, sound recordings mutually reinforce mobile, TV/cinema and games outputs. Outwardly, the paramount justification for synchronization is customer service. The Big Four music labels have recast their business organization because they *listen to the customer*. That margins are increased and dividends expanded by these means is beside the point. Serving the customer is portrayed as being all. This is another example of the wider phenomenon of traditional capitalist organizations learning from smaller 'neat' or 'cool' capitalist companies to provide strong brand loyalty and supplier affiliation through pyramid deals (see Rojek 2007: 115–34; McGuigan 2009).

The success of Viacom's Music Television (MTV) alerted music corporations to the financial potential in bundling. MTV has a market of 340 million in 140 countries. It operates through over 100 international affiliates, such as MTV Latino, MTV Europe, MTV Brazil, MTV Mandarin, MTV Australia, MTV New Zealand, MTV Africa and MTV Asia. Targeted at the 12–24 age group, MTV is financed by advertising. The network is recognized by the music industry as a prime highway for the promotion of new releases and setting youth agendas (Banks 1996, 1997). MTV's fusion advertising-based music and video is a model for streaming networks and pyramid supply structured around a subscription model.

Of late, the term 'pyramid deal' has fallen into bad odour in business circles as a result of the Bernie Madoff confidence scam in the financial sector.[1] The sense in which I wish to use it in this book refers not to illegal trading, but to multi-layered corporate organization. At the apex of the pyramid corporation is a board of governors and executors who dictate strategy. However, the corporation works through calculated devolution in which various brands situated at the base of the pyramid are designed and run for segmented markets. Since each brand is located as a brick in the whole structure, it is assumed that the trading functions of each part will ordinarily be mutually reinforcing. Trade in the music division must achieve an acceptable margin through either direct sales or synergy with other divisions, such as promotions, video, public relations, television and film.

As an example, consider the industry leader: the Vivendi Group. Vivendi is a French-owned entertainment conglomerate, situated in seventy-seven countries, with revenues of 25,392 million euros and a workforce of over 42,000 (2008). It is a 100% owner of UMG, the biggest music corporation in the world, and Groupe Canal+, France's premium TV theme channel producer and a major investor in European film. In addition, Vivendi has a controlling interest in Activision-Blizzard, a major online and console games producer, SFR, the second largest telecommunications operator in France, and Maroc Telecom, the largest fixed line and mobile telecom operator and internet access provider in Morocco. Furthermore, it has a 20% stake in NBC Universal, which is involved in the production of TV, films and theme parks (see Figure 6.1). The main bricks of production and trading are therefore music, film and TV, games and mobile/internet telecommunications. In 2007 Vivendi launched ZAOZA, a mobile entertainment distribution subsidiary, which seeks to exploit group content and relay the content of other groups through franchising and subscription models.

The business strategy focuses on exploiting the opportunities provided by digital technology to provide synergy between the entertainment and telecommunications industries. The Vivendi model builds strong brands and mutually reinforcing distribution platforms. For example, Canal+ film and TV production, Activision-Blizzard Games or SFR/Maroc Telecom ringtones have UMG's back-catalogue archive to raid. New UMG recordings may be geared to promote new products in any of the three company subsidiaries. While the goal of strong brands presupposes a level of autonomy at the subsidiary level, with each division having its Managing Director and Executive directorate, group strategy is controlled by the Vivendi Board of Governors and Executives.

Other leading corporate players in the entertainment-telecommunications industry, such as AOL Time Warner, Disney, Viacom and News Corp, are experimenting with similar pyramid-type models. The bundling of services, linking

Vivendi
Governors and
Executive

Games	Music	Mobile/Fixed	Pay TV/ Cinema
Activision-Blizzard	UMG	SFR/Maroc Telecom	Canal+
			NBC Universal (20%)

Figure 6.1 Vivendi Group organizational pyramid chart

music to TV/film, games and telecommunications, is the new bedrock of corporate organization in the music industry.

The State of the Music Business Today

The contemporary music business is multi-layered, with major record companies dominating and independent music companies offering a range of niche services. The independents are small, with lower overheads, and consequently are more flexible in green-shoot development and responding to genre-busting transformations in the music business. In aggregate, the current annual turnover of the global industry is estimated to be $40 billion (McPhail 2006: 129).

Digitalization has shaken the industry to its foundations. According to Gallo (2007), album sales dropped for the seventh consecutive year in 2007. Figures provided by Nielsen SoundScan for the USA show physical album sales for 2006 at 363.9 million, down 6.5% on 2005. Back-catalogue sales were down 8.1%. In contrast, digital album sales (5.5% of the market) increased, with Warner controlling 23.9% of the market, UMG 27.4%, Sony-BMG 24% and EMI 10%.

This has produced many consequences. Artists have undertaken a recasting of the traditional musician's role. In particular, the notion of creativity has been expanded to encompass production and distribution functions that have traditionally been regarded as the preserve of management. The business success of Radiohead's In Rainbows has set the bar in the industry. One must not underestimate the technical difficulties involved in advertising digital downloads, providing zip files, collecting online revenues and managing rights. The business merit of In Rainbows is that it demonstrates that these difficulties are soluble. Even allowing for revenue seepage through illegal downloading, the zip release was hugely profitable.

Music corporations have also been forced to rethink production models and re-gear their portfolio of services. All of the Big Four have invested heavily in digital download delivery systems and opened franchise arrangements with online filing and streaming companies like iTunes, Amazon, Last.fm and Spotify. They have developed CRM initiatives to create a 'Big Buddy' link with consumers that enable them to extract key market data and deployed them hand-in-hand with DRM strategies. The aim is not to *occupy* a place in the digital market; it is to colonize it. The market for physical sales is declining but it is unlikely to vanish. There is considerable loyalty to vinyl and CD as commodity forms. However, the future lies in the direction of the expansion of the digital market and bundling music with multi-media platforms.

The partnership of UMG and Sony-BMG to launch VEVO is a sign of the emergence of a new cross-collateralized business partnership model in the music industry. VEVO is responsible for all mobile sales. Far more than the digital download of the front- and back-catalogues is involved. VEVO oversees licensing arrangements with digital distributors like Apple, YouTube and Amazon and manages ringtone, subscription and kiosk sales.

Because digital downloads allow consumers to purchase single tracks, the market for album sales, which had been a staple of the music business since the 1960s, will continue to contract for the foreseeable future. The focus of managerial control will cease to be on singles or albums and will move to intellectual property: that is, music files that can be used for a variety of purposes, covering entertainment, advertising, promotion, brand-building, education and health.

Because intellectual property extends to performance as well as recording, music labels are likely to expand their management function to represent their artists directly in tours and promotions. We have already noted that the ticket prices charged by headline acts have vaulted during the last decade (pp. 39–40).

The recorded music business is exceptionally adaptable. In the 1970s and 1980s, home taping did not kill recorded music. Nor will the digital revolution. New models of authorized downloading, combined with ramping up litigation against illegal downloaders, are the industry's future. Conglomeration of music majors is likely to continue as record companies struggle to rationalize assets and cut overheads. Direct, global digital provision from performers, of the type pioneered by Radiohead's *In Rainbows*, is deemed to be a success. It will be expanded and consolidated to become a niche in the music retail business. However, because financial management skills rarely coalesce smoothly with skills of musical creativity, the direct involvement of artists in retail supply will probably be limited. Illegal digital consumption can never be effectively policed. Because of this, substantial revenue seepage will continue and grow. The cachet of live performance, and the revenue from ticket sales, will partly offset the seepage problem. Of more significance will be the evolution of bundling intellectual property rights to cover multiple platforms of delivery. Revenue opportunities here are not negligible. In 2003, the ringtone business was worth $3.5 billion (Kusek and Leonhard 2005: 70).

DRM initiatives are necessary, but, by the lights of current policing and technology capacities, unenforceable. The creation of victims and martyrs is one thing. Of deeper damage to the credibility of DRM initiatives is the fact that they do not touch, and are normally viewed as being *unable to touch*, the vast majority of unauthorized downloaders.

CRM initiatives have more capacity. The Big Buddy principle undermines orthodox concepts of alienation and exploitation by appearing to turn the exploitative agent into a pal. There is a sort of spiritual revivalism going on here. Portraying your portal as a gateway into a 'one world' global community of boundless recommendations, listings and direct participation revives the essence of the communard utopianism of the 1960s and early 1970s. Potentially, the commercial pay-off is considerable. It hooks subscribers into a compelling business model when their defences are down, because the accent is upon inclusion, empathy and engagement. The information that they release is compatible with innumerable extractive permutations of data-mining.

Of course, in time, consumers may develop reactions to these virtual communities with greater cynicism or scepticism. But from the standpoint of the CRM strategists, a bird in the hand is worth two in the bush. CRM offers multi-media development opportunities, access to free (licensed) recordings and a basis for re-educating subscribers about the perils of unauthorized downloading. As such, it is likely to figure as the lead initiative in managing the unauthorized download challenge.

Yet the subtext of DRM and CRM initiatives is that the music business is intent upon appropriating a mode of distribution and exchange that is currently free (P2P exchange) and outlawing it in favour of a subscription model. Open exchange of a commodity after point of sale is therefore replaced with some form of licensing arrangement. In effect, the music corporation seeks to extend copyright into services that are currently organized around the principle of fair use. They aim to appropriate an area of exchange that has been researched and developed out of their control in order to subject it to their ownership and will. I shall return to develop this point in greater detail in the Conclusion.

7

Artists, Managers and Audiences

Pop music is a people business. It is constructed around transactions of emotional labour between artists, managers and audiences. Traditionally, the star system in the pop music business has positioned the composer and performer as the fountainhead of creativity. As a result, pop and rock stars have been showered with rewards and lionized as icons of glamour. Rock gods like Mick Jagger, Robert Plant, Gene Simmons and Steve Tyler enjoyed immense wealth and a cornucopia of sexual encounters. This has distorted the importance of the star at the expense of developing a balanced reading of the collaborative process involved in recording, writing and performing.

By way of a small corrective, Auslander's (2006: 66) account of the calculated theatricality of glam rock powerfully demonstrates the power of artist and management collaborations to prepare and manipulate audience reactions and appetites. The bedrock of glam rock consisted of costume, cosmetics, hairstyle and sexual ambiguity. In reaction to the communard utopianism of hippie culture and the pomp of progressive rock, glam rock made a fetish out of quotidian display, camp ambivalence, unapologetic consumption and an unquenchable thirst for excess. The glam rock look of futuristic, colourful clothing and dramatic make-up contrasted with the denim jeans, T-shirt and 'natural' look of progressive rockers. Drugs were used not as a means of gaining transcendental insight, but as a practical lifestyle accessory.

This was an artfully crafted presentation nucleated around a strategy of generational rupture promoted and aestheticized by managers and artists. In London and New York during the early 1970s, Tony Defries's company, MainMan, which represented David Bowie, deliberately cultivated a roster of music designed to signify a generational break with the 1960s and pursued a business ethos of extravagance and expense accounts to create the illusion of pharaonic wealth (Napier-Bell 2002: 169).

In the mid-1970s the genre of punk emerged and developed an ambivalent reaction to the glam rock moment. Many elements in it were attracted to the image of financial extravagance. But the style of punk was more conventionally political, organized around class and the display of authenticity, rather than sexual ambiguity and style. Punk took mundane domestic items from commodity culture, like the safety pin, ripped T-shirts and bin liners, and glamorously appropriated them. The Sex Pistols were encouraged to behave like Caliban's children by their manager, Malcolm McLaren. McLaren was the proprietor of Sex, a kinky clothes store on Chelsea's King's Road. Drawing on the analysis of class and commodity culture from French Situationist authors like Guy Debord, McLaren encouraged The Sex Pistols to cultivate hatred as an aesthetic in order to give the bourgeoisie a bloody lip and thus to gain publicity and make a fortune.

In both of these cases the logic and impact of glam rock and punk would have been entirely different without the input of charismatic managers who acted as lifestyle architects, not just for the artists they represented but also for the audience. Yet the manager is an absent figure in academic studies of popular music. If he or she features in the literature, this is in terms of a narrow consideration of that individual's technical role. Thus, Baskerville and Baskerville (2010: 176–95) categorize the pop manager's role as involving controlling finances (including accounting and contractual matters), managing presentation (including stage presence and media), developing peripheral income (merchandising, franchising) and managing personnel (including the artist). Typically, in return, they receive a royalty of 10–25% gross. What is largely absent in the technical description is an account of the manager as a social institution: that is, a structure of power and system of mythology that generate social energy, contribute artistically and marshal behaviour.

Until relatively recently, the same was true of the audience. Simon Frith's influential book *Performing Rites* (1996) has no chapter on the audience, nor does the term figure in the index. Instead, his focus is upon songs as texts, the meaning of music, genre rules and popular aesthetics. These are perfectly respectable and valid topics for academic study. But in neglecting the shape, desire, organization and intelligence of the audience, they cast an unduly narrow-angle lens upon what Henry Jenkins (2006) terms 'participatory culture'. Elsewhere, Jenkins (1992) berates the sociology of consumption for holding stereotypical, predominantly passive, readings of fans. Jenkins calls for an approach to the study of fans that regards them positively as fertile agents. He introduces the term 'textual poachers' to refer to the active part that fans play in appropriating and redefining received texts, whether they be songs, videos, adverts, TV footage or other items of commodified culture.

Then there is the question of the artist. Because artists are the composers and performers of music, the academic literature has awarded them a privileged place (Longhurst 2007). But musical articulation is not simply a matter of the charisma and creative ideas of composers and performers. Musicians are also positioned by managers and wider social and economic forces. They are recognized by audiences and their texts are re-materialized in exchanges of fashion, lifestyle forms and identity/counter-identity formation. The analysis of musical genres clearly reveals a complex pattern of interplay between artists, managers and audiences (to say nothing of the parts played by technology and the media, which will be the subject of the next chapter) (Bennett 2001).

Artists

The relational model pictures artists and musicians as situated in a field of scarcity in which they behave creatively to expand access over limited resources. This is a different approach from the extreme agency position, which is to behold artists as supremely creative individuals, and the extreme structuralist position, which attests that creativity is the product of antagonisms of class, gender, race or integral forces, genetically distributed, in the human brain. The relational model does not deny the influence of structural energies. To be sure, the concept of *habitus* is designed to encapsulate the insight that individuals are variably positioned in relation to scarcity. Differences here encompass genetic, social, cultural, economic and political factors. Nor does the relational approach deny the idea of agency. Indeed Bourdieu's (1993: 59–61) account of creative agency in the arts explicitly presents artists as bent upon maximizing their self-interest by accumulating cultural capital. Through this means, their access to scarce resources is increased. The relational model thus offers a technically superior account to approaches to popular music that naïvely regard it to be the product of individual talent or the reflection of structural forces. Instead, the relational approach examines creative agency as situated in the play between *habitus* and field.

The question then is: can one plausibly regard the music of Elvis Presley, The Beatles, The Doors, Marvin Gaye, Michael Jackson, Nirvana, Ice-T, Jay-Z or Coldplay simply as a matter of personal struggle, located in conditions of scarcity, to maximize access to limited resources? Jason Toynbee (2000: 37) convincingly criticizes the relational approach for under-estimating the significance of altruism in pop music and proposes that any worthwhile approach must commence by analysing artistic agency as a mixture between 'a struggle for individual position and a utopian drive to make the world better through music'. This is why it is correct to view the careers of some artists as constituting a cultural biography of collective time and space, a 'structure of feeling', in Raymond Williams's (1961, 1977) phrase, as well as a history of an individual subject. In the 1960s and early 1970s, the work of Marvin Gaye, Diana Ross and The Supremes and The Temptations at Tamala Motown crystallized common issues in the field of the civil rights movement; just as Michael Jackson's *Thriller* (1982) represented the transition and acceptance of Afro-Americans into public life and the national theatre of strategic influence. More than the result of *habitus* was reflected here. It was the intersection of *habitus* with field that ultimately gave supreme force to this music.

To illustrate these points about artistic agency, let us briefly examine three case studies:

(1) *Janis Joplin.* Joplin was born in Port Arthur, Texas, in 1943, the daughter of an engineer and a registrar at a business college. The family were religious. Joplin saw herself as an ugly duckling and was alienated from the values of white, middle-class America. At school she was treated as a misfit and complained of bullying (Friedman 1989; Amburn 1994; Echols 2000). She found refuge in the blues tradition, especially the recordings of Bessie Smith, Leadbelly and Odetta.

She enrolled at the University of Texas at Austin, where her interest in the blues was complemented by exposure to the poetry, fiction and lifestyle values of the Beat Generation. The writings of Jack Kerouac, Allen Ginsberg, William Boroughs and the legend of Neal Cassady provided a repertoire of models and representations of white American counterculture that Joplin devoured.

In 1963 she dropped out of university and migrated to the home of Beat culture, North Beach, San Francisco. Here she recorded some demos and developed a dependency upon drugs (amphetamines, alcohol and occasionally heroin). Health problems forced her to return to Texas, where she enrolled as a sociology major at Lamar University. She punctuated her study with local gigging, notably in Austin, where liberal traditions were perhaps stronger than elsewhere in Texas. Her bluesy, raw singing style attracted the attention of a San Francisco-based band, Big Brother and the Holding Company, who recruited her to front them. The band gigged mainly in West Coast venues. They signed an abortive record deal with Mainstream Records in Chicago before their first album was released by Columbia in 1967. In the same year their performance at the Monterey Festival won plaudits. The band acquired Bob Dylan's manager, Albert Grossman, to take care of business affairs.

During this period Joplin re-acquired a substance abuse habit. On-stage drunkenness was accompanied by teasing and candid displays of pent-up sexuality. In 1966, frictions in the band resulted in Joplin leaving to pursue a solo career.

Her substance abuse problems escalated. By 1969 she was a heroin addict and her performance at Woodstock, supplemented by alcohol, was so variable that the footage was never included in the film.

In 1970 she recorded *Pearl*, her most commercially successful album, which included the Kris Kristofferson song 'Me and Bobby McGee'. During the recording of this album in Los Angeles, Joplin was found dead, at 27, in her room at the Landmark Motor Hotel, the victim of a heroin overdose.

Joplin's *habitus* was white, middle-class Southern American. As with Jim Morrison, the traditional authoritarian combination of patriarchy and religion that were the central pillars of this background could not cope with the expectations explosion of the 1960s. As Joplin and Morrison reached adulthood, they encountered an expanding field of counterculture in which old family models, business practices and belief systems were impugned for being outmoded and irrelevant. Countercultural theorists like R. D. Laing (1970, 1995) argued that the modern family is a type of imprisonment, extorting submission in return for financial security and status; the work ethic produces a treadmill of punishing obligations and decayed aspiration; and the military-industrial state is out of control, masquerading in liberation wars that are actually exercises in terrorism (Viet Nam) and imposing neurotic, paranoid values and beliefs on the population. The Civil Rights movement exposed a shameless white American history of lynchings, racial harassment and organized white supremacy in business and all walks of public life. Joplin's music articulated widespread feelings of injustice, repression and guilt. She assimilated the conventions of the blues tradition and redefined and expanded them to cover the new cultural issues based around resistance and opposition in white youth culture.

(2) *Michael Jackson*. Apart from *Their Greatest Hits* by The Eagles (1976), which continues to clock up year-on-year sales, the best-selling album of all time

remains *Thriller* by Michael Jackson (1982). The album was number 1 in the USA for thirty-seven weeks, won eight Grammy awards and has sold an estimated 50 million copies. Jackson, who died aged 50 in 2009, had a career of extremes. Internationally famous at the age of 11, as the lead singer of The Jackson Five, his solo career spanned everything from being a poster boy for African-American upward mobility and a symbol of a supposedly post-racist America, to being the butt of allegations of child molestation and the embodiment of morbid eccentricity and pathological conspicuous consumption (Taraborrelli 2004; Halperin 2009).

The Jackson Five were a boy band before the concept of boy band had been invented. Michael was born into humble circumstances in Gary, Indiana. Managed by their father Joe, a strict disciplinarian, The Jackson Five developed a stage act crafted around synchronized singing and dancing. Signed by Motown, they achieved their first hit, a number 1, in 1969: 'I Want You Back'.

Jackson weathered the *Sturm und Drang* of being a child star, before leaving the rigid business control of his father to enter the more liberal orbit of producer Quincy Jones. Jackson met Jones on the set of *The Wiz* (1978), in which he played the part of the Scarecrow. Jones was far more than a record producer. He acted as a substitute father figure, distinctly more tolerant and imaginative than the tyrannical Joe. Jones provided Michael with a sustaining sense of collaboration and musical purpose. With Jones at the tiller, Jackson produced two stand-out albums, *Off the Wall* (1979) and *Thriller* (1982). The unprecedented commercial success of both transformed Jackson from the lead singer in a boy band into a global, boundary-breaking superstar. The adult Jackson was the perfect postmodern pop showman. His tailored blazers, false eyebrows, coiffured hair, lipstick and improbable prosthetic nose matched his apparently bizarre behaviour: wearing surgical masks in the street, dangling his child from a balcony in Berlin, inviting unchaperoned boys back to his Neverland ranch, and travelling with a personal magician in his retinue. Jackson's life and music consisted of a combination of contradictory elements. He fused the black rhythm and blues tradition with white rock. He identified with Afro-American culture yet consorted with white Hollywood aristocracy, such as Elizabeth Taylor and Macaulay Culkin, and recorded with the godfather of the 1960s pop revolution and the 'British invasion', Paul McCartney. He supported authenticity and solidarity yet cultivated a personal lifestyle which was widely castigated for its artificiality and separation from the ordinary considerations of everyday life. He spoke about feeding the world, and privately gave considerable support to his favoured charities. Yet in 2003, the damaging Martin Bashir TV documentary revealed Jackson to be a dedicated, tasteless consumer of overpriced, vulgar reproductions and household fittings. In one trip, Jackson casually spent over $6 million on everything from glass urns to gargantuan marble chess-sets.

At about the time of the release of *Thriller*, the studied postmodern hybridity of Jackson's music found a notorious referent in Jackson's own body. His skin colour started to lighten, an effect, he claimed, of the skin disease vitiligo, and his Afro-American physical features – his nose, chin, eyelids and lips – appeared to slowly morph into characteristics of the Caucasian type. Soon thereafter, Jackson's eccentricities became press staples. We have already referred to his relationship with his pet chimp, Bubbles, and his purported intention to purchase the skeleton of the Elephant Man. The press devoted acres of column space to these as well as to Jackson's spendthrift ways, his habit of filling Neverland with dolls and mannequins, his increasing dependence on a team of advisers for business and health matters, his androgynous appearance and Peter Pan complex.

What were the reasons behind the success of Jackson's albums in the late 1970s and early 1980s? The music was released on the coat-tails of the Civil Rights movement, in which the central battles of racial equality appeared to have been formally won (i.e. in the sense of legal recognition of equality). It emerged between the meltdown of the rhetoric of welfarism in America and the rise of the neo-liberal reinvention of the minimalist state, global deregulation and the return to an ideology of unlimited personal freedom for the successful. *Off the Wall* and *Thriller* supplied the soundtrack for the crescendo of guilt-free consumption that typified the Studio 54 era (Haden-Guest 1997). It was a culture based in private abundance and public want. Jackson's music was caught up in the climate of materialism and personal success. It reflected these values. The production values and dance routines were slick. The driving beat supported lyrics that revolved around the themes of *making it*, *proving* it and *doing it*. The politics were naïve. Jackson's music made a virtue of direction, but after the success of *Thriller*, the direction in which he was heading was never entirely clear. He supported racial harmony. He even talked about adopting a child from every continent. His main Californian residence, Neverland, was designed as a tribute to the world of J.M. Barrie's Peter Pan, in which childhood innocence reigned supreme and growing old was banished. Yet the traders who operated sub-prime, credit default swap, hedge fund and collateralized debt obligation deals also partied to 'Don't Stop 'Til You Get Enough', 'Rock with You', 'Beat It' and 'Billie Jean'.

Of course, so did millions of others. The formula that Quincy Jones and Jackson discovered in these albums appeared to overcome the contradictions of class, race and gender to achieve a transcendent sense of collectivity. Yet other than displaying action and championing direction, it was never really apparent what Jackson stood for. In private he donated time and money to charity, especially to causes related to children. However, his music became more pompous, self-regarding and disconnected from reality. When he performed 'Earth Song' at the 1996 Brit Awards, Jarvis Cocker disrupted the performance by climbing onto the stage, a protest at a singer whom he regarded as having become a pretentious bore living in a bubble of errant self-approval.

In 2005, the climacteric of Jackson's career was the court trial in Santa Maria, California, in which he faced highly public investigations of abusing a 13-year-old boy during visits to the Neverland ranch, giving alcohol to a child and engaging in a conspiracy to cover up his illegal sexual practices. The media had a field-day with Jackson's court-room behaviour, which included attending court in his pyjamas and, on one occasion, with an emergency room doctor in attendance.

Since his untimely and unexpected death, Jackson's career has been partially rehabilitated. The cloak of the accused child molester has slipped from his shoulders. He is now mourned as a lost, victimized superstar. After 11, his chart success deprived him of a normal childhood and his personal judgement became warped with show-biz values and press intrusion. His life was insulated from the real world by a team of business, style and health advisers who told him what to wear, the deals he should sign and the pills he needed to take to get sleep. Jackson, who had been publicly accused of being a sexual deviant, preying upon minors, took on a posthumous existence as a victim of bloodsuckers and press hounds.

(3) *Coldplay.* Currently, Coldplay are the world's biggest band. Their last album release, *Viva La Vida*, was the best-performing iTunes download album of 2008, selling 500,000 copies digitally and 2 million CDs (*Variety*, 2.12.2008). Since 1998, when they were formed, the band have sold over 50 million albums worldwide (*www.contactmusic.com*). The International Federation of the Phonographic Industry (IFPI) reported that in 2005 Coldplay's previous album release, *X&Y*, was the year's best-seller, with 8.3 million units globally. Although their debut album, *Parachutes*, was released in 2000, Coldplay are most properly described as a post-9/11 band. That is, their music reflects the emotional regime and themes of global hazard, unpredictability and risk that became pre-eminent in the West after the attacks on the World Trade Center in 2001. Paradoxically, in view of the title of their first album release, it is music for people who feel, emotionally, that they are living *without* a parachute or a safety net. While Chris Martin, the front man, is a supporter of Oxfam's 'Make Trade Fair' campaign and the band participated in 'Make Poverty History', Coldplay are more politically low-key than their punk/grunge predecessors or global rivals U2. That is not to say that their politics is absent. Rather it is restrained and not in your face. Perhaps this reflects the class origins of the band members. Not to mince words, Coldplay are a bourgeois band.

Chris Martin's father and mother worked, respectively, as a chartered accountant and a music teacher. He was a boarder at Sherborne School in Dorset. Drummer Will Champion's father is Professor of Archaeology at the University of Southampton. The band were formed when all four members were studying at University College, London. There are thoughtful, polite, fragile, intimate qualities to their music that in some critical circles have been denigrated as a sign of repression or passive aggression. Coldplay come across as well-oiled performers. The naked emotion of a Janis Joplin concert or the exotic exhibitionism of Michael Jackson do not figure in their repertoire.

When Martin sings 'You're in control, is there anywhere you wanna go?' at the start of *Square One*, the opening song of *X&Y*, he addresses an audience the majority of whom do not feel in personal control. He is appealing to people who feel that the world is too big and the people who are formally in control are bluffing.

It is music that appeals to those who feel comparatively helpless and powerless. This is not a criticism of the band's music. Unlike the counterculture bands of the 1960s and the punk movement of the 1970s, there is no momentum of a plausible alternative behind Coldplay's music. Coldplay do not provide music for *making it*, *proving it* or *doing it*. Their sound is more introspective and reflective.

Earlier, I reproached Michael Jackson for not having a clear sense of political direction. Coldplay's direction is also unclear. It is not a matter of failing to express a clear path and hold a tenable vision of life as it might be. Rather, it is a matter of a type of music that follows endlessly forking paths. 'They got the guns, but we got the numbers,' sang Jim Morrison. Coldplay button-hole anyone who is 'lost and lonely too' and 'waiting till the shine wears off'.

There is an acceptance and resignation about the music – an emotional expectation that in the end nothing lasts, so that trying to transform things is pointless. The title song of *Viva La Vida* is about someone who 'used to rule the world'. The certainties of pre-9/11 are exposed as having feet of clay. In '42', a reference to the novels of the late Douglas Adams in which the number is the super-computer's answer to The Ultimate Question, Coldplay refer to the 'dead who are not dead', but who are 'just living in my head'; and 'since I fell for that spell, I am living there as well'. This is the dream-like world of Ground Zero in which the living 'think they might be a ghost' who 'didn't get to heaven but made it close'. The *habitus* of Coldplay involves being in touch with personal vulnerability. This intersects powerfully with the current field of civic culture, which is haunted by the shadows of terrorism, global warming and financial meltdown.

The digital revolution has given artists new opportunities to produce and exchange music independently of corporations and managers. Keith Negus (1999: 177) argued that in the era of the rock superstar, the picture of the music business as a flint-hearted Goliath and the recording star as David was always an exaggeration. For him, a more balanced approach recognizes that while the music business has considerable power over production and distribution, they are locked in a war of manoeuvre to cede control to superstars whom they can ill afford to lose. With the rise of laptop recording technology, declining costs of synthesizers and samplers and online exchange, the balance of power has tilted in favour of unknown artists as well as superstars. As evidence, consider the record contract. Traditional contracts specify the date of delivery, royalties, escalator clauses, cost control, creative control, publishing rights, tour support, video provision, promotional duties and the geographical territories of exclusive marketing, distribution and point of sale.

The crux of traditional contracts is the assignment of copyright. Copyright was introduced nearly three centuries ago. During this time the essential meaning of the term has remained the same. Copyright means the assignment of permission to make copies of a given work. Copyright owners depend upon the revenue generated from the assignment of copyright to cover costs. Thus, record companies assign an advance to musicians on the mutual understanding that the advance will be recouped when the given work is sold (Goldstein 2003; Bielstein 2006).

A variety of issues are raised by the question of copyright. Contracts assigning shared copyright to the record corporation and the musician set the mould for labour relations in the music business until the 1970s. As Caves (2000) and Hesmondhalgh (2002) note, a series of high-profile disputes about rip-off record contracts in the 1980s and 1990s broke this mould. These disputes tended to centre on five general issues:

(1) *Advances and royalties.* In the 1970s typical royalty rates were 7 to 9%. As a result of various legal challenges, the royalty for entry-level musicians has risen to 11–13%, whereas middle-range acts typically command between 14 and 16%. Major stars have much higher clout, commanding royalties of between 20 and 25%. In general, established musicians can expect to be offered an escalator clause in their

contract which provides for an increase in royalty rates tied to achieving agreed target points in record sales.

(2) *Creative control and cost control.* In 1994 George Michael legally challenged his fifteen-year eight-album contract with Sony (signed in 1988) on the grounds that it amounted to 'professional slavery', leaving him with limited control over his career. Michael alleged that he had deliberately decided to play down his sultry sexual image for the promotion of 'Listen Without Prejudice' (1990), but was rebuked by Sony executives after the album sold only 5 million copies (after 14 million sales worldwide of his 1988 album, *Faith*). This case challenged the principle of issuing an advance against copyright on the grounds that it leads to unreasonable infringement of artistic freedom.

(3) *Promotional duties.* Contracts may specify tours, videos, TV chat show interviews and a variety of other promotional exercises to support 'physical' sales. These are set out in a list of obligations with contracted times and duties. The details are often disputed by musicians, who argue that promotional duties are excessive and interfere with creativity.

(4) *Publishing and intellectual property rights.* Publishing and intellectual property rights to recorded music are assigned for distribution by the record corporation. This can lead to disputes as to whether the corporation distributes rights in the best interests of the musician. Sampling has unleashed a raft of issues having to do with monopoly control of rights. A landmark case in music copyright law is the action of the largest country music publisher in the world, Acuff-Rose Music, against the assertion of fair use by the controversial rap group 2 Live Crew. Acuff-Rose had acquired rights to 'Oh, Pretty Woman' (1964) composed by Roy Orbison and William Dees. The legal issue turned on alleged copyright infringement for unsolicited use of a version of the song on a 2 Live Crew album. Now copyright infringement is a much-contested concept in the law. A version of a song may be very different from a copy. For example, the version may involve changing lyrics, altering rhythm and outright parody. In the case of the action brought by Acuff-Rose, the ruling found in favour of 2 Live Crew. Namely, the rappers were found to have parodied the original so forcefully that the allegation that their recording constituted a copy or near impression was not corroborated (Goldstein 2003: 1–3).

(5) *Terms of delivery issues.* This refers to stipulated delivery dates of master copies to the record company and enforcement of multi-album deals. The Mamas and the Papas broke up in 1968, but were forced by their record label, Dunhill Records, to re-form to record and release one further contracted album (1971's *People Like Us*). Similarly, The Clash understood that their record contract with CBS was a five-year, five-album deal. But the terms of the record contract were unclear whether a double album constituted a single album or two albums. So the two-album *London Calling* (1979) and the three-album *Sandinista* (1980) became objects of dispute between the band and the record company. Peter Jenner, the band's manager, who took over from Bernie Rhodes in 1979, commented:

The contract was the biggest mess I've ever seen. It had obviously been cobbled together really quickly, bits of paper stuck everywhere. They'd left out the crucial clause about double-albums. But on the other hand Joe [Strummer] had told me that it was a five album deal. I thought: 'That's cool: a five year, five album deal.' But when you looked deeper you saw that CBS at any time could ask for an additional album in any year. So in fact, it's a ten album or ten year deal, with another clause that can take it up to thirteen albums. (Quoted in Salewicz 2006: 301)

Another notorious case is David Bowie's contract with MainMan. The contract classified Bowie as an employee of the company, with all of his earnings accruing to the employer in return for an allowance to cover expenses. The relationship was inherently exploitative, although, as Stevenson (2006: 90) remarks, given that Bowie's expenses extended to covering his infamous drug use in the early 1970s and to supporting his entourage, it does not necessarily follow that the arrangement always worked in MainMan's favour. In 1975 Bowie parted with MainMan, although the contract still entitled the company to 50% of his earnings from *Hunky Dory* to *David Live*, and 16% until 1982. In 1981 Bowie applied for a tax exemption certificate as a Swiss resident, which relieved most of his future earnings from a high tax burden.

The examples of the bad contracts signed by Bowie and The Clash are far from isolated. They became part of the pop legend of rip-off culture in the music business that left its mark on the *habitus* of subsequent artists. This created a backlash from new, smaller companies that held up the major corporations as an example of fat-cat exploitation.

Thus, the indie record boom of the late 1970s and 1980s tried to develop new contractual relations between record companies and artists. Deals were often structured on a 50/50 share of profits and reliant on high trust relations between record company executives and artists. They were also commonly on a record-by-record basis, leaving artists free to move on if they judged it best suited them to do so. Independent labels attempted to break the stranglehold that major labels held over distribution by creating their own retail networks. All of this reinforced the independence of artists.

As Hesmondalgh (1998; 2002: 170–1) notes, the indie bubble burst after the major companies went bankrupt, artists became frustrated with limited production and promotion budgets and the major companies developed strategies of conglomeration. However, the ethos of artistic independence has not disintegrated. The digital revolution revitalized it by freeing the musician from the studio and redefining the laptop as a staple compositional tool. Traditionally, route one for musicians to be discovered was the A&R (Artists and Repertoire) man, who scouted pubs, clubs and other musical venues for talent. MySpace, Facebook and YouTube have seriously undermined this system.

Artists have always been conscious that music is also intellectual property. However, the saturation of music in pop culture has produced the meltdown of boundaries and the coalescence of genres and traditions. This cultural de-differentiation has led to several notorious copyright infringement cases in pop music where 'borrowings' and cut and paste jobs have been done on a subconscious level. George Harrison was judged to have 'unconsciously' violated the copyright of The Chiffons' record 'He's So Fine', composed by Ronald Mack, and owned by Bright Tunes Music Corp; in 2003 The Flaming Lips agreed to split the royalties on their composition 'Flight Test' with Yusuf Islam (formerly known as Cat Stevens), after Islam successfully argued that the melody bore comparison with the Stevens composition 'Father and Son'; in 2008 Joe Satriani sued Coldplay for allegedly 'recycling' substantial portions of his song 'If I Could Fly' – the case was dismissed in 2009, with media rumours of an out-of-court settlement.

Disputes over intellectual property in the pop music business are not limited to questions of copyright over compositions. Between 1978 and 2006 The Beatles launched a series of trademark infringement lawsuits against the Apple Corporation. The issue turned upon the use by Apple of The Beatles' Apple logo, which was alleged to violate the rights of the copyright holders.

The examples show how issues of agency are always located in a structure of habit and practice that can mould the choice and action of artists. Doubtless George Harrison and The Flaming Lips did not consciously steal from The Chiffons or Yusuf Islam (Cat Stevens). Mere immersion in pop culture was the root of the problem.

Paradoxically, the onslaught of cultural de-differentiation and the new business opportunities that it has created have boosted artistic consciousness of the economic value of copyright control. Today, artists are far more aware that music is intellectual property that can be sold to advertisers, ringtone companies, game manufacturers, political parties seeking rousing campaign anthems and a variety of other outlets.

Currently, the market benchmark is what has come to be known as the 'P. Diddy Model'. The rapper, record company mogul, restaurateur and fashion designer and activist Sean Coombs, formerly known as Puff Daddy, parallels the Vivendi business model in his career. That is, he structures his various commercial activities as synchronized, mutually reinforcing ventures. His music videos and rap records are vehicles for product placement exercises for his clothes line, restaurants and fragrance brands. The music sells a lifestyle, and P. Diddy markets and supplies the main pathways of lifestyle achievement. The music reinforces the clothes line, which in turn reinforces the fragrance brands, which in turn boosts the restaurants, and so on.

It would be an error to conclude that artists have entered artistic and commercial nirvana. What is at issue here is a set of balance of power relationships that, at present, have moved in favour of artists. The power of global multinationals in respect of marketing, franchising, exploiting the back-catalogue and sponsorship deals is not lost on contemporary artists. This is one reason why Lily Allen and The Arctic Monkeys, to name two examples, switched to London Records (part of WMG) and EMI, respectively, after breaking through with free demos and MySpace broadcasts. Artists see themselves as creative agents. Nowadays they may be more interested in the commercial side of their operations, but most view it as taking second place behind composing and playing. Hence the persistence of the framework of relations between record corporations, managers and distribution networks which 'takes care of the business'. Notwithstanding this, in recent years, as a result of the digital revolution and the increased artistic know-how about contracts and multi-layered business models (involving sponsorship and merchandising arrangements of various kinds), the framework has been radically revised.

Managers

If the revised framework has repositioned artists, it has also called upon pop managers radically to recast their role. Traditionally, pop managers have provided leadership and administrative functions. Following Burns (1978), it is helpful to distinguish between two general types of leadership (Table 7.1). *Transactional* leadership refers to exchange transactions between leaders and social networks in which they are located. This type of leadership operates within well-defined parameters of transactions. Thus, if an employee achieves agreed target objectives, he or she can expect promotion. If a client provides the agreed financial reward, a service is reciprocated. Transactional leaders aim to fulfil transparent agreed objectives within the field in which they are located. That is, they attempt to achieve a 'business as usual' ethos.

In contrast, *transformational* leadership refers to a process of example or direction in which people are motivated to maximize their potential. It involves transmitting confidence, commitment to a strong achievement mode and holding a compelling vision of good practice and coherent goals. Bass and Avolio (1990) extend the category by adding the qualities of idealized vision, inspirational motivation, intellectual stimulation and individualized consideration.

In pop music, transactional managers have generally restricted themselves to the prudent running of business affairs. This involves managing the financial relations of clients diligently, overseeing contracts, exploring franchises and sponsorship opportunities, negotiating and supervising transactions with the media and creating and maintaining a general climate of probity and fair dealing to enable artists to get on with the creative work of composition and performance. As a result, transactional managers have tended to be back-room boys. Typical examples include John Reid, who managed Elton John from 1970 to 1998 and Queen from 1975 to 1978; Tim Collins, who managed the hard rock band Aerosmith between 1984 and 1996; Caresse Henry, who managed Madonna between 1991 and 2004; and Paul McGuinness, manager of U2.

Transactional managers sometimes step out into the limelight to handle client controversy or questions about industry standards. John Reid and Paul McGuinness have certainly done that when the occasion demands. But in general,

Table 7.1 Pop music leadership models

	Transactional	Transformational
Public face	Low key	High profile
Duties	Administrative/supportive	Administrative/inspirational
Status	Back-room boy	Unofficial band member
Percentage	10/25	25/50
Ideology	Consolidator	Change agent
Organization	Divides and devolves power	Monopolizes power

they have a low profile and, publicly at least, defer to their clients in matters of creative control.

The situation with transformational managers is quite different. They utilize the mechanics of the system of pop music stardom to present themselves as celebrities by association with, and direct influence over, the clients whom they represent. Thus, Allen Klein, who took over as the manager of The Beatles after the death of Brian Epstein, extracted unprecedented royalty rates from EMI, reformed the business culture of Apple and enlisted the American producer Phil Spector to work on the Let It Be tapes. Kit Lambert, the manager of The Who, invented the concept of the 'rock opera' and prevailed upon Pete Townshend, the main songwriter in the group, to compose Tommy. Malcolm McLaren, manager of The Sex Pistols, coached the band on the correct (insolent) attitude to strike with the press and astutely staged concerts and record contract signings as 'spectacles' designed to maximize public disbelief and galvanize media attention. Indeed, McLaren styled himself as the management guru of punk, who conditioned the fashion, style of interaction and music.

Transformational pop managers appropriate the musical creativity of the artists whom they represent and extend it to cover managerial functions. Hence, Albert Grossman (manager of Bob Dylan, Janis Joplin, John Lee Hooker and The Band), Peter Grant (who represented Led Zeppelin, Janis Joplin, Terry Reid and Bad Company) and Andrew Loog Oldham (who managed The Rolling Stones, The Small Faces and Marianne Faithfull) lived the rock and roll lifestyle. Simon Napier-Bell (2002), who in his time managed The Yardbirds, Wham!, Japan, Tyrannosaurus Rex and Asia, correctly identified illegal drugs as a major component of this lifestyle. In the case of Lambert and Oldham, illegal drugs eventually played havoc with their abilities to manage. Illegal drug use was part of the risk ethos favoured by the counterculture between the 1960s and 1980s.

Colonel Tom Parker, who managed Elvis Presley, was an old-style transformational impresario who in many ways set the bar for the leadership model until the 1980s. Parker's management style has been described as 'a cross between P.T.Barnum and W.C. Fields' (Nash 1995: 52). Parker signed Presley in 1954. He acted as a personal manager, adopting a fatherly role over Elvis while masterminding his career trajectory. He is credited with toning down Presley's stage act and choice of material, emphasizing the need to be polite and respectable. Parker's transformational management style concentrated power in the hands of the manager. In the words of Lamar Fike, a member of the so-called 'Memphis Mafia' who surrounded Presley:

> When the Colonel signed deals, he would discuss them with Elvis first. Well, in a fashion he would discuss things with Elvis. But he would never ask Elvis's permission. He would just say, 'Do you want to do it?' Elvis would say, 'Yeah.' And then the Colonel would go make the deal. The important thing is that the Colonel had total freedom to make any deal he wanted. Elvis would say, 'Take care of it. Bring me the paper, I'll sign it and go do the show.' Elvis signed the contracts blind. He didn't know what they were. He just signed them. (Quoted in Nash 1995: 60)

Marsh (2002) reports that Parker took an 'outrageous' 50% commission of Presley's recordings and 80% of earnings from merchandising. The controversial buy-out contracts that the Colonel negotiated in 1973, which assigned all master tapes and royalty rights to RCA, apportioned $4,650,000 to Presley and $6,200,000 to Parker (Dickerson 2001: 194).

Parker adopted the habitual manner of a fairground showman (Barnum) and grouchy wise-acre (Fields). He was flamboyant and publicity-seeking, with a ruthless determination to dominate every scintilla of Presley's music career, tour schedule, film performances and public image. His was a Svengali-like iteration of the transformational impresario role. Elements from it were clearly borrowed by Kit Lambert, Andrew Loog Oldham, Albert Grossman and Malcolm McLaren.

Bespoke Aggregation

By the 1990s a new type of transformational manager was emerging, as exemplified by Simon Fuller and Simon Cowell. This new type is hardly publicity-shy, but claims transactional privilege in respect of superior business competence in applying transformational philosophy to the modern world of consumption and entertainment. Simon Fuller originally came to prominence after managing Paul Hardcastle's hit single '19' (1984). He progressed to manage Annie Lennox, masterminded The Spice Girls and invented *Pop Idol* and *American Idol*. The *Idol* franchise has been a huge global hit. *American Idol* is currently the number 1 TV show in the Nielsen Ratings. Through his connection with Victoria Beckham of The Spice Girls he commandeered the transfer of David Beckham from Real Madrid to Los Angeles Galaxy. He refers to his own production and management company, 19 Entertainment, as a 'bespoke aggregator' (*Guardian*, 28 October 2009). By this term he means a company that adopts standards of flexible professionalism to entertainment management, takes the whole of pop culture as its remit and builds cross-collateral capital between business enterprises.

Thus, in 2009 Fuller ploughed some of the revenues from *Pop Idol* and his pop music management enterprise into film production (his latest project at the time of writing is producing *Bel Ami*, with Uma Thurman in the lead role) and fashion through the creation of Fashionair, an online fashion and entertainment platform with an audience of 500 e-tailers and 22 million consumers. In 2009 19 Entertainment also acquired a 51% stake in *Storm Model*, which represents Kate Moss, Eva Herzigova, Lily Cole, Carla Bruni and Jourdan Dunn among its leading models.

Bespoke aggregation tailors one aspect of pop enterprise, say the guitar powers of a band, and connects it with other aspects, such as merchandising guitar brands, ringtones, fashion, television jingles, and so on. The purpose is to build a suit of cultural capital, so that each activity that the artist (or enterprise) pursues reinforces and strengthens the other threads in the material.

A powerful example of bespoke aggregation today in pop is the *Got Talent* and *Idol* franchises. They are not just about musical talent. Rather they are organized to build cross-collateral capital by using prime-time competition between artists to boost television revenue (through advertising income), generate a profit stream by premium rate calls voting for artists, nurture a market for recorded music (the winner of *Got Talent* produces an album – generally for the Christmas market – which is part-owned by the franchise production company) and road-test genres of music.

Simon Cowell owns Syco, the production company that controls the *Got Talent* franchise. He began his music career as an A&R executive, signing Sinitta and creating a successful partnership with the Stock, Aitken and Waterman Hit Factory. However, the meteoric success that has been his since the turn of the century reflects the extension and elaboration of his role as a TV talent/reality show producer and talent judge, and the recording deal for the artists that he represents with Sony-BMG.

The crucial and defining element in the careers of Fuller and Cowell is the realization that music is a multi-media phenomenon. Fuller invented the *Pop Idol* TV format, which has been franchised throughout the world, notably in the USA with *American Idol*, which has been running since 2002. The *Pop Idol* format scores highly in viewer ratings and is a magnet for revenue from sponsors, telephone phone lines and music and youth merchandising advertisers.

Cowell came to the attention of television audiences as the acerbic judge on Fuller's *Pop Idol* and *American Idol* shows. He has gone on to develop his own TV reality/talent format shows, with *The X Factor* and *Got Talent* franchises. The business model that Cowell has created through his company Syco is audacious. The *Got Talent* franchise merges talent shows and reality TV models. Performers are amateurs who are encouraged to audition, selected by a panel of researchers and perform on television for free. The pre-selection stage is erased in the TV broadcast in favour of the convenient illusion that performers have come in off the street to face Simon Cowell and his panel of celebrity judges. The television audience vote for their favourite performers, paying a premium phone rate for the privilege. The acts are road-tested for several weeks in conditions of free market research, until the winner emerges. The act is then signed to Syco. Subsequent Syco recordings are released in partnership with Sony-BMG. Syco therefore controls a product that has been subject to prolonged market research and conclusively identified as popular with consumers.

The rise to stardom of each performer is presented as an open process, involving the audience, who freely vote for their preferred entertainer and performers, who are merely amateurs. Actually, the *Got Talent* format is designed to turn amateurs into professionals, since the point of winning the *Got Talent* shows is to pursue a career in the entertainment business. For the successful acts, the shows are like public auditions in which the choice of material and presentation skills are honed to perfection. The commercial production and management of the music are a closed circle since Syco is responsible for the public inception of the acts, controls the market research campaign which occurs through the audience voting procedures and retains a percentage of the earnings of the eventual winner through a production/distribution deal with Sony-BMG.

Not surprisingly, it is a massive business success. In December 2007 Syco celebrated holding the number 1 spot in three of the UK sales charts. It held the top three albums in the album charts with Leona Lewis, Shayne Ward and Westlife; it was at numbers 1 and 3 in the DVD chart with the *X Factor* DVD and Shayne Ward longform DVD; and it had Leona Lewis entering her sixth week at the top of the singles chart with 'Bleeding Love'. This is to say nothing of the additional money deriving to Syco through international sales, franchising and merchandising deals. The personal rewards that follow this level of market saturation are significant. In 2009, Susan Boyle, the runner-up of *Britain's Got Talent* and a Syco/Sony artist, achieved the best-selling debut album in UK chart history, with 410,000 sales. At the time of writing, US sales are projected to be 1 million.

In 2009 the *Forbes* business magazine named Simon Cowell as the highest paid man on prime-time television, with earnings of $75 million in 2008–9. This reflects Cowell's involvement as the lynchpin of the judging panel for *American Idol*, which, despite falling ratings, was listed as the top US TV show in 2009, with 27 million viewers; and his role as the creator of *America's Got Talent*, franchised to the NBC network.

Pursuing the centrality of a competent business ethic in commercial success, Cowell emphasizes the pivotal importance of the manager in creating pop stardom. As he puts it:

> Managers make things happen because they have track records, because they have time to talk to many different labels, and because they have a history of success . . . a good manager is an absolute necessity, because I have never, ever met anyone in my life who got a record deal by sending in an unsolicited tape. (Cowell 2003: 260)

This suggests that the transactional model of pop management has been eclipsed by the transformational model. However, modern pop managers are not an adjunct of the band, in the way that Andrew Loog Oldham, Peter Grant and Kit Lambert were. Nor do they live the rock and roll lifestyle. They are corporate executives, in the most successful cases running multi-media entertainment corporations. They maintain professional distance from the acts they manage, yet place severe conditions on permitting artistic licence to flourish. Fuller and Cowell micro-manage the look of the performer, the choice of material, musical arrangements and television promotion. The most complete expression of this style of pop management is the boy band.

The Boy Band Phenomenon

Strictly speaking, there is nothing new in the boy band. In 1966 Bob Rafelson and Bert Schneider invented the television series *The Monkees* and recruited the four band members. The group's recordings were supervised by the song publisher and rock producer Don Kirshner, who contracted compositions and managed the recording process (initially using session musicians). Initially, The Monkees were a packaged band. However, gradually they objected to Kirshner's style of management and choice of material. They started writing their own songs and parted company with Kirshner in 1967, citing artistic control as the main grievance. Other precursors of the modern boy band were The Jackson Five and The Osmonds.

The catalyst for the growth of the phenomenon in the 1980s was the success of Michael Jackson's highly choreographed style of performance. His method of singing and dancing was copied and elaborated by groups like Take That (managed by Nigel Martin Smith), Boyzone and Westlife (managed by Louis Walsh), The Backstreet Boys (launched by record producer Lou Pearlman) and New Kids On the Block (created by Maurice Starr). Martin Smith, Walsh, Pearlman and Starr are examples of modern transformational pop impresarios. They micro-manage every note that the band sing, every iota of the record (including the choice of material), merchandising and distribution, and issues of stage dress and physical appearance.

The boy band is a powerful example of Weber's (1922) second meaning of charisma: that is, mediated charisma – the management of mass responses of intoxication and devotion to essentially packaged agents of entertainment. The operation of the boy band is restricted to the entertainment sphere. Evidence from the world of the girl band suggests that when they move out of this sphere into the political or charity arena the results can be counter-productive. Geri Halliwell's role as a UN goodwill ambassador, which started in 1999, is widely regarded as unsuccessful. It is not a question of personal sincerity; rather it is a matter of whether her Spice Girl background is a genuine asset in the world of celebrity diplomacy. This is a matter of the social response to the artist and the management of the artist. In other words, it is a matter of audiences.

Audiences

Shallow readings of Weber's (1922) account of charisma rarely get beyond submitting that authority derives from extraordinary qualities innate in the individual or mediated by third parties. The accent is upon the influence of nature and management, or an amalgam of the two. Yet Weber is unambiguous that extraordinary qualities are not merely asserted by individuals who throw their hat into the ring as potential leaders. In order to possess social force, these qualities must also be recognized by others. Leaders require followers, just as followers require leaders. The relationship between the two is not straightforward.

This has sometimes been glossed over in audience reception perspectives that portray the audience as the outcome of media machinations. As we saw in Chapter 2 (pp. 71–5), Adorno's (1991, 2009) account of the culture industry is a case in point. It presents the audience as situated under capitalism to respond to pop music in programmatic ways. Within the field of audience research this perspective has been strenuously attacked. Commentators emphasize the multi-dimensionality of audience responses to pop music and correlate variations with issues of discrimination, motivation, aesthetic judgement, class and other types of power (Cavicchi 1998; Schroder 2000; Hesmondhalgh 2007). The Frankfurt School hypothesis that the masses subsist passively in a state of false consciousness was indigestible in an era that witnessed the rise of the counterculture, the expansion of higher education and the critical sharpening of the mass media. One result in the analysis of pop music audiences was that the balance of research gravitated to a view of fans as intrinsically interpretative, creative, capable, practical, competent agents (Fiske 1992; Jenkins 1992). However, since the mid-1990s something of a backlash against 'the active audience' perspective on fans has been evident.

In an important summative article, Sonia Livingstone (1998) holds that the pitfalls of regarding audiences as active agents are as considerable as viewing them as passive, plastic respondents. According to her, audience studies must be triangulated around three dimensions: *production* (the capacity of audiences to interpret and make meanings), *text* (the format of cultural stimuli, such as songs and performances) and *context* (the socio-economic conditions of scarcity in which the production, exchange and consumption of pop music are situated). Utilizing elements from the work of Alexander and Giesen (1987), Livingstone contends that the various contributions to the relationships between production, text and context in audience relations can be usefully classified into five positions, as shown in Table 7.2.

This corresponds to the structure/agency continuum discussed in Part I of this book. Hegemonic/objective structuralist perspectives posit the individual as ideologically grounded. Conversely, instrumental/interpretative individual approaches postulate the individual as an autonomous, reflexive agent. Social constructivism is a halfway house between the two poles. It depicts the individual as located in a condition of socio-economic and cultural scarcity and analyses personal agency as a consequence of this state of affairs. That is, the practice of the individual agent (in this case, the fan) is analysed as conditioned by the intersection of *habitus* with field.

Generally speaking, audience studies has clearly moved away from the default setting of the passive/plastic audience in commodified, consumer culture, outlined by the Frankfurt School. According to Cornel Sandvoss (2005: 154), the first wave of critical reaction was signalled by Stuart Hall's (1980) widely cited discussion of encoding/decoding. Hall's paper examined textual production and consumption through the problematic of ideology. He maintained that the production and reception of texts are positioned to privilege hegemony. Resistance occurs, but it takes place in a theatre in which white, male, capitalist interests are hegemonic.

Within audience studies, Hall's work stirred a swarm of interest in matters of textual coding and decoding. John Fiske (1992), in particular, is credited with developing the idea of the active audience: that is, a perspective on fans that views them as skilled consumers of texts who are immensely adept in adding, subtracting and reformulating meaning through interpretation and practice. However, the question of context, especially the role of hegemony, was neglected.

The second wave was influenced by relationism (Thornton 1995). As we have seen (pp. 89–94), relationism disavows bipolar approaches to questions of production, exchange and consumption. Instead what it offers is a more granular reading of power that encompasses local, regional, subcultural and hybrid distinctions. Audiences continue to be viewed as active agents. But the remit of agency is widened and fleshed out to include distinctions relating to *habitus* and

Table 7.2 Production, text and context in audience relations

Position	Audience function
Instrumental/individual	Free market consumers
Interpretative/individual	Creative
Social constructivism	Citizen receivers
Hegemonic	Potentially resistant
Objective structuralism	Duped mass

field that the first wave under-scored. Livingstone's (1998) stress on the centrality of production, texts and context in audience studies is developed from a different perspective, but it fetches up with the same conclusion. Namely, audiences are capable, reflexive agents who conduct themselves in fields of cultural and economic scarcity that influence how texts (in this case, songs, performances, artist information) are exchanged, interpreted and consumed.

As with the subcultural take on the analysis of pop, ethnographic research on the audience is fruitful because it clarifies the basis of group formation, the representative codes that define social inclusion and exclusion, the relationship between identity and markers of distinction, the codes of innovation and routine of textual poaching, and much else besides. Conversely, it is subject to the same objection made of subculturalism. Namely, it is only too tempting to pursue the accumulation of ethnographic data as an end in itself, so that the dynamics between production, text and context are, in effect, summarily addressed.

The most promising way of reorienting the analysis of audiences in pop music studies is to draw upon the manifest strengths of ethnographic traditions and attempt to fuse them with broader questions of production, text and context. In this respect, Rentfrow and Gosling's (2007) research into musical genres and representations of personality characteristics with a sample of university students in Texas, and Rentfrow et al.'s (2009) subsequent study among a sample of students in England into representations of taste, class and race, throw up some interesting pointers. They discovered that consumers have robust and well-defined stereotypes of the correlations between fan base and musical genre. For example, fans of rock and electronica are typically rated high on psychometric scales measuring Extraversion and Openness, moderate on Agreeableness and low on Conscientiousness and Emotional Stability. Fans of rap and pop have broadly similar ratings, with the exceptions of being valued as high on Extraversion and moderate on Emotional Stability.

Strong correlations are also apparent in perceptions of the relationships between musical taste and the contexts of class and race (see Table 7.3). On the basis of these findings, rap appears to have replaced rock as 'the people's music'. As we shall see presently, it is the working-class preference, irrespective of ethnic background. The typical rock fan is now middle-class. Rock does not figure in the top three ratings of upper-middle or upper-class respondents. This is a major difference from the 1960s and 1970s, when black music played second fiddle to pop and stadium rock.

Table 7.3 Fan base of music genres: correlation with class

Class base	Music genre ranking
Working class	(1) Rap; (2) Pop; (3) Rock
Lower middle	(1) Rap; (2) Pop; (3) Electronica
Middle	(1) Rock; (2) Rap; (3) Jazz
Upper middle	(1) Classical; (2) Jazz; (3) Rap
Upper	(1) Classical; (2) Jazz; (3) Pop

© Renfrow et al. (2009). Reprinted by permission of SAGE.

Proto-Markets and Genre Markets: The Black Culture Industry

The question of the relationship between race and musical taste is complex. The power of music corporations and the mass media means that audiences inevitably operate within a context dominated by selective information and commercial imperatives. The musical taste of fans is far from supreme. The story told by Thomas Frank (1997) and Jim McGuigan (2009) of the co-option of many aspects of the counterculture by corporate culture was reprised in the punk, post-punk, new romantic, grunge and electronica eras.

Tim Wall (2003: 111–12) has pointed to the influence of music corporations and pop management in constructing taste cultures and finessing genre markets among audiences. The term *genre market* refers to the ensemble of production, exchange and consumption associated with a particular musical genre, such as rock, pop, reggae, rap, hip hop, electronica, house, acid, and so on. The distinctive features of genre markets is that they constitute commodified fields of musical articulation, in which performers are managed by pop impresarios and music is promoted, marketed and exchanged on the back of imperative commercial interests. The question of how genre markets emerge from popular culture is complex. The analytic challenge is to preserve the empowerment of the audience while engaging with the lifestyle-architectural aspects of taste cultures and the mechanics of commodification.

Of help in understanding the dynamics involved here is Jason Toynbee's (2000: 26–9) concept of the *proto-market*: that is, fields of music production and consumption that are not fully commodified. Pub rock bands, college bands and dance music networks are not organized around the principle of financial exchange. In proto-markets performers act as mouthpieces and songs as anthems for the mobilization of sentiment and the expression of solidarity. In the mid- to late 1970s the whole London punk scene was organized around pubs like The Hope & Anchor and The Dublin Castle, while in New York the parallel scene revolved around clubs like CBGB's and Max's Kansas City. These venues were performance hubs where not only music, but entire 'vibe tribe' lifestyles were enacted and copied. As we have seen (pp. 75, 128), Miege (1989) maintains that the organization of popular music is founded in an over-supply of composers and performers. Because of this, there is always a large pool of labourers to take up the cudgel and strike for the new musical genre and youth movement of the day. Proto-markets are defined in opposition to the commercial values of the mass market. But there are limits to the life-span of proto-markets.

The pop music business is an intensively commodified culture. As such, the privileging of distinction over exchange value is the proto-market's downfall. As Keith Negus (1992: 48–51) recounts, proto-markets inevitably become magnets for the A&R department of music corporations. It is here that music companies discover the raw talent of the next big stars and contract them cheaply, micro-manage performance and commodify output. Although proto-markets are compatible with cultural seepage, they are subject to strong pressures of being subsumed under corporate control.

In a controversial book analysing Motown and post-Motown forms of black popular music as represented by Michael Jackson and the artist formerly known as Prince, Ellis Cashmore (1997) argues that black music is commodified to fulfil the business requirements of white-dominated music corporations. He would see black proto-markets pupating rapidly into corporate control because the entire field of black music is a genre market that is ultimately subject to white corporate domination. This raises difficult questions about the autonomy of black composers and performers. The logic of Cashmore's argument is that white cultural pre-eminence condemns their musical output to act as a parody of racial stereotypes. For Cashmore, successful black pop music genres are tolerated, providing they conform to familiar racial canons that ultimately confirm the ascendancy of white culture. For example, James Brown was required to be the proverbial 'sex machine'; The Jackson Five offered a politically neutral form of music for the electronic post-Minstrel age; and Diana Ross and the Supremes represented black female power, but in a form that did not materially challenge white priority.

To some extent, Curtis Mayfield and Marvin Gaye were black superstars who bucked the trend. Mayfield's (1972) soundtrack to the blaxploitation film *Superfly* (1972) and Marvin Gaye's album *What's Going On* (1971) confront racism, injustice and inequality in American life. Both are held to be classics in modern black consciousness music that challenge white complacency and provide a megaphone for black anger. However, Gaye's divorce from Anna Ruby Gordy, the elder sister of Berry Gordy, the founder of Motown Records, and protracted problems with substance abuse, were factors in his reversion to a black Lothario image, which he maintained until his sudden death in 1984.

Leaving aside the reggae boom of the late 1970s, which was more international, the next burst of metropolitan black consciousness music was the rap revolution of the 1980s. This was bound up with globalization, the de-escalation of welfare reforms and de-industrialization. For an interlude it appeared to be the unmediated voice of authentic black American youth culture. The music of Grandmaster Flash, Public Enemy, Eazy-E, Ice Cube, Queen Latifah, Snoop Dog, Run DMC, 2Pac and black indie record labels like Ruthless Records, Death Row Records, Sugar Hill, Cheetah and Interscope was direct, indignant and pulled no punches on questions of police corruption, racial abuse and urban squalor. Briefly, it promised to lever a transformation from corporate power and the star system to the local level and the articulation of black popular values and opinion. Rap stars cultivated a public image of being from the neighbourhood, speaking for ordinary ethnic minorities and releasing their work through black-owned independent record labels.

However, as with the punk indie boom in the late 1970s and early 1980s, this turned out to be a mirage. The odds were, and remain, heavily stacked in favour of the big corporate players. In the words of Chang (2007: 443):

> At the beginning of the new millennium, five . . . companies – Vivendi Universal, Sony, AOL TimeWarner, Bertelsmann and EMI – controlled 80 percent of the music industry. Another, Viacom, owned both MTV and BET. To Chuck D, the forces that controlled hip-hop looked like this: 'You got five corporations that control retail. You got four who are the dominant record labels. Then you got three radio outlets who own all the stations. You got two television networks and you got one video outlet. I call it 5-4-3-2-1. Boom!'

Table 7.4 Fan base of music genres: correlation with race

Race type	Music genre ranking
White	(1) Pop; (2) Rap; (3) Electronica
Asian	(1) Pop; (2) Rap; (3) Classical
Black	(1) Rap; (2) Jazz; (3) Pop
Mixed black	(1) Rap; (2) Jazz; (3) Pop

© Renfrow et al. (2009). Reprinted by permission of SAGE.

The *fin de siècle* witnessed a domino effect upon the autonomy of indie rap labels and distributors. Ruthless Records is now a division of Epic; Death Row Records was auctioned to the entertainment development company WIDEawake; and Interscope is now owned by UMG. Rappers like P. Diddy, Lil' Kim, Jay-Z, Ice Cube, 50 Cent and Def Jam – to name but a few – are separated from their fan base by the walls of stardom, including, most obviously, financial success and calling cards to the power elite. In 2006 P. Diddy was declared the richest person in hip hop, with an estimated fortune of $346 million (*www.euroweb.com*). His structure of product diversification, which uses the P Diddy brand in several, mutually reinforcing avenues of business activity, has already been referred to as a model for artists in the music business (p. 160).

Rap is now so mainstream that it is one of the major divisions of the 'Big Four' music corporations. Rentfrow et al.'s (2009) research found that pop and rap are the top-rated music genres of people from white and Asian backgrounds. Typically, black and mixed black groups rate rap and jazz more highly (see Table 7.4).

This level of popularity prompts questions about the potential of rap and hip hop radically to articulate black consciousness and demands for distributive justice and eschew the temptations of parody.

Fan Silo Cultures

Dan Laughey (2006: 117–21) argues that nowadays it is an error to conceive of music audiences in terms of the narrow metrics of concert-going or the consumption of recorded CDs. MTV, illegal downloading, streaming, talent/reality TV, dance, drugs, fashion, bespoke aggregation and other axes of musical production, exchange and consumption mean that music is consumed at many nodes of pop culture. In terms of understanding the meaning of pop music among audiences in everyday life, it is now necessary to situate the commodity of music in multi-media pathways of data production, exchange and distribution. The logic of consumer culture has stretched the application and meaning of music from the CD and the concert arena and extended it to advertising, ringtones, product placement, MTV and education.

In this respect, Ian Condry's (2006: 113) analysis of Japanese rap fans and consumer culture supplies intriguing signals. He convincingly shows how Japanese fans deploy rap to work through ethnic contradictions between Japanese notions of social inclusion and the diversifying effects of globalization. Besides this, his analysis of postwar Japanese pop and consumer culture tells a tale that is familiar to students of Western society. Pop and consumer relations are marked by an accentuated tendency to commodify consumer culture and regiment consumer experience *via* engagement with multi-media rather than resistance to these pressurized through collective organization. Condry (2006: 123) holds that postwar consumer culture in Japan is subject to a process of 'massification'. That is, commodification is ubiquitous and inexorable. The result, just as Adorno (2009) proposed, is the standardization of pop music and the homogenization of consumer culture. Within Japanese youth culture, individuals and groups addicted to commodity culture and the regimentation of consumption are called *shinjin-rui*, connoting conspicuous consumers whose leisure practice and taste cultures are regarded to be deeply inscribed by advertising, the emulation of celebrities and groups who possess distinction, and other consumer stimulants. Figuratively speaking, this consumption experience is ruled by a 'brand manual'. This extends into participation in pop culture as fans of the latest concoction of the music industry, such as boy bands, girl bands or torch singers.

However, contra Adorno (1991, 2009), this is not the only, or even the chief, consequence of massification. Drawing upon ethnographic work on Japanese youth subcultures, Condry (2006: 217) refers to the converse expansion of what he calls *otaku*. As with the *shinjin-rui*, the context for the emergence and expansion of *otaku* is massification. As we have seen, the *shinjin-rui* is an audience that produce meanings that *converge* with the taste texts manufactured by symbolic creators and commercial impresarios in the music business. In contrast, the key word to comprehend the relationship between the *otaku*, consumer culture and the music business is *accumulation*. The *otaku* are consumers, including pop music fans, who are indifferent to the taste cultures of the *shinjin-rui* and cultivate silo 'home-worlds', utilizing resources from the media such as comic books, science fiction, amateur radio, message boards and blog sites.

Otaku is a term meaning home. It carries various nuances, of which the most relevant for our purposes are respect, a lack of intimacy between 'me' and 'you', a mania for accumulation and the practice of psychological exclusion. Behaviourally speaking, *otaku* individuals and groups have the following characteristics:

(a) *codes of social exclusion*: organized around jargon, knowledge bases, types of dress;
(b) *conditional participation*: based upon the principle of limiting interpersonal warmth, beyond acknowledging others as fellow *otaku*; and
(c) *non-hierarchy*: codes of exclusion and the practice of conditional participation do not presuppose judgements of superiority. *Otaku* are somewhat judgemental and self-righteous. They will automatically dismiss individuals and groups representing other *otaku* clusters as 'weirdos' and reject the entire *shinjin-rui* genre as objectionable. But these are strictly judgements of cultural difference. They carry no evaluative connotation of either superiority or inferiority.

The *otaku* are silos of consumption. Their *raison d'être* is not to accumulate data about their selected area of interest in order to acquire distinction. Rather, they accumulate data as an end in itself. Thus hip hop *otaku* retrieve and process from multi-media sites all of the data relating to Jay-Z, 50 Cent, Timbaland, Akon or related performers just as material accumulates in a silo.

Silo culture is compatible with the pop monadism that we referred to in Chapter

2 (pp. 31–3). Immersed in the perfect storm of contemporary pop culture, the monad confronts a world of fragmenting boundaries and musical coalescence – in short, a world of massive cultural de-differentiation. Building a silo of pop culture is a perfectly rational response to feelings of being overwhelmed and engulfed. It may appear to be retreating from the fray. Actually, it is a way of *asserting* control.

The rise of the *otaku* is symptomatic of broader changes in advanced global consumer pop cultures. Their relationship with consumer culture is not based upon withdrawal, distinction, the development of a counterculture or adherence to a brand manual. It is the result of the over-determination of consumer culture: that is, a structure of multiple limits and pressures that develops internally consistent forces which overwhelm the individual. Building a silo of data about a cultural commodity or experience provides the psychological comforts of grounding and self-regulation. Being an *otaku* is a never-ending game of data consumption and asserting boundaries.

Currently, Jay-Z tops the *Forbes* 2009 Hip-Hop Cash Kings list. Being a Jay-Z *otaku* is not necessarily primarily based in having a passion for his music. The primary base is having an encyclopaedic knowledge of the media data streams and information mills relating to Jay-Z. Knowing everything there is to know about Jay-Z is the fulcrum of personal identity and group membership.

Condry (2006: 127) therefore queries Bourdieu's (1984, 1990) characterization of consumption as driven by a search for distinction. In Condry's view this applies to merely some sections of consumer society. The over-determination of consumer culture has up-ended the hierarchy upon which the characterization of distinction relies. In Condry's (2006: 128) words:

> One of the driving forces behind the rise of *otaku* is the abundance of cultural goods, 'more and more things came out'. The increasing diversity of niche cultures and an erosion of their hierarchical ordering can be partly related to the expansion of consumer options. This expansion is itself an outgrowth of corporate, national and global economic policies often predicated on an ideal of so-called consumer-led growth, as well as broad-based shifts from Fordist methods of production to flexible accumulation.

The over-determination of consumer culture weakens the concept of taste hierarchies and creates the space for the development of silo fan cultures. In a silo, one is at 'home', defended from the rapidly changing conditions and unstable arrangements of the outside world. The *otaku* fan is not exactly detached from the world, since what makes the silo secure and comforting is the protected base that it offers to accumulate selected data from outside. By the same token the *otaku* observe a firm distinction between the 'home' and the exterior, the silo of safety and the wilderness of uncertainty and potential danger.

Condry's (2006) account of the *otaku* may be implying something much more important about the development of silo fan cultures as a response to the over-determination of consumer culture. If consumer culture is experienced as a 'perfect storm', it makes sense to go to ground and develop emotions of grounding and control by accumulating expertise about one selected commodified product. As such, it can be interpreted as a way of acquiring specialized knowledge and a depth perspective in contrast to the general data streams and superficial responses that characterize the common audience reaction to cultural de-differentiation.

I have tried to suggest what this wider application of *otaku* culture in relation to Western music audiences might look like. To hypothesize about the rise of fan silo culture as a response to consumer culture is one thing. Manifestly, the topic demands further empirical research. However, even as a hypothesis, the notion of fan silo cultures offers a corrective to over-enthusiastic applications and extensions of relationist and structuralist models of consumer behaviour. Fan cultures are not necessarily reponses to the search for difference and distinction in the manner interpreted by Sarah Thornton (1995) and Phil Jackson (1994). Nor are they inevitably consumer robots blindly following the cues of the culture industry (Adorno 2009). They may appropriate and apply music as a form of lifestyle security that they apply in conjunction with other multi-media data to produce affirming emotions of control and ordering. The exploration of this hypothesis requires us to follow Livingstone (1998) in methodologically framing fan behaviour in terms of the triangulation of production, text and context.

Technology and Media

Imagine music without electronic amplification or wireless transmission. It is irretrievably territorialized. It is embedded in sound lagoons, marked by local conditions, micro-cultures and regional personalities. The subject matter of songs reflects the parochial nature of composition and performance. It deals with folklore. The subjects are episodic. They might relate to an unexpected, bountiful harvest, an enthralling jade or a blackguard at court; an indentured slave who suffers the cat-o'-nine-tails at the hands of his plantation master or the aftermath of an insurrection against a frontier stockade; the life of a noble steed or an apparition of Christ in a delta grotto.

There is no sense of consistent historical or social analysis. The text is the spoken word. Audience texts and interpretation are based in speech, not print. Music is bound by folklore and is obsessively ritualized, in Attali's (1977) sense of the term. It travels via an oral tradition of troubadours and wandering minstrels. In doing so it naturally borrows from other traditions. Notions of global or network music lie far beyond the horizon. It is appropriate to speak of a technology to this music. But by contemporary standards it is enormously restricted, being confined to the voice, string, percussion and wind.

Robert Briffault's (1965: 76–9) discussion of the Moorish tradition of the medieval *jongleur* observed that songs travelled quickly. A composition from Egypt or Morocco might become popular in Paris or Cologne faster than it took for a work of literature to cross the Rhine. The wandering minstrel tradition infiltrates polyglot cultures with music from distant lands. The involvement of *jongleurs* in military campaigns and marches through conquered territories extends and elaborates this tradition. Yet often the music was not exactly instantly accessible. Polyglot courts employed bilingual Mozarabians, Jews and Mudehars to translate foreign lyrics and unfamiliar cultural ideas and nuances. The reaction to music was not informed by recorded sound with the attendant issues of collaborative teamwork in engineering sounds and producing the basis for comparison between performance and archival fidelity and transmission quality. It is dependent wholly upon performance: the face and body of the musician before you, the notes and chords as they are directly heard. As a means of connection between audiences and performers this was exceedingly hit or miss. If a performance bombed, there was no CD or online music file to compare *how the music should have sounded*. Everything turned on the one-off performance and local acoustics. Both were necessarily associated with considerable variability, which plainly hindered the development of common technical standards and a mass audience. Additionally, the context of parochial conditions, high rates of mortality, restricted travel opportunities and the technologies of the day set boundaries on musical production and texts. However creative one is, compared with synthesizers, samplers, electric keyboards, electric guitars and amplification, there is only so much that can be done with the technology of the voice, strings, percussion and wind.

Electricity unutterably changes the production, exchange and consumption of popular music. Sonically, it transforms common hearing and appreciation of pitch, tone, timbre, cadence, metre and rhythm. Recording makes performance and reception universal. There are no bum notes in the world of vinyl recordings or music files. Indeed, studio recording offers opportunities of sonic perfection that in the long run, as Glenn Gould (1984) remarked, threaten to make live performance redundant.[1] Inevitably, composition and performance are more collaborative since they draw upon archives of recorded music and the specialized skills of studio personnel.

Perforce, the exchange of music continues to involve oral traditions. Yet now it is vastly extended by supplements from pop music print media, MTV, DVD, radio and the worldwide web. Electronic media expose the field of exchange based around the technologies of voice, string percussion and wind as small, awkward and as redundant as a box of clogs in the age of the superjet. To be sure, a global audience only becomes *technically* possible with wireless transmission. In addition to the tune-picking of local tourists, the Himalayan people who, we noted (Chapter 3), were fully conversant with the lyrics and music of Ralph McTell's song 'Streets of London' had certainly encountered broadcast versions in their mountain settlements. Electricity permits us to speak of global pop anthems: 'All You Need Is Love', 'Blowin' in the Wind', 'Brown Sugar', 'Thriller', 'Billie Jean', 'One', 'Speed of Sound'. Electricity also enables audiences to be more discerning. For recorded music can be played regardless of social settings, *ad infinitum*. It is therefore possible for consumers to repeatedly assess the worth of venerable recordings against new sounds and new technologies. EMI's 2009 release of The Beatles' re-mastered back-catalogue claimed to offer consumers the original music *as it was meant to be*, compared with the 'dull' approximations of their vinyl and CD forebears.

The consumption of music occurs in ways that would have been beyond the wildest dreams of Beethoven, Chopin or, come to that, Jimi Hendrix, Janis Joplin, Jim Morrison, John Lennon or Kurt Cobain. Domestic sound systems reproduce the standards of the recording studio. Personal sound systems make popular music totally mobile. Blogging sites and web-based servers like Facebook, Twitter, MySpace, Last.fm and iLike make the notions of the folk and the popular developed by Herder, Bretano and the Brothers Grimm seem quaint and to belong truly to another age – to 'pre-history', in fact. Globalization and network society allow cultural monads to engage in encoding and decoding practice in relation to popular music and popular culture on a laptop or mobile phone in any social setting.

The postwar music business was founded upon a rigid division between artists and consumers. The introduction of sequencing, sampling, scratching, Garageband, MIDI and VST systems make composing and performing available to anyone who is literate in basic computer skills. Nor is this rightly described as a matter of dumbing down. Laptops have been turned into indispensable ingredients of the chart-topping pop combo. As sonic tools, they are as cherished and necessary as electric guitars, pianos and drum kits. The latitude for reproducing and modifying recorded music has been significantly expanded. The computer and synthesizer allow music to be cut, sampled and spliced in the home to concoct innumerable ambient settings and emulate voice, string, wind and percussion in various ways.[2]

While technology has augmented the productive role of consumers in interpreting and modifying texts, it has also transformed the context of consumption. The digital revolution enlarges the utility of the web as a browsing and retail system. Music is streamed, ripped and copied by P2P platforms without money ever changing hands. Correspondingly, the significance of the music print media as a hub of exchange and the record store as a setting in which music fans gather, browse, exchange information and buy recorded music has declined.

The larger chains, such as Virgin, adopted their own strategies of bespoke aggregation: that is, by adding coffee shops, magazine and book sections, DVD stalls, game sections and musical instrument sales sections to the conventional CD counter. They were unable to overcome the challenge of web-based retailing, especially as the latter was able to cut point-of-sale price by radically scaling back on the overheads involved in running a high-street retail megastore.

Electricity changed everything. The production and exchange of music ceased to be imprisoned by regional grids and grated allegories. For sonic communication, free global exchange was analogous to photosynthesis. It was a nursery for experiments in hybridity that produced world music. It permitted different musical forms to be appreciated and transferred from tradition to tradition, context to context, to swim from inland source to the sea. It decoupled sonic composition and performance from musical training. It made sheet music obsolescent by making vinyl and later CD formats weightless, and encrypted data the primary medium of exchange. It made recorded sound reproducible and subject to perpetual revision. It amplified what hitherto was scarcely audible.

Wolfgang Schivelbusch (1988) writes about what he calls 'the industrialization of light'. With electric illumination, age-old distinctions between night and day evaporated. One could read comfortably in the night; one could parley face-to-face after sunset; one could make love with the lights on! Retailing was reinvented by electric light display in shop windows and counter space. Streets and waterways became safely navigable betwixt dusk and dawn. The smell of tallow, wick and gas, which were the staples of private and public illumination before the age of electricity, and which must have impregnated atmospheric space and social relations, was replaced with odourless light.

The effect of electrified sound upon the production, exchange and consumption of popular music was no less dramatic. In the nineteenth century, following Schivelbusch, it is right to speak of 'the industrialization of sound'. Everything indeed changed. It was not just a matter of the recording, performance and retailing of sound, it was also a question of how texts were represented, exchanged and interpreted. Originally, the medium of music was oral culture. People would tell each other about the music of this or that *jongleur* or minstrel. The defect of oral culture is twofold. In the first place, it is restrained by locality. Music can never become global in a context in which word of its merits and defects is limited to capricious exchange or other unmonitored conversations. Secondly, oral traditions are prone to distortion. When it comes to recounting the virtues and vices of this or that performer, there is many a slip between cup and lip. Oral culture is capable of transferring enormous truths and penetrating insights. However, because it provides no reliable means for independent verification it often produces tales that say more about the chronicler than the chronicle. Electricity transforms the representation of music from oral to visual culture. Speech culture remains an important conduit for exchanging data about music. But print, celluloid, television, video and web-based transmission subject speech to a new independent discipline. It is one thing to be told of the guitar licks of Albert Lee, Eddie Van Halen, Slash, The Edge, Johnny Marr or Johnny Buckland. But seeing is believing. Visual playbacks of these players transform literacy about popular music because they constitute an electric archive that can be applied for entertainment *and* instruction.

The pop press created new media avatars in the form of pop journos like Cameron Crowe, David Fricke and Robert Christgau with *Rolling Stone*; Jon Landau, Sandy Pearlman and Richard Meltzer with *Crawdaddy!*; Dave Marsh, Greil Marcus, Penny Valentine, Lester Bangs and Lisa Robinson with *Creem*; Ray Coleman, Chris Welch, Richard Williams, Jon Savage, Simon Reynolds and David Stubbs with *Melody Maker*; Nick Kent, Ian MacDonald, Mick Farren, Tony Parsons, Julie Burchill, Barney Hoskins, Paolo Hewitt, Charles Shaar Murray and Ben Knowles with NME; Keith Altham, Caroline Coon, Vivienne Goldman, Steve Lamacq and Mary Anne Hobbs with *Sounds*; and Nick Logan, Paul Morley, Fiona Russell Powell and Ian Penman with *The Face*. They supplied audiences with news of the latest sounds, thought pieces on performers and musical genres and, crucially, reviews of the latest recorded releases and photographs of musicians. To a generation raised on the internet, it is hard to convey the influence exerted on readers in campus coffee bars and suburban bedrooms by a trusted pop journo's five-star record review of the latest release of an established or new artist. Before iTunes (which enables buyers to listen to samples of their intended purchase before buying), streaming, ripping, premium service on YouTube, video file-sharing on Google, MySpace and Last.fm and the proliferation of analogous online communities, an enthusiastic thought piece or record review by Lester Bangs, Cameron Crowe, Nick Kent, Paul Morley or Ian MacDonald made all the difference.

The subjects of music technology and mass media deserve book-length treatments. In a study of this type, whose purpose is to provide a sociological survey of the general mode of production rather than a detailed, granular account of constituents, it suffices to offer some brief case notes regarding the effects of technology and mass media. But before coming to specific cases, what is the general theoretical position on the relationship between technology and popular music?

Theodore Gracyk's Thesis: Technology Rocks

The first sound recording was made in 1877. The phonograph quickly moved from being an adjunct transcribing performance to a full-scale genre in its own right. Playback fidelity – that is, the capacity of the recording system to reproduce the truth of a recording – became a factor in choices of consumption. Laing (1991) contends that the invention of the phonograph replaced the connection between the audience and the professional musician with a 'new physical object', the playback system: that is, the phonograph and, later, the gramophone. In the domestic context, popular music became, so to speak, faceless. For playback was now mechanical, erasing the age-old necessity for the physical presence of the singer. This changed the character of listening. The focus switched from absorbing the presence and aura of the live performer to achieving repeatable playback purity. Thus, Gelatt (1977: 222) and Sanjek (1988: 63, 131–2) document the efforts of phonographic companies and radio corporations that, commencing from the 1920s, began to engineer high-fidelity recording and transmission.

Technology also became fundamental in the production of pop music. From the earliest days, the recording of live performance involved the manipulation of cylinders and discs by the sound recordist. Theodore Gracyk's (1996) thesis holds that, unlike earlier pop musical forms, notably folk, country and the blues, technology is the *precondition* for pop and rock. In other words, the latter are impossible without the industrialization of sound. What does Gracyk mean by this?

Realist interpretations of pop submit that recording is the mirror of performance. The recording is the natural extension of the skills of the composer and the performer. Theodore Gracyk's argument is that pop genres are anti-realist and anti-naturalist. That is, they are not, by any tenable reckoning, the natural reflection of the skills of the composer and musician, nor can they be produced and reproduced in natural settings. Through multi-tracking, over-dubbing, echo and other production devices, the studio sculpts recorded sound effects that are not natural. Realism is not tenable because it idealizes the creativity of composers and musicians and downplays the technological principles that structure sound (Gracyk 1996: 71).

In this respect the introduction of magnetic tape in 1949 was a considerable breakthrough. Simultaneously, it boosted sonic quality and lowered recording cost. This brought the possibility of recording down from the level of big studios to independent entrepreneurs and small recording studios. Presley's Sun recordings, made between 1953 and 1955, reflected the wider dissemination of recording opportunities facilitated by the new technology of magnetic tape. The use of echo, fading, phasing and reverberation in Presley's recording on 'Mystery Train' (1955) disrupts natural auditory codes as a calculated part of the production process. Marsh (1982: 28) observes that the use of magnetic tape in the Sun sessions allowed songs to be immediately played back, analysed and, at minimal cost (studio time), re-recorded. Studio recording liberated musicians in two ways. Firstly, it freed them from the fickle nature of the audience, whose approval/disapproval response was perfectly capable of wrecking performance. Secondly, it made musicians independent of the songwriter, since it offered ample opportunities for jamming and improvisation.

As to the instrumental qualities of tape in multi-tracking, over-dubbing, time-delay and distortion effects, Jason Toynbee (2000: 80–1) is right to categorize the industry response as extremely conservative. Between 1949 and the early 1960s, magnetic tape was chiefly used as a low-cost means of recording sound. Yet the sonic potential of magnetic tape and the studio setting was an irresistible resource in the development of creative labour and pop music. 'Tomorrow Never Knows' (1966) and 'A Day in the Life' (1967) by The Beatles would be impossible to compose outside the studio or to play naturally on stage. They are more properly described as studio sounds. The same is true for The Beach Boys' 'Good Vibrations' (1966) and 'Heroes and Villains' (1967), and the music of Frank Zappa, Pink Floyd, Led Zeppelin, U2, Abba, Kayne West, Foxy Brown, Queen Latifah, Lil' Kim, Beyoncé, Jay-Z and, to be sure, practically all of the catalogue of pop and rock recorded since the late 1950s.

A corollary of consumer recognition of the fundamental importance of technology and the creative labour of technicians in recording sound is the emergence of the studio as a setting of cultural distinction. Thus, certain studios became globally famous for producing certain kinds of sound. Abbey Road and Trident Studios (London), Sun Studios (Memphis), Motown (Detroit) and RCA Studio B (Nashville) are much-cited examples.

According to Schmidt-Horning (2004: 710), by the mid-1950s, the introduction of magnetic tape and improvements in microphone technology created the advent of 'The Sound-Man Artist': that is, a professional technician skilled in the art of selecting and placing the microphone in the recording studio. As three-channel stereo was replaced by four-, eight-, sixteen- and twenty-four-track recording, the importance of the Sound Man Artist in engineering was dramatically increased. Multi-track recording allowed engineers to record instruments on separate tracks. This produced new opportunities for technical intervention, especially in the area of sound mixing, using echo chambers, program equalizers and multiple dubbing (Kealy 1979; Pinch and Bijsterveld 2004).

It is not for nothing, therefore, that Gracyk (1996: 38) insists on claiming a 'symbiotic relationship' between pop and recording technology. Properly understood, pop recordings are not immediate. They are synthetic, sculpted forms. The main actors in the cycle of synthesis are (a) professional songwriters, (b) record producers and (c) record engineers. These participants collaborate with composers and players in the production cycle. Music publicists, photographers and marketing personnel are accessories in the same process with specialized functions at the levels of visual culture and media dissemination.

In the formularized pop of contemporary TV talent/reality pop, these players are hardly side-men. In his autobiography, Simon Cowell (2003) makes no bones about the pivotal role of professional songwriters and producers (notably Stock, Aitken and Waterman) in creating contemporary chart success. Cowell's model is to use professional specialists to micro-manage raw talent and turn it into pop stardom. Spontaneity is the enemy. Nothing is left to chance. The choice of material, the arrangement of the songs and the dress, hairstyle and cosmetics of the singer are all centrally co-ordinated and planned. The accent is upon the intensive control of all aspects of the production cycle.

With respect to the dynamics of technical production, sampling and scratching in dance music take this as far as the technology currently allows it to go. They layer and fuse musical fragments from different eras, separate genres and distinct cultures to 'create', as Simon Reynolds (1998: 368) puts it, 'a timewarping pseudo-event, something that could never possibly have happened. Different acoustic spaces and recording "auras" are forced into uncanny adjacence. You could call it "deconstruction of the metaphysics of presence"; you could also call it "magic". It's a kind of time travel, or séance.'

The influence of technology is not confined to the process of production. It also encompasses exchange and consumption. Tim Wall (2003: 41–9) distinguishes four different technological layers in the production, exchange and consumption of music:

(1) *The creation of musical sound.* Until the 1920s, acoustic performance was the script for recorded sound. The options for producers and engineers to doctor sound were strictly confined. Record companies took a back seat in the evolution of electrical microphones and speakers. Popular playback formats were subject to the technical constraints of a four-minute format centred upon acoustic voice, string, wind and percussion (Morton 2000). The limitations of recording technologies privileged the single as the primary commodity form in popular music.

(2) *The recording of music.* The introduction of microphones and speakers in the 1920s multiplied the demand for technocrats, notably record producers and sound engineers, to manipulate the recording process and the production of recorded sound. Microgroove technologies on 12 inch recordings (1940), the introduction of magnetic tape (1949) and the replacement of 78 rpm recording discs with 7 inch and 12 inch microgroove records increased the potential for amplification (1950), and the introduction of stereo (1960) extended the palette of recording effects by increasing the volume of data that could be recorded. In doing so, it enhanced the synthetic qualities of pop and rock, separating it definitively from naturalism.

(3) *The distribution of music.* By 1920, radio established itself as the main network for the distribution of popular music. The use of recorded music as the backing track for sound films in the 1930s widened the popular music audience. The introduction of FM in 1955 improved sound quality.

Changes in the material commodity form of recorded music were also crucial. In 1965 the development of the portable radio increased the accessibility of playback systems and freed popular music listening from fixed settings. The introduction of the LP in 1950 transformed the meaning of recorded playback. The 12 inch format provided greater scope for narrative content, the development of character and the range of emotions. In 1980 cassette sales out-performed vinyl sales. By 1990 digital formats like the mini disc and compact disc became the main material commodity form. By the new century, the internet and digital mobile systems emerged as main highways for cost-effective distribution.

(4) *The consumption of music.* Radio, transistor radios, compact discs, mini discs, car systems, the ghetto blaster and digital files have made access ubiquitous. In the mid-1980s the introduction of the laptop provided sophisticated playback and low-cost

recording systems. With the introduction of the web it was possible to download copyrighted music (theoretically, at no cost) and exchange domestically produced items. The introduction of digital platforms like MySpace, YouTube and Twitter provided internet junctions compatible with the free global exchange of music.

Technology does not *determine* the trajectory of development in pop composition, performance and consumption. On the other hand it is a major and indispensable structural element in the production, exchange and consumption of pop. It positions people in relation to resources and is associated with propensities for certain types of social action. It is no exaggeration to hold that pop is situated at the intersection between technology and the emotions.

We can illustrate this further by examining some brief case studies of this intersection: (a) amplification; (b) sampling and scratching; and (c) long-player technology.

Amplification

The amplification of voice, guitars and keyboards was a practical solution devised by singers and players who struggled to be heard in the big band/dancehall stage settings of the late 1930s and 1940s. The Rickenbacker electric guitar was commercially available from 1931. Fender electric guitars appeared in the market in the mid-1940s. The electric guitar replaced hollow guitar interiors with a solid piece of wood that allowed the vibration of the instrument's guitar strings to be amplified through the magnetic qualities of the pickup system. Initially, as may be inferred from what I have already said, the main market was musicians in dance band orchestras. However, the dramatic sonic and stage potentials of pickups for auditory dissonance and visual spectacle were soon realized by popular musicians, who foregrounded the instrument in arrangements and mixes with the intent of 'articulating' the preoccupations of youth culture. In the words of Hegarty (2008: 59–60):

> Rock 'n' roll is the first music that consistently works with loudness:
> this was music to be played loud, as an assertion of youth identity. . . .
> Electricity, primarily through amplification, signifies. It is not just loudness,
> but the connotation of loudness, of aggression (particularly in the form of
> the electric guitar). It also allows the development of musical meaning, as
> notes are bent, stretched, made to vibrate.

Amplification has instant auditory impact, in the way that a gun report makes you start and brings you up short. But it also broadens the palette of what can be played because amplitude reframes the pattern of sound waves. It supports electric sound with new dimensions of pitch, duration and timbre. The application of distortion and feedback by Jimi Hendrix, Neil Young, Johnny Buckland and innumerable other musicians is intrinsic to the rock genre. It generates a specific emotional response. It is attained not by lyrics or harmony. It is the result of something as technologically prosaic as over-loading an amplifier so that the signal destabilizes. Axiomatically, feedback and distortion are cogent sonic expressions of the inchoate, conflicting emotions of adolescence.

Amplification is also consonant with minimalism. The pre-electronic magnification of sound required the multiplication of instruments and musicians. A string quartet is not as loud as an orchestra because the latter has more players and more sound-making machines. Electronic amplification concentrates this effect in one player or a small ensemble connected to a keyboard or an electric guitar. Deep Purple or Iron Maiden can achieve the same auditory impact as the London Symphony Orchestra or the New York Philharmonic.

The resultant consolidation of the star as the focal point of audiences intensifies the commodification of pop music. For the amplification of sound privileges players and makes strong psychological links between virtuosos and stars. It accentuates the focal position of the vocalist by relaying every breath and vocal inflection. Moreover, it makes feature players out of members of the ensemble by supporting extended solos and trademark licks. The electric guitar performances of virtuosos like Jimi Hendrix and Jimmy Page combine virtuosity with technology to enhance the message of masculine presence (Waksman 1999: 246–7).

Edison patented the microphone in 1886. It revolutionized vocal performance by eliminating the need for lead vocalists to sing at a high range in order to be heard above the band. By the late 1920s, condenser and ribbon fixed-stand microphones replaced the megaphone. Equipped with the asset of greater sonic capacity, vocalists could extend the range of emotions conveyed in a song by making the smallest sigh or whisper audible. By leaning in on the microphone for soft and low notes, and backing off on high or loud notes, performers were able to create powerful vocal effects. This was not simply a matter of auditory production and response. The microphone became an indispensable visual component of performance. Frank Sinatra was one of the first lead singers to realize the amorous and erotic potential of the microphone with the Tommy Dorsey Band. He compared it to 'a geisha girl' and developed a detailed repertoire of stage mannerisms and caresses to employ it as a key prop in vocal performance (Shaw 1968: 47; Lahr 1988: 17).

Microphone technology eventually produced headsets that offered new ways of combining stage mobility with amplification and gave consumers the opportunity to listen to music in any spatial setting. Contemporary rap and hip hop apply the microphone as the chief instrument in composition and performance (Weitzer and Kurbin 2009).

The fundamental importance of technology requires us to recast our thinking about the use of creative labour power in the creation of music. The importance of the Sound Man Artist alerts us to the collaborative nature of creative labour in producing sounds. But this is hardly confined to the recording studio.

In their path-breaking work on Robert Moog and the invention of the Moog synthesizer, Pinch and Trocco (2002) demonstrate how a musical instrument acted as an influence in the organization of sound production and consumption communities. The Moog breached many of the taken-for-granted conventions shared by musicians, engineers and audiences. In turn, it acted as the basis for revision and innovation to reappropriate control from technology. The work of Pinch and Trocco introduces the idea of the instrument as a 'non-human agent' in the production, exchange and consumption of music. If you like, the Moog is the technical expression of the much wider processes of cultural de-differentiation that we have explored elsewhere in the book. Musically speaking, it allowed everything to happen, every genre and tradition to be accumulated and cross-fertilized, *in one place*.

Sound is the crossroads of exchange between technology, which has a standardizing and universalizing impulse, and culture, which cultivates and personalizes resources. Thus, Théberge (1997: 191) speaks of this as the 'personalization of sound'. Take the case of the tinkering of musical instruments. Tinkering is an interesting type of creative labour in the music industry because it involves the expenditure of 'surplus' creative labour power in transforming the meaning, use and effect of ready-made instruments. Oldenzeil (2001) argues that this activity should be understood as a sub-type of resistance to mass consumerism. For this reason, it has been an important element in the DIY, non-corporate ethic pursued by many exponents in the punk and heavy metal genres (Waksman 1999, 2004).

From the earliest days in the 1930s and 1940s, modifying electric guitars to change amplification and sound waves in the post-work settings of garages and backyards was commonplace. Eddie Van Halen (of Van Halen) and Greg Ginn (of Black Flag) are contemporary guitar virtuosos who have invested considerable creative labour in reconfiguring their instruments. Van Halen built his own guitars, customized them by combining a Gibson Humbucker pickup with a Stratocaster body and rewired the pickup to his own specifications. Ginn experimented with a range of pickups and rewired the guitar to bypass the tone and volume controls in order to push volume and feedback to extremes. The pronounced physicality of his sound and playing style is credited with the emergence of a new style of slam-dancing in audiences (Waksman 2004: 691–2).

Sampling and Scratching

The technology of reproduction combined with accessibility has multiplied options for borrowing and piracy from recorded works. The progressive industrialization of sound creates the technological basis for the perpetual cannibalization of recorded music. This is a matter of redefining creativity as appropriation. The extraction, isolation and recalibration of notes and licks may be untraceable. As such, questions of originality and plagiarism are currently being radically debated and revised.

What does sampling entail? The invention of digital sampling in the mid-1980s permits chunks of recorded sound to be converted into binary information that instructs a sound recording system to reconstruct the material rather than *replay* it. Playback quality matches that of the best analogue system. Creative labour input here is not limited to composition and playing notes. At the heart of sampling is experimentation with the relationships between technology and a database. It allows inscribed codes to be reprogrammed. Strictly speaking, output is not in the hands of an *auteur*, a composer-God. The technology explicitly introduces a random element that is universally distributed. Re-composition utilizes chance and contingency as compositional resources. Assembling layers of sound may be what the artist does. But the production of layers are technologically cloned and modified.

Artists used to be viewed as thinking reeds. They made meaning from the *zeitgeist*, or spirit of the times. The metaphor of the thinking reed is still applicable to hip hop, house and techno performers. But their creative labour is also portrayed and recognized as unabashedly commonplace. Before they are thinking reeds they are shoppers in the supermarket of sound. Indeed, the prosaic aspect of their creative labour input positively contributes to the popular recognition of their work as credible, competent and relevant.

As such, the dance music of Howie B, Beck and DJ Shadow has been censured by purists and labelled as inauthentic. In response to this it might be objected that it is unduly restrictive to confine technology to a bit part in the composition and performance of popular music. Using playback modification technology creatively elevates the sampler as an agent of sound production that rivals the importance of the Sound Man Artist in the postwar production of music. For sampling expropriates the choices made by the Sound Man Artist and reconfigures them. Thus, it makes living labour out of dead labour. Of course, this is one of the secrets behind its appeal.

Scratching may be defined as the real-time application of direct physical labour to modify discs to produce new sonic values. It applies speed shifts, phasing, repetition and simple manual manipulation to doctor sound recordings. Scratching developed in radical black club culture in the mid-1970s. The turntable was redefined to make scratch the backbone of house, techno, jungle, trip hop and swingbeat. The role of the DJ was recast in two important ways. Firstly, DJs were redefined as sonic pirates, seizing contraband from the galleons of mainstream recorded music sent out by the executives of record corporations. Secondly, their creative labour was extended from selecting recordings and playing them, to effectively acting as an underground accompanist. Cutler (2008: 138–55) coins the term *plunderphonia* to describe this process. The technology brings sonic *bricolage* and Pop Art within the reach of anyone who can afford a sampler, a turntable and an amplification system.

For *aficionados*, sampling and scratching are idiomatic of widening access. They realize the democratic potential inherent in rock. The keyboard and MIDI system brings composition and performance within the reach of the audience. The gramophone and 12 inch record are creatively stripped of their commodity status and turned into craft instruments. Sampling and scratching are evidence of a profound alteration in the chain of production, exchange and consumption. Traditional aesthetic notions of hierarchy between producers and consumers are obliterated.

Adjusting and stretching notes, reconfiguring recorded sound, transforming cadence and pitch become legitimate creative inputs. In the words of Cutler (2008: 152), 'leakage, seepage, adoption, osmosis, abstraction, contagion . . . describe the life of the sound work today'. Music is not just composed, it is cannibalized, thus collapsing not merely conventional distinctions between artists and audiences, but external frames of time and space.

Long-Player Technology

Earlier, we saw that the invention of the gramophone created a new genre in the music business: an object for playing recorded discs. This set in motion a demand for engineering perfect high fidelity so that the commodity accurately replays the sonic articulation of music as it was originally made (Gelatt 1977; Sanjek 1988). Gramophone design was also made more competitive as suppliers sought to produce not merely the best sound quality systems, but also the most ornamental, distinctive visual designs. The Danish company Bang & Olufsen, founded in 1925, became a market leader in this respect. Their audio website (*www.bang-olufsen.com*) may be referred to for examples of product designs that seek to combine audio-visual distinction in playback systems. Thus, the mass-produced commodity uses dead labour to produce listening replay qualities that are experienced as live and personal. For every listening experience is unique and mediated through the time-bound response of an individual to the recording device.

One crucial break-through in the history of listening technology was the long-player disc. Long-player technology is a comparatively recent invention. Columbia Records first demonstrated its 'Revolutionary Disk Marvel' to press corps in June 1948. After the Second World War, in relatively short order, the introduction of the 33⅓ rpm microgroove album and two-/three-channel stereo recording revolutionized the record business (Elborough 2008: 19). In one fell swoop, it offered longer playing time and higher fidelity (Schmidt-Horning 2004: 708–9). The 12 inch vinyl disc, invented in 1930, was more versatile and durable than the shellac-based 78s that it replaced. Vinyl is robust and malleable and allows narrower grooves to be cut into the surface. Shellac is a resin secreted by Asian tree insects. The grooves are wider and layered with fillers to reduce erosion from the heavy steel needles. Hence the problem of hiss in 78 rpm playback formats.

The war provided the spur to the introduction of 12 inch 33⅓ long-players. The outbreak of hostilities in Asia severed the supply lines of shellac to the rich metropolitan markets of the West. The result was a major shortage in the supply of the chief resource (above carbon and a collection of abrasive fillers such as emery powder and limestone) in disc production.

The technical advantages of vinyl recordings over shellac are indisputable. The average life-span of a shellac disc is between 75 and 125 plays. Vinyl 12 inch albums have an indefinite shelf life, and are cheaper, lighter and easier to store. In addition, playing time is longer.

Until the emergence of compact discs in the early 1980s, vinyl LPs were the financial backbone of the music business. As we saw in Chapter 5 (pp. 126–8), the postwar industrial planning strategy of the major record corporations privileged the LP as the technological foundation of artistic expression and the primary revenue source for recorded music. The LP offered unprecedented inter-linked opportunities for design and artistic development.

One example of this is the sleeve cover. Album sleeves encouraged new combinations of music with images, typographic design and text that redefined record purchase into a broader pop art experience (Barzun 1977; Day 2000). The sleeve ceased to be a mere accessory of packaging and became designed and identified as an artwork. With the emergence of rock bands in the 1960s this connection was solidified and extended by the art school origins of many musicians. Similarly, during the punk era the theory of aesthetic outrage and 'King Mob' *bricolage* style of album and fashion by punk designers Jamie Reid and Vivienne Westwood was indebted to the writings of the French Situationists (Frith and Horne

1987: 42–8, 130–1). Peter Blake's (1967) image for *Sgt Pepper's Lonely Hearts Club Band* by The Beatles, Andy Warhol's (1971) zipper design for *Sticky Fingers* by The Rolling Stones, Roger Dean's album covers for Yes, Asia, Rick Wakeman and Uriah Heep, Jamie Reid's celebrated cover for *Never Mind the Bollocks* by The Sex Pistols, which built upon his ground-breaking design for the single 'God Save the Queen' (both 1977), Brian Duffy's album photos for David Bowie, notably the cover image of *Aladdin Sane* (1973), Robert Mapplethorpe's stark black and white image of Patti Smith for the album *Horses* (1975) and Peter Saville's sleeve designs for Joy Division and New Order are acknowledged totems of pop culture.

Album artwork must synchronize with recorded music. Here the opportunities that long-playing records offered for narrative and character development, evolving settings and moods, were unparalleled in the history of recorded sound. Most people think of the concept album as the invention of The Beatles, The Beach Boys, Bob Dylan, The Who, Frank Zappa, David Bowie, Joni Mitchell, Pink Floyd or The Kinks. Each of them released albums that explicitly told a story. The Who's *Tommy* (1969) and *Quadrophenia* (1973) and Pink Floyd's *The Dark Side of the Moon* (1973) and *The Wall* (1979 were conceived and performed as rock operas.

Yet Frank Sinatra's LP *In the Wee Small Hours* (1955) has a prior claim, being a suite of songs deliberately designed to evoke a late-night mood of isolation, *amor fati* and melancholy (Rojek 2004: 43–4). The music has been appropriately compared to the visual representations of alienation and loneliness conveyed in the paint canvases of Edward Hopper (Elborough 2008: 135). Artistically, Sinatra was clearly striving to provide personal insight into his tempestuous relationship with Ava Gardener, but also, very clearly, he wanted to comment upon wider issues, having to do with the plight and dilemmas of adult masculinity in America during the Cold War era.

By the 1980s the reign of the LP over the music industry was fraying. In Britain Bow Wow Wow's first single release, 'C30, C60, C90, Go!' (1980), captured the challenge of home taping to the dominance of the LP. Tape cassette prices of recorded albums were lower than LPs. But of course, the illegal challenge provided by home taping made the technology even more alluring. Home taping was free and the commercial provision of high-density converter systems, first for vinyl to tape recording, and later to mini disc recording, produced high-quality results at low cost.

The introduction of the Sony Walkman in 1979 provided a massive fillip for cassette sales. In contrast to vinyl 12 inch formats, cassettes were lighter, could fit into your pocket, were easier to store and could be re-recorded. The convenience and price of the product conferred compelling market advantage. By the end of the 1980s, tape sales outstripped vinyl. In the USA in 1987, 63% of all albums sold were on tape. At the peak in 1989, pre-recorded tape sales reached 83 million. By 1989 sales of the Walkman were 50 million and, within three years, the figure doubled (Elborough 2008: 368, 371).

The emergence of CDs in the early 1980s pushed vinyl back from the mainstream to the backwater category of specialist sales. Analogue sound is reproduced by etching the groove on vinyl and transcribing the sound wave. In contrast, digital sound is sampled and transcribed as digital data that is then reconstructed to provide higher-fidelity results.

Although the CD massively eroded vinyl sales, it paradoxically extended the life-span of the LP format, since CD re-issues of vinyl releases created a demand among consumers to replace their entire record collection with versions possessing purportedly higher sound qualities. In 1986 in Japan, CD sales surpassed LP sales, with the USA following suit in 1988. Record corporations were able to exploit the back-catalogue while aggressively marketing front-list digital recordings at developmental costs that were estimated to be less than half of analogue recordings. By 1992 back-catalogue sales amounted to 40% of CD turnover (Elborough 2008: 382, 389). Back-catalogue CD sales were enhanced through re-packaging devices that offered consumers out-takes and additional extras.

The digital web revolution has produced another twist in this story. As I have noted repeatedly throughout the book, music files are weightless, high quality and can be wirelessly downloaded into a variety of hand-held or desk-top devices. The premium for illegal suppliers and consumers is huge and the risks of detection are negligible. Additionally, Wifi downloading is compatible with mobility and multi-media activity. So listening to the latest market-priced album release of an artist on your iPhone, BlackBerry or Facebook can occur in conjunction with perusing an illegal film ripped via Bit-Torrent, or watching the latest print or TV news via Google. The multi-media opportunities of digital surpass those of vinyl in every respect, bar one.

Hip hop, house and techno have given vinyl a new lease of life as a craft instrument. With just two turntables and a microphone they have defined an entirely new way of producing music (Brewster and Broughton 1999: 227–8). Sampling and snatching created new DJ stars, such as Grandmixer DXT, Grandmaster Flash, Grand Wizard Theodore, Larry Levan, Ron Hardy, Norman Cook (Fatboy Slim), Sasha and Alfredo Fiorito.

The presence of the turntable DJ began to rival that of the electric guitar virtuoso in the mythology of popular culture. Interestingly, the vinyl listening experience has been totally reframed. At the peak of vinyl sales, singles and albums were listened to in the domestic setting or, by the standards of today, fairly restrained collective settings, such as coffee bars, student junior common rooms and discos. Club dance culture makes the listening experience loud, collective and intertwined with dancing. The listening experience is knitted to movement and, often, the consumption of drugs.

Reynolds (1998: 264) identifies physical energy, the relaxation of inhibitions, the atmosphere of non-judgemental social inclusion and good-natured bonhomie to be the trademarks of 1990s dance culture (which peaked between 1998 and 2000). It has been replaced by the revival of neo-garage bands like The Hives, The Holloways, The Strokes, The White Stripes, Florence and the Machine, the post-9/11 music of Coldplay, Eels, Pavement and Vampire Weekend, the off-the-wall folk of Devendra Banhart and Joanna Newsom, and microhouse, which imposes an aesthetic of minimalism and restraint upon the tempo of house. In general, contemporary dance culture is awash with experimentation and sound cannibalism, but lacks the clear sense of propulsion that it had in the late 1990s. Yet the mood of multi-media transmission and non-judgemental collective inclusion persists. Some of the most genre-busting new challenges are the result of technology rather than artistic innovation.

Thus, the rise of digital music produces fresh challenges to DJ-driven club culture. Digital DJing is expanding in popularity. The digital format allows more music to be sourced and stored, and offers greater control over production since the sounds can be burned direct from the computer or wired to an iPod. Software such as Traktor, Final Scratch Ableton Live or PCDJ provides new opportunities for cueing and mixing music. Moreover, the internet means that performance is potentially deterritorialized and globalized. Twin turntables using vinyl are still widespread in club culture. But the digital revolution looks set to provide a major, increasing challenge. As with the question of illegal downloading, the ground has far from settled. However, the sensible money must be on a digital future, with vinyl being pushed to the margins, just as with the CD revolution in the vinyl LP market back in the 1980s.

Music Media

Following the work of Stuart Hall (1980) on encoding and decoding, it has become conventional to regard representation as integral to cultural practice. As such, the production, exchange and consumption of pop music texts are now automatically understood to involve coded meanings and effects. As we have observed (pp. 104–8), the textualist approach prioritizes decoding as the main task of pop music analysis. In the hands of most commentators on pop, textual analysis must relate music practice to the context of social regulation and the balance of social and economic forces (Hebdige 1979; Grossberg 1992, 1997). The mass media are of pivotal importance in the business of cultural inscription. They follow an operational logic that both reflects pop and invests it with specific denotations and connotations.

Music media consist of five basic components: music print, radio, television, film and the internet (Frith 2001: 39–45). Music print and radio have their origins in the postwar era. In the UK by 1939, it is estimated that the radio reached an audience of 34 million people (Laughey 2006: 77). Research into listening habits discovered that 75% of UK radio audience devoted 16% of their listening time to dance band music (Greenwood 1986: 4).

Music and dance magazines also emerged in this period. *Melody Maker*, which was closely associated with the Mecca Leisure Group, was founded in 1926; *Danceland* in 1927; *Billboard*, founded in 1894, boosted circulation by publishing the charts in the 1930s; and *Down Beat* appeared in 1934.

The boom period for music radio and magazines occurred between the 1950s and 1980s. In the 1960s, unlicensed pirate and so-called 'free' radio broadcasting enhanced the mystique of pop and rock by tagging it with an outlaw quality. For teenagers intent on gaining experiences denied by their parents, the efforts of the state to criminalize pirate radio acted as a powerful rallying point and *cause célèbre*. Radio provided mobile, voyeuristic access to the world of counterculture. Until the advent of MTV in 1981, it was the chief music media highway, providing listeners with immediate releases and automatic news.

Print culture, generally in the form of weekly magazine publications, provided a more reflective information gateway. It provided news, reviews, thought pieces, adverts for mainstream acts and classified ads for band recruitment and various types of merchandising. Among the new music magazines founded in this period are NME (1952), *Record Mirror* (1953), *Village Voice* (1955), *Crawdaddy!* (1966), *Rolling Stone* (1967), *Creem* (1969) and *Sounds* (1970).

Between the 1970s and 1990s, there was considerable diversification in media delivery. The establishment of MTV, the internet and illegal pirate music stations broadcasting the latest sounds, often before official release in major cities, offers music fans an unprecedented multi-media hub of direct access.

Music Print Culture

Pop and Rock print culture created the foundation for new music subcultures organized around textual avatars using the music press as platforms for proclaiming about music, politics and many other aspects of lifestyle architecture. In the era before the web, their enthusiasms and musings were widely devoured and fastidiously imitated. In school classrooms, university refectories and bars, urban and suburban coffee shops and drinking places, they set trends.

By way of illustration, consider three legendary textual avatars from the 1970s, 1980s and the present day.

Lester Bangs

Born in 1948, and dead in 1982 from an accidental drug overdose at the age of just 33, Bangs became a legend among pop journo avatars in the 1970s. A mentor for the *Rolling Stone* tyro and later Hollywood film director Cameron Crowe, and revered by second-wave British pop journo avatars like Nick Kent, Mick Farren and Barney Hoskyns as the original and premier scribe of the so-called 'punk aesthetic', Bangs produced copy mainly for *Rolling Stone*, *Creem* and *Village Voice* (DeRogatis 2000; Heylin 2007: 2–7). He also wrote for *Fusion*, *Teenage Wasteland*, *Penthouse*, *Playboy*, *Recording World*, *Chicago Tribune*, *Los Angeles Herald-Examiner* and NME (Bangs 1988) . A scion of the direct, free-association style of the Beats and Hunter S. Thompson's gonzo style of journalism, he was the public embodiment of the avid music fan who believed in the music and abominated hype. This carried over into an appetite for alcohol, painkillers and illegal drugs that emulated the casual, careless excess of the hardened rock star. Bangs was a crucial figure in symbolizing the journalist who did not simply write about pop and rock stars, but fraternized and partied with them. Yet he also took care to maintain the moral high ground as a judge of what he saw going on around him.

A sterling and implacable opponent of the commodification of rock and pop, a genre that he scathingly denounced as 'homogenized margarine' (*www.furious. com/Perfect/lesterbangs3.html*), Bangs regarded punk to be the ultimate populist art form. In his view, it was the crystallization of democratic art since it requires conviction, attitude, passion and no more than basic three-chord proficiency to make searching artistic statements. In addition, pop is an extremely adhesive form that brings together fashion, politics, film, fine art, design, architecture, literature, television and print. For Bangs, popular music possesses the unique democratic quality of *making connections* (Heylin 1993: 32–3).

Bangs was a beacon for pop journo avatars and apprentices because he achieved prominence as a spokesman of the crowd. The archetypal rock and roll model is a rags to riches story: Presley born in a wooden shack to dirt-poor parents in Tupelo, Mississippi; James Brown born into extreme poverty and a society of racial intolerance in Barnwell, South Carolina; The Beatles raised in the terraced streets of working-class Liverpool; David Bowie, the son of a cinema usherette and promotions officer for Barnardo's, born in Brixton, London and relocated at age 6 to the unfashionable outer suburb of Bromley.

Bangs had all the credentials. He came from nowhere. He had no history or pocket-book of contacts in the music business to pull strings for him. He was born in Escondido, California, to a mother who was a devoted Jehovah's Witness and a father who had done time in prison. When Bangs was 9, his father deserted the family. His first break was an unsolicited, spoiling review of the MC5 debut album, *Kick Out the Jams*. He sent it to *Rolling Stone* in 1969, achieved publication and his career was launched.

Bangs was abrasively scornful of the fantasy individualism and communard utopianism of the 1960s. Before the Manhattan new wave got off the block, Bangs raved about the mainline emotion of The Stooges, The Velvet Underground and Lou Reed (DeRogitas 2000) and looked forward to the overthrow of the cosseted rock aristocracy. With the new wave breakthrough of The Ramones and Television in 1977, Bangs relocated to Manhattan. Despite having staunch claims to have anticipated the punk revolution, he lived through the new wave revolution as a sort of prophet without honour. His physical appearance, dress and scorn of 'attitude' did not fit the part of the new wave role model. The undistinguished book that he wrote on Blondie was matched with a half-cocked book-length effort to critically evaluate Rod Stewart. Yet his reviews, thought pieces and rants were widely recognized, even by his enemies, as frequently inspirational.

What made Bangs a luminous presence in the history of pop journalism is an unaffected eye for pomposity and an unerring ear for honesty.

The stirrup to his career was the bloated self-satisfaction and indulgence of the 1970s rock aristocracy. He despised this. Bangs could spot a phoney at a hundred paces. His stance was that of the regular rock fan, unmoved by rock business management hype and stadium testosterone, with their 'hectares of fans' (Castles 2008: 145), who perpetually had a gimlet eye fixed on pop music as a true passionate statement.

Nick Kent

The most exotic of pop journo avatars, Nick Kent was primarily active in the 1970s and early 1980s. Arguably, he was the chief ornament in the wildly talented collection of staffers and freelancers at NME in its heyday, including Mick Farren, Charles Shaar Murray, Ian MacDonald, Tony Tyler, Ian Penman, Tony Parsons, Julie Birchill and Max Bell. Looking back, Kent's journalistic beat was to patrol the aftershock of the fantasy individualism and communard utopianism of the 1960s with long retrospective pieces on Brian Wilson, Syd Barrett, Nick Drake and The Rolling Stones (Kent 2007). In the days of news soundbites, puff pieces and one-page features, sustained evaluations of major figures in pop and rock were unusual and distinctive. He supplemented this with reviews and thought pieces on the emerging sounds of the day, notably Elvis Costello, Guns 'n' Roses, Iggy Pop and Morrissey.

That Kent chose to focus on high-profile casualties of the era, like Brian Jones, Syd Barrett, Nick Drake, Brian Wilson and Sid Vicious, added to the romantic, vaguely fey quality of his work and public image. In the 1970s his lifestyle emulated the star system that he chronicled. He took drugs with Keith Richards, dated Chrissie Hynde, was physically threatened by John Bonham and, bizarrely, Bob Marley, hung out with Iggy Pop and Mick Jagger, was invited by Malcolm McLaren to play guitar with The Sex Pistols and briefly had a band of his own called The Subterraneans (Kent 2010).

There is a decidedly voyeuristic element to his journalism. Kent not only relished writing about the stars, he wanted to consort and dally with them. In doing so, he employed a style of writing that many people today find narrowly masculinist. As Kent (2010: 149–50) himself puts it, in Hemingwayesque vein, the rock scene is saturated with 'surreal people living surreal, action-packed lives . . . rock writing [is] fundamentally an action medium that best came to life when the writer was right in the thick of that action and yet removed enough to comprehend its possible consequences.'

Doomed youth – another echo with Hemingway (and Byron) – is the leitmotif of his writing. Thus, Elvis Presley was addicted to 'fame and medication', with 'a low attention span', 'bad taste' in friends and 'horrendous' eating habits; Jim Morrison took 'perverse delight in starting riots'; Keith Richards 'adored getting high'; Sid Vicious was 'clueless, devoid of a fully formed personality and a borderline psychotic'; Liam Gallagher has assembled a lifestyle around 'drunken loutishness'; Courtney Love is 'a celebrity unfit mother'; and Pete Doherty and Whitney Houston are 'slowly disintegrating before our very eyes' (Kent 2007: 465–67).

These are figures who, as the legend has it of the blues genius Robert Johnson, make a pact with the Devil at the crossroads to have everything they want in this world but at the price of their soul in the afterlife. For Kent, the allure of popular music is not just the song but the star. Despite his disapproval of the celebrity cultures surrounding David Bowie, Jimmy Page and Iggy Pop, Kent clearly adored being the writer with the band.

It is the exact reversal of the priorities of his mentor, Lester Bangs. In Bangs-World it is the music that matters and the idol that is usually fake. Kent-World eschews Bangs's puritanism to relish the vanity, veracity and vapidity of the star. In this world, what fans aspire to be is their idols. Here is Kent (2007: xiv) describing what drew him in the first place to the world of popular music:

> As a teenager – moving around the country at the behest of my father's work locations, feeling shy and awkward and experiencing few solid friendships along the way – I developed fantasy relationships with my favourite rock and pop stars of the time. . . . I used to imagine their lives were perfect in every way.

And again, upon seeing The Rolling Stones for the first time as a schoolboy in 1964:

> I was twelve, they were only weeks away from being the biggest thing to hit England since the bubonic plague – and, oh, I will never forget it. They looked simply out of this world, like a new delinquent aristocracy, they played music of a stunning arrogance and unbridled potency. And they had Brian Jones . . . he looked to me like a young man who has everything –

charm, beauty, grace, success, infamy – every wondrous virtue this world could hope to offer, and for a long time afterwards his vision epitomized everything I in turn could hope to aspire to. (Kent 2007: 126)

The focus on Jones, the doomed narcissist, says it all. Kent was fixated on the brilliant star whose fate was to burn brightly and then implode. Whether commenting on a harrowingly disassociated Brian Wilson reclusively thumping out tunes on a piano in his Californian mansion with his feet in a sand box, Syd Barrett, drug-fried and unable to sustain a meaningful conversation, or Nick Drake, an introspective troubadour who slowly disappeared into the same thin air that characterized his wispy voice and nonchalant guitar style, Kent provides little portraits of perfection turned bad.

Despite the accent on decadence and progress, Kent is a profoundly conservative author. He doesn't merely comment about pop and rock celebrity, he passes sentence upon it. For example, here is his judgement upon the rise of MTV in the 1980s: 'A cultural abomination robbing young minds of their God-given right to let music run riot with their own imaginations by force feeding them with crass video images to appease their dwindling attention spans instead' (Kent 2010: 361). No prisoners are taken there. Somewhere behind the fixation with narcotic excess and attraction to amorality is a backbone of solid British middle-class values. It is no surprise that Kent emerged from a career meltdown in the 1980s and a long battle with heroin addiction to find marriage, family life and God.

Simon Reynolds

Reynolds is one of the most accomplished and interesting pop journalists working today. Born in the UK in 1963, he moved to New York in 1994. He got off the mark with fanzine culture, notably *Monitor*, which he co-founded in 1984, while he was reading history at Oxford.

His copy has been featured in *Melody Maker*, *The New York Times*, *Village Voice*, *Rolling Stone*, *Artforum*, *Spin*, *The Guardian*, *Mojo*, *The Wire* and *Uncut*. A distinctive feature of his pop journalism is the extensive use of social theory, notably the writings of Adorno, Bataille, Barthes, Baudrillard, Gramsci, Kristeva, Debord, Guattari and Deleuze.

Citing inspiration from post-punk bands like Scritti Politti, Gang of Four and The Pop Group, Reynolds examines popular music as inherently politicized. Thus, punk and post-punk are primarily analysed not on the aesthetic dimension, but as critical reactions to the culture of defeatism produced by the New Right, while the music of dance culture is systematically investigated as connected up with the politics of embodiment. For Reynolds, the intense generational involvement with punk, post-punk and dance culture articulates a particular kind of political engagement, far removed from both fantasy individualism and communard utopianism. It was appealing because after the New Right politics of globalization, deregulation and laissez-faire revivalism with respect to questions of social inequality and environmentalism and the collapse of Soviet-style communism, the music 'mobilize[d] a kind of exodus from the mainstream – an exit from the social, from history itself, even – through the creation of an underground culture based around self-loss and transcendence' (Reynolds 2009: 421).

As with Lester Bangs, a writer about whom he is occasionally less than hospitable (Reynolds 2006: 73; 2007: 80), Reynolds sees the democratic potential of popular music to *permeate* popular culture to be one of the main attractions for studying it. For him, everything connects with pop music. Studying it is therefore not merely addressing the aesthetics of form, it is a routeway into all aspects of pop culture.

Reynolds's (1998, 2006, 2007) writings on post-punk, electronica, techno, jungle, rave, microhouse and dubstep reveal a passion for theory and mapping genre. Bangs and Kent were critical of celebrity rock culture, yet enraptured by it. Reynolds is not centrally interested in celebrity. He treats it as a symptom of context and a much wider *conversation* about culture. The gap between the star and the audience is far more abbreviated than in the writings of Bangs or Kent. In the work of these writers, the music is compartmentalized from the rest of society and culture and explored as an end in itself. Punk vilifies precisely these qualities as sheer navel-gazing. Much of the energy and impact of punk music derived from bringing society back in. Reynolds approves of this. But utilizing his interest in cultural and social theory, his take on popular music is that 'music [is]n't extreme *enough*' (Reynolds 2009: 414, emphasis in the original). This suggests the glimmer of a more full-blown position on the place of music in cultural politics. To date, Reynolds has yet to elaborate it.

In recent work (Reynolds 2006, 2009), he comes close to matching the position of Adorno and the Frankfurt School that popular music is a distraction in popular culture. In his words:

> . . . all this incredibly intense involvement in music that my generation had – all this chasing the future through music, searching for utopia through music – might have been a deflection from actually changing anything. Maybe we should have put our energy into politics. . . . But, you know, serious political involvement is really hard work and kinda dreary: endless meetings and organizational drudgery, scheming and means-to-end compromises. Music can seem a lot more pure. It's more immediate; more glamorous too. The results are 'total' in a way that things rarely can be in real-world politics. It's quite a bleak verdict, perhaps, but you could see rock culture as a whole as being a way of living within capitalism while remaining opposed to it. (Reynolds 2009: 431)

This amounts to a reassertion of the old 1970s slogan that 'the personal is political'. Pop and rock are remiss in not changing the world totally. We still have tin-pot leaders, jobs-worths hunkered in dreary bureaucracies, hunger, poverty, ignorance, misery and want. At the same time, pop and rock can change *your* world utterly, providing intimations of an identity and solidarity not yet seen, which can, nevertheless, be life-changing.

MTV and MTV2

Television producers cottoned on early to the mass appeal of popular music broadcasts. *American Bandstand* (1952–89), *Soul Train* (1971–2006), *Thank Your Lucky Stars* (1961–6), *Ready, Steady, Go* (1963–6), *Shindig* (1964–6), *Top of the Pops*

(1964–2005), *The Tube* (1982–8) and *Rapido* (1988–92), achieved cult status via conventional terrestrial channels of transmission. Not until the age of cable and satellite, and, critically, the emergence of MTV, did the potential of television and music as an international multi-media platform start to be realized. In contrast to music print culture, MTV offers multiple texts organized around a perpetual twenty-four hour a day, seven days a week rotation of music videos and magazine-style news items, celebrity bulletins and audience participation slots. Targeted at the 12–34 demographic, the channel derives its main revenue streams from advertising and record labels. The format has been described as 'the biggest continuous advertising network in the world', since the videos operate as commercials designed to sell albums and offer a cornucopia of product placement opportunities (Pettegrew 1995).

MTV, the premier global music video channel, was launched in the USA in 1981 by Warner Media. It was an overnight sensation, gaining an audience of 24 million viewers in less than three years and offering the 12–34 age group continuous access to music videos and acting as a magnet for investors from advertising and the music business (Sayre and King 2003: 186). Global affiliates grew like Topsy. MTV Europe, MTV Australia and MTV Japan were launched in 1987; MTV Latin America in 1993 and MTV Asia in 1995.

Now owned by the video syndication giant Viacom, the channel has diversified its output. With the rise of the internet, which rapidly established itself as 'the celestial jukebox', MTV dropped its public image as the first contact point in youth culture for consuming music video and mixed up the programme schedule with reality and celebrity shows (Burkart and McCourt 2006). Music videos now comprise, on average, three hours of transmission per day, compared with eight in 2000. Today, MTV is transmitted via satellite worldwide, reaching an estimated audience of 340 million households in 140 countries (Fung 2006: 72). It is the world's third-largest televison network, broadcasting to one third of the world's TV-viewing households. Countries outside the USA now account for 80% of its market (McPhail 2006: 134).

MTV2 was launched in 1996 based on a programme schedule of innovative and alternative music video rotation with a higher profile of metropolitan black music. It was a response to the changing youth consumer demographic that migrated from mainstream rock and pop towards rap and techno. However, even here, a programme schedule of music videos proved to be insufficient to grab the youth market. The rise of internet broadcasting provided a more accessible, flexible gateway of communication that offered opportunities for direct audience participation. MTV2 responded by supplementing music video transmission with news, competition shows, sit-coms, youth-oriented documentaries and live concert broadcasts.

Upon its explosive irruption into pop culture, MTV was fêted by leading cultural critics as the realization of the democratic, participatory potential of television transmission. Before going on to consider evidence for the place of MTV in contemporary culture, it is necessary briefly to review this period, since it reveals broader defects that lie in wait in responding gratuitously to changes in the technology of media pop culture that are instantly seen as 'apocalyptic' or 'progressive'.

The most noted exponent was the poststructuralist theorist John Fiske. Catching the wave of the MTV revolution in music multi-media, he (1986: 74) pronounced MTV to be 'the only original art form' in broadcast TV (Fiske 1986: 74). How so?

Fiske builds his argument in the form of a trio of bold theses. He submits that the originality of MTV rests upon the following features:

1 Privileging the signifier over the signified: the medium of MTV, which prioritizes embodiment, plasticity and contradiction, has more cultural impact than the pop music that it plays.
2 The 'openness' of textual structure: MTV is compatible with an array of programming, a diversity of sounds and unfamiliar multi-media permutations of sound and music.
3 Its capacity to build 'a non-conventional, possibly oppositional audience' (Fiske 1986: 74).

Fiske (1986: 75) contends that MTV is 'anti-capitalist', because while orthodox TV schedules operate in 'the plain of the signified' (programmes with content), it promotes the signifier as 'a form of resistance to the mainstream' (programmes are triumphantly polysemic). In today's terminology, Fiske asserts that MTV is the scene-changing technological articulation of what Charles Taylor (2004) later calls 'the social imaginary': that is, popular resistance to social control and popular assent to liberty.

Whereas Taylor sees resistance and the pursuit of freedom to be the products of practical struggle, Fiske regards them as the dividend of technology. On this reckoning, MTV is the child of capitalism. It bears the birthmarks of the social and economic relations of the mode of production that created it. Yet it pushes capitalism to breaking point and, according to Fiske, *beyond*, by producing a technological medium that allows communication without frontiers and perpetuates cultural over-determination. MTV exposes the incapacity of the capitalist mode of production to contain the energies that it unleashes. As a result, the frames of social ordering that permit the capitalist order of everyday life break down.

Drawing an explicit comparison between MTV and punk, Fiske (1986: 76) asserts: 'MTV is the safety pin through the nose, the army uniform worn to deny authority. It takes the iconography of the social world and . . . uses it to resist the social.'

Upon what does this case rest? One must recall that Fiske's position derives from the ascendant poststructuralist/postmodern fashion of the day, which defiantly turned its back on the traditional idea of finite meaning in culture and instead stressed the interplay of texts and the implosion of meaning. In particular, he was leaning heavily on Jean Baudrillard's (1980, 1983) writings regarding the relationship between the media and what Baudrillard termed 'the ecstasy of communication': that is, the saturation of the airwaves with collage, contradiction, fragmentation, quotation, multiple channels/viewpoints and non-unity.

Adorno (2006, 2009) maintains that the culture industry requires a helmsman to be at the wheel in order to guide people into conditioned responses. The bland acceptance of *unfreedom as freedom* is the precondition of pseudo-individualization.

The reproduction of this condition requires a network of authority. With respect to popular music, Adorno regards music corporations to be direct, unremitting agents in this process. Behind them is class power, specifically ruling class power.

For Baudrillard and Fiske this is no longer tenable. Capitalism has entered a perfect storm, created by the technological forces that it greedily but rashly conjures forth, which leaves no pilot at the wheel. Social development is unplanned and uncontrolled. MTV offers a perpetual combination of video with music, and so connects the mind with the body to continuously signify pleasure as a self-supporting end, disenchantment with the routines of capitalist everyday life and sensual stimulation without authority or judgement.

So, for Fiske, MTV signifies the end point of capitalism. In effect, and revealingly, he proposes that the termination of capitalism resides in a surfeit of consumption. But this is not the consumption of hard commodities like cars, clothes or computers. It is the consumption of images. The death of capitalism is not achieved by workers waging revolutionary struggle to seize the means of production. It is achieved by well-fed Western consumers sitting in their living rooms and student dormitories and turning on to the procession of images and sounds that MTV supposedly allows to run wild on screen. Fiske (1986: 75) does not mince words here: 'MTV is orgasm – where signifiers explode in pleasure in the body in an excess of the physical. No ideology, no social control can organize an orgasm. Only freedom can.'

Several things make this argument look rather feeble and dated today. Three points need to be made.

To begin with, MTV/MTV2 is neither a random nor a spontaneous cultural force. On the contrary, it is a business, now wholly owned by Viacom, which is a division of the American entertainment conglomerate National Amusements, Inc. As we shall see presently, the position of MTV/MTV2 in the National Amusements/Viacom business structure corresponds to the standard bespoke agglomeration pattern of multiple, mutually reinforcing brands: that is, the business model applied by major global corporations like Vivendi and Rupert Murdoch's News Corporation. From today's vantage point it is absurd to label MTV/MTV2 as anti-capitalist. The people who control it are fully cognizant of the need to deliver audience approval and win ratings wars. This is why, since the mid-1990s, MTV has rationed music video transmission in response to the supply challenge created by the rise of online music (Burkart and McCourt 2006). The producers of MTV are not in it together with the consumers in some sort of orgiastic mind trip. On the contrary, their ultimate objective is to make as much money as they can, as rapidly as they can. The money may be made from advertising or franchise deals. But its ultimate source is the consumer.

One aspect of this is the iconography of MTV. Against Fiske, the imagery broadcast by MTV, especially visual data of a sexual nature, is conventional. Heterosexual norms predominate and at most, argues Stanley Aronowitz (1994: 27), they are 'suggestive', rather than 'explicit' or 'kinky'. In other words, the iconography does not break with everyday life. Rather, it exaggerates and glamourizes commonplace imagery.

Implicitly, this takes issue with Fiske's second dimension of MTV, namely the openness of the text. What Aronowitz is saying is that the diet of MTV videos is subject to closure. The iconography must resonate with everyday life. Since everyday life is a product of capitalism, it is not clear how MTV video can be properly described as 'anti-capitalist'.

Goodwin (1993) pushes further the idea of the commercial basis of MTV. He claims that the music video should not be considered as an artwork. Even though the form allows for artistic statements, the purpose of the music video is first and foremost to advertise the song. It is a closed medium in the sense that it is aimed at an audience that has been monitored via market research, for the purposes of cable adoption, home rental sales and to purchase the audio recording. In a vein that is reminiscent of Adorno's thought on the place of typification and repetitive tonality in the contemporary pop song, Goodwin (1993: 83) speculates on a homology between the construction of the pop song and video. That is, the pop song is organized around 'conventions of tonality' that resemble 'the realist system' of visual appearances in cinema. The point strikes at Fiske's first and third dimensions of MTV, namely the proposition that MTV privileges the signifier (Goodwin argues that it delivers the signified, which is produced by the unequal relations of property under capitalism) and elicits an unconventional response in the audience (Goodwin sees the resemblance between the organization of tonality in the song and the idiom or cinematic realism as entirely *conventional*).

Secondly, it is far-fetched to propose a link, let alone imply an iron logic, between the streamed rotation of musical images and sounds and the practice of anti-capitalist resistance. Why should Fiske privilege anti-capitalist resistance as the consequence of MTV? He supplies no evidence of the radicalizing effect of MTV. Indeed, it would be unreasonable for him to do so, since he cites 'openness' as a core dimension of MTV as a medium of communication. An open text cannot be, at one and the same time, subject to closed readings. Hence, it might be objected that Fiske's privileging of an anti-capitalist response is arbitrary. If one examines the medium from the perspective of the cultivation of youth silo cultures in contemporary society, it could just as well be held that MTV is an iteration of mass consumerism.

Indeed, this is the case made by Hardt (1986: 64), who, à la the Frankfurt School, argues that MTV is a visual and aural technology that 'overpowers the eye and ear' and aims for compliance to the rule of capital. Against Fiske's proposition that MTV is anti-capitalist, Hardt maintains that it is completely faithful to the logic of capitalist accumulation. That is, it emphasizes hedonism over organization, personal difference over solidarity and meaninglessness over rational planning and struggle. What is needed to adjudicate over these matters is empirical studies of the effects of MTV on audiences. These studies were only born later, and were not available to the media and communication theorists of the 1980s. I will come to consider some of them below. Before doing so it is necessary to turn to another issue relating to the competence of Fiske's account. This brings me to my third point.

Fiske's (1986) argument is woefully ethnocentric. It celebrates empowerment and freedom, but completely glosses over the thorny relationship between MTV, the unequal power relations in globalization and the fact of cultural imperialism. Banks (1996, 1997) presents an opposing view. According to him, MTV is an exemplar of cultural homogenization. He quotes Tom Freston, the president of

MTV Networks: 'Our goal is to be in every home in the world' (Banks 1997: 44). For Banks, MTV is not innocuous. It is a colonizing force. It promotes an Anglo-American diet of youth culture to a global market and seeks to normalize it from the tip of the Northern, to the tail of the Southern, hemisphere. The motivation behind this is unabashedly commercial: 'MTV's plans to develop an international youth culture based on consumerism provide a receptive audience to advertisers seeking to sell their products to upscale youth everywhere' (Banks 1997: 58).

Banks's position is now itself widely regarded to be problematic. Nevertheless, in pointing to the inherently unequal relation between MTV producers and the MTV audience, he supplies a necessary and cogent corrective to Fiske's argument. There is a business logic behind MTV that aspires to global domination. It is capitalist down to its bootstraps. But it does not quite work in the manner envisaged by Banks.

What, then, is the relationship between MTV and globalization today? Recent work on the penetration of MTV culture into markets in the emerging and developing world suggests that MTV does not result in cultural homogenization. In China and India, MTV prospers only if it accommodates to, and promotes, indigenous music and directly engages with youth subcultures (Cullity 2002; Juluri 2002; Fung 2006).

It was only when MTV India realized that it had to 'Indianize' aspects of the programme schedule to maximize ratings that market share expanded. The process of Indianization was hardly tokenistic. Cullity (2002: 413) and Juluri (2002: 380) maintain that MTV participated directly in the liberalization of Indian economy and society by presenting a calculated 'Cool India' image and arena for youth culture. Western values were not rebuffed. Rather, they were mediated through positive presentations of Indian cultural institutions and youth networks. The effect was to *increase* Indian national identity rather than dilute it with globalizing images of The Backstreet Boys, The Notorious B.I.G., Westlife and The Spice Girls. Needless to say, this is the exact opposite of the cultural homogenization thesis propounded by Banks (1996, 1997).

The case of MTV China is of particular note. *Prima facie*, it might be supposed that Red China would either be hostile to global capital or seek to subdue it under the ruling ideas of Communist ideology. Conversely, global capital might be expected to exploit counter-hegemonic local divisions by promoting the capitalist alternative with maximum volume. In reality, MTV China has pursued an accumulation strategy that designs and transmits programmes with 'Chinese characteristics'. In addition to employing Chinese VJs, and featuring Chinese musical material, MTV has co-operated with the mobile phone campaign of the Korean high-tech company Samsung to launch college singing contests to promote the Samsung brand in Chinese campuses. MTV created the programme 'yue ding yue zheng' to allow young people to select songs on TV for friends via the mobile phone. MTV is therefore inviting Chinese youth to adopt a tactical approach to high-tech Western culture. For Fung, MTV China has adroitly exploited an accumulation strategy that makes a virtue of hybridization. In his words:

> It is not that the global capital kowtows to Chinese authorities; or that the
> state backs down to allow their entry. Both these arguments are simple. The

state for its part is not reluctant to accept globalization, and the political and economic forces are not inherently contradictory. Nowadays, transnational media corporations and the Chinese authorities work in tandem to produce a state–global media complex. (Fung 2006: 84)

Hybridization means that the Chinese state supports strategic multinational globalization and, in return, global capital bolsters the state. Integral to the idea of a state–global media context are notions of friction and contradiction. But rather than Banks's (1996, 1997) view that MTV is a motorway truck crushing local opposition to create cultural conformity, Fung's state–global media points to a more complex frame of analysis having to do with shifting positions, changing balances of power, tactical brokering and conditional alliances.

National Amusements, Inc.

The most powerful argument against the thesis that MTV is anti-capitalist rests upon the question of ownership and control. MTV and MTV2 are owned by the American global entertainment corporation Viacom. It is part of a rich, interlocking portfolio of entertainment companies in the Viacom group, including BET Entertainment, Paramount Pictures and Paramount Home Entertainment.

Viacom was created in 1971 as a spin-off from the music and TV giant Columbia Broadcasting System (CBS). It purchased MTV in 1986 and presided over the channel's most aggressive era of global expansion. A year later, National Amusements, Inc. acquired an 83% stake in Viacom. In 1994 National Amusements, Inc. merged Viacom with Paramount Communications. Although the corporation trades as a self-contained entity, it is owned and controlled by National Amusements, Inc. As such, it is part of a massive force of bespoke agglomeration in the global entertainment industry. You would never know this from the corporate website. It is low-tech – bizarrely so for such a high-tech giant – and pitchforks the traditional role of the corporation as a humble movie distributor, rather than one of the biggest entertainment corporations in the world. Talk about a shrinking violet.

So what is National Amusements, Inc.? The privately owned company was created in 1936 as a motion picture exhibition company. It owns movie theatre assets in the USA, the UK, the Russian Federation, Argentina, Brazil and Chile. At the time of writing, the controlling stockholder is the 85-year-old Sumner Redstone, who has nominated his daughter Shari to succeed him. Despite corporate restructuring activity to finance debt caused by the global recession between 2009 and 2010, the Redstone family are estimated to hold at least 85% of shares.

National Amusements split Viacom from CBS because it defined the latter as a slow-growth business based in saturated market share, whereas the former was designated a high-growth business based in a volatile, but expanding market (Table 8.1).

These are huge global entertainment brands. In 2008, the revenue of CBS was $13.9 billion, with total assets of $16.89 billion. In the same year the revenue for Viacom was $14.6 billion, with total assets of $22.38 billion.

The economic recession of 2009–10 produced a dip in revenue streams and

Table 8.1 National Amusements, Inc.

CBS	Viacom
CBS TV	MTV
CBS Radio	MTV2
CBS Records	CMT
CW Television Network	BET
Simon & Schuster	Spike
	Gametrailers
	Harmonix
	Paramount Pictures
	Nickelodeon Movies

forced the Redstone family to divest assets. Both companies are currently in the midst of significant corporate restructuring. The 2009 company report indicated that income to CBS plunged by 52%. Viacom achieved a higher than expected profit of 15%, assisted by strong sales of Transformers, GI Joe, The Beatles Rock Band video game and fees from MTV. However, global advertising revenue fell by 4%, film sales were down by 6% and DVD revenue declined by 21%. In 2010 the Redstone family sold assets to restructure a $1.6 billion debt, but retain overwhelming ownership and control of stock (Li 2009).

National Amusements, Inc. holds an extraordinary portfolio of interlocking entertainment brands that span, television, film, games, music and publishing. Poststructuralist writers in the 1980s and 1990s referred to the 'play' of texts. In the case of National Amusements, Inc. this play is not exactly defined from the centre, for there is a sense in which the various texts that it produces are polysemic. That is, the meanings that producers assign to them are not infallible, nor can they be contained. They are inflected and subverted through the exchange of communication with other elements in the media and audiences. Nonetheless, the corporation is in an immensely powerful position to corral the texts that it produces into an interlocking grid. For example, film interconnects with the music industry (through the soundtrack of the film), publishing (the book of the movie), television (home video, sales and rentals) and games.

The fact that National Amusements, Inc. was hurt by the economic recession of 2009–10 proves that the corporation does not always get things right. Just like any other commodity, the contours of media production are subject to market laws of supply and demand. Viacom may provide the base of interaction in that, for example, The Beatles Rock Band game provides a platform upon which responses and developments are constructred. However, the various elements in the construction of responses, the relation of *habitus* and field to reflexive consciousness, the reflexes of power struggles within audiences and their further development in the form of new positions, and so on, also exercise influence upon Viacom, namely in their advertising, marketing and distribution campaigns and design issues in the market renewal of the game. With this accepted, the fact remains that National Amusements, Inc. has enormous global power to use marketing, advertising and cross-sales strategies to discipline demand.

The Internet

It is estimated that there are over 80,000 websites in the world devoted to music (McPhail 2006: 135). These fall into five categories:

1   *Advertising platforms.* The websites of the Big Four and indies that advertise front-catalogue and back-catalogue holdings. News blogs regarding recording and touring are often part of these sites. The main objective is to use the site as a marketing and distribution channel for commercial purposes. CRM features as a prominent means of building online communities and reinforcing brand loyalty.
2   *Celebrity sites.* The official websites of solo artists and bands that provide news, tour dates, free downloads, ringtones, mailing lists and 'community' access to the online store (selling CDs, music files, DVDs, MP3s, books, T-shirts and accessories).
3   *Social networking sites.* Online communities that exchange music blogs, tour details, messaging services, photos and hit-list recommendations. They also allow musicians to exchange downloads for the purposes of promotion. Examples include Facebook, MySpace, Flotones, Sonific and Haystack.
4   *Blog sites.* Individual sites in which opinions, lists, recommendations, news, commentaries, graphics, music files and videos are posted. These may be produced by people in the public eye. Simon Reynolds's 'Blissblog' (*blissout. blogspot.com*) is a good case in point. More commonly, blog sites are run by anonymous, unknown individuals.
5   *P2P exchange platforms.* These are music exchange sites dedicated to the unauthorized exchange of recorded music. Examples include Kazaa, Audiogalaxy, MusicCity, Morpheus, WinMX and Grokster. Although the record industry has applied aggressive DRM policies to eliminate these platforms, they have not achieved a successful result. Proposals to create a voluntary collective licence for P2P exchange to create an income stream to defray losses by copyright holders have been mooted, but no global system has been agreed (Kusek and Leonhard 2005: 132).

The ideology behind internet information technology is saturated with libertarian and utopian values. The crux of this is the principle of *free exchange of information.* Around this are a number of related customized practices having to do with personal autonomy, privacy, maximizing access and establishing and maintaining a community of users. Outlaw, renegade status is central to the self-image of unauthorized downloaders (Flichy 1999: 36).

The internet has affected all levels of the music business. It has eroded the power of the Big Four and independent record companies to enforce a monopoly relationship over production. Music hobbyists are now capable of generating studio-level recordings at home and exchanging them on blog sites or social network platforms. The development of cheap sequencers and music software packages enables ordinary individuals to produce effects of ensemble playing and Sound Man technologies on their laptops. This undermines the corporation's monopoly over the provision of studio time, the allocation of instruments and accompanists and the basis for claiming copyright over recordings. The balance of power has shifted in favour of amateurs and hobbyists.

By the same token, the internet has transformed the orthodox retail network in the music business so that the meaning of exchange and distribution has dramatically changed. Online authorized sales have weakened the *raison d'être* for high-street record stores. Virgin Megastores and Borders have been big brand-name casualties of net trading. But every reader of the book will also be able to name local high-street record stores that have gone under in the last five years. Unauthorized online trading has limited the growth potential of authorized online services and severely dented the balance sheets of major record corporations. The Big Four have taken severe hits in the digital revolution. The hatching of aggressive DRM strategies has, on the whole, been counter-productive and ineffective (Burkart and McCourt 2006; David 2010). CRM strategies have shown a better return. In addition they offer cross-sales potential in multinational corporations that are already organized around a bespoke aggregator model. However, the plain fact is that recorded music sales in the USA have declined from a peak of $14.6 billion in 1999 to $6.3 billion in 2009 (Kusek 2010). The trend is mirrored in all of the advanced industrial nations.

The internet offers new and serious challenges to established music media hubs. Blog sites and social network communities offer flexible, automatic and non-hierarchical driveways of communication that provide news, reviews, opinions, thought pieces, video and live broadcasts at no cost. Media hubs have responded by trying to enhance content. For example, MTV has diluted the diet of music videos and introduced documentaries, game shows and reality TV formats in a bid to retain the 12–34 demographic. The internet has lessened the division between the star and the fan by widening access. As we will see in the next chapter, this has led to reframing the star/fan relationship around the concept of co-operative labour (Baym and Burnett 2009) (see also p. 5). There are doubts about how far this reframing should be allowed to go in the analysis of popular culture and popular music, since production and exchange still presuppose inequality between the corporation/performer side and the audience/consumer side (Pinch and Bijsterfeld 2004; Terranova 2004). Nonetheless, there is now a wide measure of agreement that the digital revolution has pushed the ratio of power in favour of audiences/consumers.

Despite this, it is prudent to enter some caveats about the so-called 'internet revolution'. The internet is still available to less than 15% of the world's population. The technology is concentrated in the developed world, with North America hosting 64% and Europe 24% of capacity. To get some idea of the scale of global inequality to access we might note that there are more hosts in New York City alone than in the whole of Africa (Hesmondhalgh 2002: 215). DRM strategies may be widely assessed as ineffective and counter-productive, but they still constitute a barrier to unrestricted exchange.

For the orthodox business model pursued by the music industry cartel in the postwar period the writing is on the wall. The internet supports accessible, flexible systems of producing and exchanging recordings and communicating about music which are superior in adding value to consumers to the systems maintained by the Big Four, the music retail chains and the conventional music media.

The combination of DRM and CRM strategies has not achieved market retention. The emphasis of business policy in corporate cultures is likely to lie in the direction of 360 degree deals that extend and enforce management rights over touring, franchising and merchandising, in addition to control over traditional production and exchange rights.

What are the implications of this for the analysis of the relationship between technology, media and the audience/consumers?

Music Media, Technology and the Struggle Over Control

The history of music media and technology can be most usefully studied as a struggle over control. Adapting the work of the sociologists of science and technology Pinch and Trocco (2002) and Pinch and Bijsterveld (2004), we can picture this struggle as consisting of an intertwining between innovation and reception. Innovation refers to the research, design and introduction of new technologies; and reception refers to the assimilation and reframing of these technologies by audiences/consumers. In terms of the power relations between producers and consumers, innovation is associated with the extension of control and assimilation, with the reappropriation of control.

Again, adapting the work of Pinch and Trocco (2002) and Pinch and Bijsterveld (2004), the innovation/ reception loop can be usefully expressed thus:

(1) *Technological control over nature and society.* Music production and consumption have tended to be standardized by the introduction of technology, whether in the form of electric guitars, violas, microphones, reverberation units, mixing consoles, new forms of networking software and of mediated audio listening associated with the rise of MP3 players, iPods and car stereos, or as sampling-based genres. Technology imposes itself upon agents, creating new forms of technologically dependent cultures.

The proliferation of music print media in the 1970s and MTV and other satellite broadcast schedules in the 1980s is interpreted as closing down opportunities for developing creative labour in the production process and regimenting listening experience (Hardt 1986).

(2) *Cultural reappropriation of techology and media.* One of the difficulties with the argument that technology closes down creative labour and regiments listening responses is that technology and the response to technology are themselves products of creative labour. The turntable plays back recorded sound in a programmatic way. But the boundaries of the programme create the basis for the introduction of new commands and instructions that allow agents to act as 'boundary shifters', busting the limits of technological genre (Pinch and Trocco 2002: 313–14). Sampling and scratching are one example of boundary shift-work in which technological control has been reappropriated through cultural practice. The emergence of the internet has created new opportunities for creative labour practice by the web passengers to archive, catalogue, filter and blog music-related data, to the cost of established media music hubs, who have had to reinvent content (Baym and Burnett 2009). This has not brought 'power to the people'.

But in the measured words of Pinch and Bijsterveld (2004: 644): 'New audio and recording technologies have enabled people to re-establish some control over their direct sonic environment (though not necessarily of the music made) and thereby other aspects of daily life.'

Music technologies and media hubs frame interaction and may even be responsible for patterning behaviour, but they do not negate the struggle for control (DeNora 2000: 32–41). The present-day partial displacement of DRM strategies with CRM initiatives may be taken as evidence of belated recognition of the proposition on the part of music corporations. New digital technologies have reframed our conception of creative, sensuous labour by extending it from the composer-performer to the audience-consumer. Although this reframing is real and significant, it would be naïve to hold that the people's music is now in the hands of the people. Music corporations and media hubs are exploring various firewall strategies to regain market share. In doing so they are appropriating the unpaid labour of hobbyists and net passengers who have constructed multi-layered customs and commands of internet behaviour.

The concept of customs is bound up with a *vocabulary* of discourse, shared *needs*, transpersonal standards of *legitimate* behaviour and common *expectations*. It is tempting to emphasize the consensual nature of customs. But it is short-sighted to do so. As Edward Thompson (1991: 6) elucidates, the term refers to traditions and protocols of conduct, but it also encompasses conflicting interests and opposing claims. One of the main fronts of struggle consists of copyright holders who wish to defend intellectual property by asserting control over how internet space is used and net passengers who seek to perpetuate the notion of web space as an arena of free exchange. What is emerging most cogently from this struggle is a redefined notion of fan labour that, in turn, disrupts the traditional concepts of artists-composers as active and audiences-consumers as passive agents. In a wired-up world the old idea of an unbridgeable divide between producers and consumers is unsustainable. The next chapter takes up the questions of the meaning and ramifications of this proposition.

Part IV

Conclusion

9

Co-operative Labour, Inc.

Malcolm McLaren, the Svengali of punk, faced a big problem after The Sex Pistols broke up on the last date of a mirthless American tour in 1978, culminating in a desperate performance, consisting of just one drilled-out number at the Winterland Ballroom, San Francisco.[1] His art-school philosophy, borrowed from the Situationists with their Left Bank ruminations and pamphlets about the triumph of 'the spectacle', the 'superficial', the 'gesture' and the necessity for a politics of '*détournement*',[2] took the eventual implosion of the band as given. McLaren saw himself as a reader of the runes. In his view, pop culture and pop music are, first and foremost, resources to be *read* and, second, strategic weapons. On this reckoning, The Sex Pistols did not exactly backfire. Their demise was foretold in the Situationist chronicles. But it left the question of what to do next.

For McLaren the question was resolved by inventing a new wave band, Bow Wow Wow. This was an identikit group assembled to flag an *après*-punk *détournement* back to pre-punk values of glamour, escapism and romance. Fronted by Annabella Lwin, a 14-year-old Anglo-Burmese girl, the band were conceived in the midst of a full-scale, high-alert music business panic about the home taping boom. As ever, with his eye fixed steadfastly upon the big publicity break, McLaren penned the lyrics of their first single in praise of cassette piracy, 'C30, C60, C90, Go!' (1980). The single flopped, allegedly because EMI declined to promote it forcefully since it was judged to be an incitement to home taping. While the band moved on to gain a degree of chart success, they amount to a trifling footnote in the history of popular music.

The reason to refer to the group again here is to observe that the first McLaren-driven single was exceptionally prescient. It captured three things that had not previously co-existed: (1) a nascent redefining of the power inequality between musicians and fans; (2) the unravelling of music corporation control over the re-routing of lines of distribution; and (3) the acknowledgement of the creative labour of the audience and, by extension, the recognition that it was often most ingeniously expressed in illegal activity.

Punk was a genuine 'break' or 'rupture' in the organization of pop. It attenuated the gap between star and audience by naturalizing composition and performance as ordinary cultural accomplishments. It privileged a do-it-yourself approach to production, exchange and consumption. Three-chord songs and indie record labels were like peas in a pod. In the highwater mark of 1970s pop music culture, composition and performance were defined as the work of artists who required corporations to convey the material to the people. Now, in the moment of punk, composition and performance were understood to require no specialist training and minimal aptitude and music corporations were explicitly associated with exploitation and rip-off culture rather than technical proficiency. The 'C30, C60, C90, Go!' era of home taping carried this stage onward because it extended the concept of the audience as a creative agent. Ordinary people were able to seize copyright material from the radio or copy from vinyl and symbolically strike a blow against the privileges of the pop/rock elite and the monopoly power of record corporations. Before the technology of scratching, sequencing and sampling, cassette recording allowed playlists of copyright material to be assembled and turned common-or-garden consumers into suburban DJs.

The genre-busting music of the last thirty years, from rap to hip hop, electronica and scratching and sampling, has never strayed far from the benchmark of making and consuming music as ordinary accomplishments in pop culture. Technology has been pivotal. The use of samplers, sequencers, synthesizers and drum machines has brought composition and performance within the grasp of the novice. Computer software puts studio facilities at the fingertips of any interested laptop user. But technology has been entwined with a broader re-positioning of the fan in the music business and pop culture. Through social network communities, fans habitually engage in global exchange and maintain blogging sites and information driveways.

This extends to social networking composition rings. The thounds.com website enables someone based in London, Paris or Chicago to lay down a rhythm track and have others living in Cape Town, Accra, Hong Kong or Santiago build upon it with lyrics, brass, string or other musical accompaniments of the same kidney (Salmon 2010).

The monopoly of music corporations to exert control over the global market in recorded music and the power of the music media to act as the central data hub providing information about tours, reviews, gossip, points of view and thought pieces has been undermined. The postwar industrial planning model in the music business has been swept aside. Production, exchange and consumption have been radically decentralized. This has effects upon the conventional understanding of pop music hierarchies.

Musical literacy used to be a question of aptitude, training and schooling. This conferred high prestige upon the virtuoso. When I was young, 'Clapton is God' was commonplace wall graffiti in many a British city. It is doubtful if this sort of conflation will ever be made again in the future. Stars don't mean as much as they used to. In the 1960s and 1970s most ordinary people knew the number 1 record of the week. By the mid-1980s this was already becoming a blur; and by the present day the salience of the charts as a primary component of popular culture has atrophied.

Of course, virtuosos will always be part of the repertory. Audiences will always pay to see a sensation or a legend. Live performances have been exploited as a revenue-boosting stream in a context when cash from authorized recording sales has contracted. In 2009 the UK music royalties collecting body (PRS for Music) reported that live music revenues (including direct ticket sales, secondary ticketing and 'on the night' spend) have increased by 9.4% to £1.5 billion, but have slowed from 2008's outstanding growth of 13%. After many repeat years of decline, the industry drew solace from figures on the value of the recorded music industry, including physical and digital sales. Revenue was £1.36 billion in 2009, the same as 2008, providing evidence of a stall in the shrinkage of market share (Topping 2010). Ecstasy and group frenzy remain part of the best pop concert experiences, but the biggest pop stars no longer have the political significance or enduring social impact that they once enjoyed (Wilson 1975: 124). The pop star spokesman for a generation is past his sell-by date. Rap stars and indie celebrities speak for a niche market. They are no longer situated at the apex of a pyramid of cultural capital with the fan on the ground floor. This was the position enjoyed in the old pop music by Elvis, Dylan, Lennon, Gaye, Brown, Bowie, Rotten and Cobain. The distribution of cultural capital has changed and been redefined. The fan is now re-positioned as an active agent: that is, a source of globally transferable music, blogs, news, reviews and opinons.

The digital revolution in the production of music and data aggregation is mirrored by the online revolution. P2P exchange, ripping, streaming and other forms of unauthorized exchange make access ubiquitous. The 'C30, C60, C90, Go!' generation could scarcely have dreamt of weightless consumption, sampling technologies that enable snatches of music from different eras and settings to be fused into meaningful turbo-charged dance-based wholes, let alone the storage capacity and sonic quality of an iPod or MP3 player that permit your entire record collection to be carried around in the pocket of your blouse or jacket. The revolution in production, exchange and consumption has totally battered the music business. The assumptions of ownership and control that underpinned the postwar industrial planning epoch have been shaken to the ground. This has involved the wholesale redefinition of pop music as intellectual property.

For the music business, the name of the game has moved on from monopolizing the master-cut to asserting executive control over bespoke aggregation. This entails root-and-branch reframing of the traditional concept of what record corporations do. UMG, WMG, Sony-BMG and EMI are now best comprehended as multi-media lifestyle architects and accumulators. Increasingly, the music contracts that they negotiate are based upon so-called *360 degree deals* that assign multiple rights to areas that were previously off-limits, such as concert revenues, ringtones, merchandising agreements and endorsement deals. Instead of concentrating upon record sales, music corporations now strive to finesse comprehensive, multi-layered artist management contracts. Hence, they bundle music to television, film and game output and franchise reproduction rights to ringtone companies and advertising campaigns. They employ CRM strategies to create online communities to enlarge the subscription base for authorized downloading and gather and incubate market data for research and development initiatives. They license recordings to ad-supported, on-demand streams and other new distributor driveways. They strike partnerships with reality/talent show series like the *Idol* and *Got Talent* brands and franchises owned, respectively, by Simon Fuller and Simon Cowell. The business imperatives are to build multi-media synergy and offer flexible, *à la carte* menus of consumption.

There is nothing arbitrary about this. The digital revolution has enlarged accessibility. At no point in human history has the ease with which music is composed, performed and consumed been greater.

Paradoxically, this has resulted in a stampede of record corporations to sign up new acts in the search for the elusive pot of gold at the end of the rainbow. Simon Cowell has done more than most to stir up this process. Despite this, he laments its most obvious consequence, which is to flood the market (Cowell 2004: 309). Truly, the genie has escaped, and the efforts of music corporations and the Recording Industry Association of America (RIAA) to put it back into the bottle by, for example, ramping up DRM initatives reveal a profoundly misplaced analysis of what is going on.

Co-operative Labour

'Don't be afraid of things because they are easy to do,' reads one of the cards in Brian Eno and Peter Schmidt's amusing and ingenious 'Oblique Strategies' collection.[3] It serves as a byword for what has happened in the world of music production, consumption and celebrity pop/rock culture over the last thirty years. Sequencers, samplers, synthesizers and drum machines make ordinary people competent, credible and relevant producers of music. In addition, the seeds of the punk and post-punk ideologies which stress that music making is prosaic have taken root and flourished. Jay-Z, Chris Martin and Thom Yorke pack concert stadia throughout the world. Undoubtedly, they inspire excitement and identification. But it would be outlandish to describe them as 'gods'.

The combination of forces that produced the rock superstar culture of the 1960s and 1970s, documented by Lester Bangs, Nick Kent and others, has disintegrated. Jimi Hendrix, The Rolling Stones, The Who, Led Zeppelin and The Doors were among those at the high table in the rock star pantheon. They were spokesmen for a generation, magnets for popular fantasies of achieved celebrity.[4] However, their wealth and jet-set lifestyle drove a wedge between them and their fan base that was exploited by punk and post-punk practical theorists. What the jet-set rock star era got wrong is the true nature of the relationship between the star and the fan. This relationship is one of co-operative labour. For the star is intimately the projection of the fantasies and unsatisfied reflexes of the fan, while the fan is partly framed by the artistic expressions and media representations of the star (Castles 2008).

At the highwater mark of 1970s stadium rock, many superstars, especially in the genre of progressive music, became, in effect, self-referential. Insulated from the audience by publicists and security personnel, they inhabited a bubble of privilege that produced either grossly condescending or utterly blind responses to the enormous creativity and intense energy that goes into being a fan. In a word, the fan was treated as donkey labour: the supine source of applause, concert revenue and album sales.

It might be said that the punk era was a moment when the donkey kicked back.

The fan was recast from being thought of as a passive recipient of art to being a fully fledged creative labourer, challenging the orthodox contours of consumer behaviour by producing music without being able to play his or her instruments, and through textual poaching, home taping and other initiatives (Jenkins 1992, 2006).

Viewed historically, the superstar era of rock and pop now looks like an aberration rather than a climax. Instead of rock gods like Hendrix and Morrison, today we have Thom Yorke, Moby, KT Tunstall and Chris Martin, all of whom are known for the understatement of their personal image. Of course, superstars have not left the stage. If anyone doubts this, consider the immense global reaction to the death of Michael Jackson in June 2009. This occurred in the midst of grinding, unpopular and bloody wars in Afghanistan and Iraq and a horrendous worldwide economic recession. Yet it swept all other news from the headlines for weeks. Should anyone quibble with the hypothesis that some celebrities in popular culture act as cultural biographies of their time and place, the media reaction to the death of Jackson provides conclusive contrary evidence.

In the same year, even an old stager like Paul McCartney smashed attendance records at Boston's Fenway Park, shifted 4,000 tickets in seven seconds at the Hard Rock Hotel in Las Vegas and set a record in ticket sales for the Citi Field stadium in New York. New stars, like Rufus Wainwright, Lady Gaga and Christina Aguilera have cultivated an image of glamour and mystique that expresses high cultural capital and distance from fans. Patently, we still reside in the after-glow of the superstar era, but it is preposterous today to regard fans as docile, passive recipients of cultural capital from the penthouse of popular culture that is supposedly occupied by superstars. The perception of an unbridgeable gulf between the creative labour of superstars and fans is no longer tenable.

Baym and Burnett (2009: 434) coin the term *fan labour* to refer to the cultural capital and creative energy of fans. It means the roles that fans voluntarily play in publicizing, promoting, archiving, filtering, labelling, translating and producing popular music. So blog sites replace the centrality of music print media in setting agendas; P2P networks support the free circulation of music; a cottage industry of music production is supported by synthesizers, samplers, drum machines, laptops and web highways; and opinion formation and social network sites like MySpace and Facebook basically function as zero-cost record marts and bureaus of market research.

In the digital age, cultural consumption involves the transfer of many of the functions that were formerly the preserve of wage labour to individuals and groups that were traditionally considered to be consumers. Hence, CRM initiatives and social networking sites out-source data collection and market research functions into the realm of unpaid voluntary labour. This is presented narrowly as the liberation of fans. What is also happening is that the fans are voluntarily doing the labour of the record corporation. While fan labour may be 'pleasurably embraced', it is also a source of surplus value that is directly exploited and reappropriated through the networks of informational capital (Banks and Deuze 2009: 421; Terranova 2000, 2004: 216).

The Coming of the Second Enclosure Movement

The era of co-operative fan labour of course presents many challenges to record corporations and pop stars. The applications of DRM control machinery and the softer regulatory equipment of CRM measures to the customary practices of P2P communities are portrayed by the music business as exercises in the defence of copyright. What this blithely ignores is that the information networks that the music business seeks to prohibit are the product of the free labour of fans intent upon maximizing the latent value in the web. It is one thing to object to the exchange of materials under the rule of copyright. To proclaim an entitlement to police the space in which exchange transactions occur is qualitatively different. It is, by far, more threatening with respect to common rights and customary practices. The occupiers (servers) of web platforms and users (platform passengers) are tenants of a technology that is inherently open. The efforts of the music business to structure web exchange amount to the imposition of capitalist-property relations upon habitual customs and rights. They are 'habitual' in the sense that they were occupied and cultivated as soon as internet driveways were opened for public traffic. They have grown organically, under a not-for-profit ethic, through the acknowledgement of reciprocal rights and obligations between net passengers. Internet communication was invented and developed as open space for the cultivation of new ideas, free data exchange and discovering common interests between people who may be physically located many thousands of miles away. A series of customs, habits and mutual understandings grew up around these driveways. Because they were defined as common space by net passengers, they lent themselves to free exchange. The P2P exchange of intellectual property bound by the rule of copyright was one expression of this. In seeking to enforce control over copyright, music corporations not only seek to prevent the exchange of copyright material. They endeavour to colonize and appropriate common space and to dismantle the entire edifice of customs, habits and support networks cultivated around it. DRM and CRM initiatives are akin to a second enclosure movement in which what was free and accessible to all is earmarked for regulation and privatization.

The first enclosure movement in Britain, of the late eighteenth and early nineteenth century, involved the enforced seizure of common arable and grazing land by capitalist entrepreneurs pursuing aggressive strategies of urban-industrial accumulation. As Edward Thompson (1963: 238–9) submits, it is facile to regard this as simply the appropriation of common land or the shared means of production. Enclosure involved the deliberate, conscious eradication of the unwritten, customary and self-governing structure of entitlements, rights and ways of going about things of the pre-industrial community. It entailed the imposition of alien, written, private property rights upon free labourers. It wasn't just about a new way of owning and entitlement, it was about a new way of organizing social being and 'positioning' people in relation to scarce resources.

The attempt by the music business to dictate and police the unauthorized exchange of copyright material on the internet and to usurp and transform the structure of free exchange with subscription models amounts to a second enclosure movement. No wonder that cyber-liberties groups in favour of free speech, privacy, genuine market competition and open communication driveways resist and challenge it (Burkhart and McCourt 2006: 158). For it is the end of any semblance of the notion that the web is a common space for free exchange between autonomous net passengers. Now, common space will be turned into corporately controlled space, ultimately policed by the state, in which people are deprived of the customary entitlement of free exchange and where open space is reclassified as leasehold property: that is, only available through subscription bases.

The first enclosure movement showed that when common rights are appropriated and common space is plundered it is exceptionally difficult to win them back. For what was an abuse of class power is transformed by, so to speak, *metamorphosis* into a necessity of nature and history. Cavaliers are forgotten when Roundheads carry the day.

Enstorying, Framing and Making the Wheels Go Round

The reason why informational capital seeks to appropriate music exchange networks is that pop has become indispensable in the culture of recognition and belonging. Pop texts frame social encounters and catalogue biography. As Ruth Finnegan (1997) puts it, music is an 'enstorying' device. It affords a 'poetics' for the time (Bachelard 1964). As such, it possesses immense economic value.

Daniel Miller's (2008) social anthropology of the urban-industrial landscape pays tribute to the ordering capacity of pop music. Commenting upon the psychological and social dimensions of the urban record collection, Miller (2008: 168) documents the Proustian effect of pop in the life of one of his respondents, 'Dave':

> Music, for Dave, had extraordinary precision; it also spoke with great feeling to moments in his life. . . . As he listened again to a specific track from a CD, he could feel again that blonde's arm on the dance floor tugging him to her body; he could recall that joke he had told or the round he had bought when he first heard that particular track . . . . Music could reclaim space better than anything.

'Let me take you there, 'cause I'm going to,' as John Lennon sang in a refrain from 'Strawberry Fields Forever' (1967). The song possesses the 'shimmering' effect described by Barthes (1985) because it evokes a dreamy sensation of childhood nostalgia along many layers. To be sure, essential to the shimmering effect of popular music is the combination and condensation of multiple textual signifiers that afford the impression to listeners that everything, fleetingly 'fits' (Lévi-Strauss 1979, 1981).

Today, listening to pop music is one element in a multi-media platform that encompasses the internet, games, DVDs, television, mobile phones, eating, drinking, talking, taking recreational drugs and reading magazines and books. This directly correlates with strategies of bespoke aggregation pursued by pop merchants to provide synergized cultural capital which, of course, is designed to generate revenue. You buy your P. Diddy clothes while listening to your P. Diddy samples and sipping the Ciroc vodka endorsed by P. Diddy. In time you may even get P. Diddy degrees and diplomas as part of your education, because Sean Coombs, aka P. Diddy, announced in 2010 that he plans to open a business school in New York to train business leaders for the future.

Pop is also now widely consumed in disembedded mobile settings, on the move through MP3 or iPod headphones or car stereo systems, rather than fixed spatial settings such as the living room, the bedroom or the coffee bar. Nor is the sonic dimension prioritized. Music consumption is now widely assumed to include a visual element: 31% of videos watched on YouTube are classified under the 'Music' category. YouTube downloads one billion video files per day (Salmon 2010). The walls of the frame have indeed changed. Pop is now one aggregator in bespoke lifestyles organized along a variety of intersecting multi-media fronts.

As I noted earlier, Friedrich Nietzsche described the effect of music as 'ineffable'. From Lévi-Strauss (1979, 1981), a serviceable riposte to Nietzsche can be constructed, which is to say that music is a type of emotional language. Instead of words and sentences it consists of notes and sonemes. These enable levels of direct emotional communication that words cannot muster. The ascendancy of rap, the popularity of ringtones and the growth of streaming suggest that emotional contacts with pop are becoming abbreviated. Pop affords forms of instant belonging and recognition.

Be that as it may, there is little to support Lévi-Strauss's conjecture that the power of this effect derives from fitting a slot in the jukebox of the human brain. Its sympathetic power with modern audiences derives from its capacity to provide an emotional payload that enables people to build frames for the experience of de-differentiation that is at the heart of modern cultural life. Music both reflects and reinforces the sensuous labour of the human species in engaging with the physical and social world. The term 'labour' means more than commonsense understandings of 'work'. It embraces conjecture, dreaming, interpretation, speculating, poeticizing, and much else besides. The effect is indeed 'ineffable' because pop connects with everything: the high and the low, the cherished and the disposable, hierarchy and community, profit and loss, love and danger.

The second enclosure movement is an attempt to ring-fence popular, unauthorized digital pathways of exchanging music. At the time of writing, the situation is in flux and it is impossible to predict accurately how successful copyright holders will be in enclosing public space. What is beyond doubt is that pop's remarkable capacity to supply a poetics for framing personal and collective experience is assured. Ancient societies attributed mystical powers to mediums and medicine men who were thought to speak in tongues. As we saw earlier, music is still used to heighten experiences with the transcendental and the ineffable (pp. 95–6, 99–102). The modern world has developed a jaundiced eye with respect to magic and the practices of medicine men. However, it has not lost sympathy for the transpersonal and the transcendental. The desire to reach out and go beyond narrow forms of subjective and interpersonal experience is widespread. Pop speaks in tunes. Even a few bars and lyrical fragments of a major hit record can endow social encounters and personal reveries with poetic quality. Pop can make a sunny day out of bleak midwinter and establish empathy between strangers. In a world where people familiarly complain of the ascendency of routine, monotony, lack of excitement and timid passions, pop songs are produced and exchanged as a means of re-enchanting the world. In the age of unauthorized downloading, their contraband status merely enhances their appeal. The modern world is not lost in music. It depends upon music to make the wheels go round.

Notes

Introduction: Why 'Pop', Not 'Popular'?

1 Tin Pan Alley is the name given to the site of the biggest concentration of music publishers and songwriters in Manhattan at the end of the nineteenth century and the beginning of the twentieth century.
2 Simmel and Benjamin, writing in the early decades of the twentieth century, provide seminal contributions to the sociology of culture. Their work on modernity emphasized the conditions of flux and permanent transformation that were interpreted as characteristically modern. These ideas lead directly to the concept of cultural de-differentiation which is pivotal to the analysis of contemporary pop in this book.
3 One of the clichés of pop is that the record corporations that enable music to be recorded and distributed come, in time, to dominate and imprison artists.

Chapter 1   The Field of Pop Music Study

1 *Shorter Oxford English Dictionary*, 1992.
2 The healing power of pop is a well-trodden theme in the analysis of popular music. Miller's (2008) ethnography of a London street notes the analgesic qualities of pop in framing memory.
3 The theoretical roots of this argument – the idea of music as a disciplinary device and regime of power – lie in the work of Michel Foucault.
4 The poetic qualities of pop can be overstated. Nonetheless, in terms of the expression of strong emotions, it is remarkable how most people turn to pop for their repertoire.
5 The terms 'dominant', 'emergent' and 'residual' come from the work of Raymond Williams.
6 The term 'homology' refers to mirrors or resemblances between categorically different things. For example, the chords of heavy metal music mirror the rhythm of industrial machinery and power plants.
7 Emotional intelligence refers to the knowledge that people require to manoeuvre individuals and groups. Emotional labour refers to the skills that people use as an accomplishment to influence social encounters.

Chapter 2   The Urban-Industrial Backbeat

1 Although they continued touring and recording for some time, Brinsley Schwarz never overcame the Fillmore East public relations disaster.

2   The distinctions employed here derive from the figurational sociology of
    Norbert Elias.
3   The Birmingham School is associated with the writings of Stuart Hall, Angela
    McRobbie, Paul Gilroy, Dick Hebdige, Paul Willis, Chas Critcher and many
    others. While not exactly a coherent school, the Birmingham group adopted a
    neo-Marxist approach to culture and society. The writings of Marx, Althusser
    and especially Gramsci were central influences.

Chapter 3   Structuralist Approaches

1   The privileging of neural structure and the mode of production refer,
    respectively, to the work of Lévi-Strauss and Marx.
2   The treatment of Carnival as a break or inversion of the rules of everyday life is
    reminiscent of the thought of Mikhail Bakhtin.
3   The politics of this time were certainly on the left. But it had more to do with
    resistance and challenging power than conventional socialist models of social
    construction.

Chapter 4   Agency Approaches

1   Neat capitalism refers to activist, socially responsible forms of appropriation.
    Making money is linked to empowering the consumer through education,
    advocacy, and so on. The term is related to the recent concept of philanthro-
    capitalism, which refers to a socially caring form of capitalist organization.
    Although I have been using the term 'neat capitalism' in my work for some
    time, these days I prefer 'smart capitalism'.
2   In the UK the death of the Essex teenager Leah Betts in 1995 after taking an
    Ecstasy tablet precipitated a full-scale moral panic. Subsequently, her death
    was found to be caused by water intoxication.
3   The concept of 'staged authenticity' was coined and analysed most fruitfully by
    my friend Dean MacCannell in his book *The Tourist* (1975).

Part III   The Mode of Production

1   Allocative mechanisms refer to the institutions of class, gender, race,
    occupational groupings and the state which position people separately in
    relation to scarcity.

Chapter 5   Roots

1   Parker has become infamous as a domineering manager. While most
    commentators now accept that Presley saw Parker as an avuncular
    figure whom he trusted with his business affairs, there is no doubt that
    the Colonel produced advantageous contracts which privileged his role
    and committed the singer to a punishing and artistically negligible film
    career.
2   Sinatra was deplored by returning servicemen. They were critical of him for

avoiding war service and saw him as having a pampered life surrounded by adoring female fans while they risked their lives abroad.

Chapter 6   Corporations and Independents

1   Bernie Madoff is a former American stockbroker, investment adviser and non-executive chairman of NASDAQ who was found guilty of a massive securities fraud, involving money laundering, false statements and perjury. He is currently serving a 150-year prison sentence.

Chapter 8   Technology and Media

1   Gould reasoned that the technical perfection of recorded sound would make live performance superfluous. What this left out of the reckoning was the audience connection to the physical presence of artists and performers. Ironically, as the price of recorded music has come down to nearly zero (through unauthorized downloading), the price of concert tickets has risen and the market for live performances by superstars has expanded.
2   Technically, it offers to make a virtuoso of anyone who can type and has the inclination to compose and play.

Chapter 9   Co-operative Labour, Inc.

1   The band were at loggerheads both with each other and with their management. The implosion of The Sex Pistols was inevitable because they celebrated and legitimated a philosophy of righteous destruction. Even so, the collapse of the band accelerated the development of post-punk initiatives, because The Sex Pistols had become the primary symbol of punk.
2   The concept of *détournement* means a deviation or reaction in an artwork or social movement that stands meanings on their head. It was a prominent concept in Situationist writing.
3   First published in 1975, 'Oblique Strategies' is a series of cards that act as *aides-mémoire* or triggers to action.
4   An achieved celebrity is an individual who acquires fame by reason of his or her talents and accomplishments.

References

Adorno, T. (1941) 'On Popular Music'. *Studies in Philosophy and Social Science*, IX: 17–48.

Adorno, T. (1947) *Composing for Films*. Oxford: Oxford University Press.

Adorno, T. (1967) *Prisms*. Cambridge, MA: MIT Press.

Adorno, T. (1973) *Philosophy of Modern Music*. New York: Seabury.

Adorno, T. (1978) 'On the Social Situation of Music'. *Telos*, 35: 129–65.

Adorno, T. (1991) *The Culture Industry*. London: Routledge.

Adorno, T. (1998) *Critical Models: Interventions and Catchwords*. New York: Columbia University Press.

Adorno, T. (2006) *History and Freedom*. Cambridge: Polity.

Adorno, T. (2009) *Current of Music*. Cambridge: Polity.

Adorno, T. and Horkheimer, M. (1979) *Dialectic of Enlightenment*. London: Verso.

Alexander, J. and Giesen, B. (1987) 'From Reduction to Linkage', in J. Alexander, B. Giesen, R. Munch and N. Smelser (eds), *The Micro–Macro Link*. Berkeley: University of California Press, 1–42.

Allen, K. (2008) 'Home Copying – Burnt into the Teenage Psyche'. *The Guardian*, 7 April.

Amburn, E. (1994) *Pearl: Obsessions and Passions of Janis Joplin*. New York: Time-Warner.

Amoaku, W.K. (1985) 'Toward a Definition of Traditional African Music: A Look at the Ewe of Ghana', in I.V. Jackson (ed.), *More Than Drumming*. Westport, CT: Greenwood, 31–40.

Anderson, B. (2004) 'Recorded Music and Practices of Remembering'. *Social and Cultural Geography*, 5(1): 3–19.

Aristotle (2000) *Politics*. New York: Dover.

Aristotle (2005) *Poetics*. Cambridge, MA: Harvard University Press.

Aronowitz, S. (1994) *Dead Artists, Live Theories*. New York: Routledge.

Attali, J. (1977) *Noise: The Political Economy of Music*. Minneapolis: University of Minnesota Press.

Attali, J. (2002) 'Making Sense of Noise (an Interview with Ian Simmons)' (http://www.nthposition.com).

Auslander, P. (2006) *Performing Glam Rock*. Ann Arbor: University of Michigan Press.

Bachelard, G. (1964) *The Poetics of Space*. New York: Viking.

Bakhtin, M. (1968) *Rabelais and His World*. Cambridge, MA: MIT Press.

Bangs, L. (1988) *Psychotic Reactions and Carburettor Dung*. New York: Anchor.

Banks, J. (1996) *Monopoly Television: MTV's Quest to Control Music*. Boulder, CO: Westview.

Banks, J. (1997) 'MTV and the Globalization of Popular Culutre'. *International Communication Gazette*, 59(1): 43–60.

Banks, J. and Deuze, M. (2009) 'Co-creative Labour?' *International Journal of Cultural Studies*, 12(5): 419–32.

Barthes, R. (1975) *The Pleasure of the Text*. New York: Hill & Wang.

Barthes, R. (1985) *The Responsibility of Forms: Critical Essays on Music, Art and Representation*. New York: Hill & Wang.

Barthes, R. (1990) *Image–Music–Text*. London: HarperCollins.

Barthes, R. (1991) *S/Z*. New York: Farrar, Straus & Giroux.

Barthes, R. (1993) *Mythologies*. New York: Vintage.

Barthes, R. (1997) *Elements of Semiology*. New York: Atlantic.

Barzun, J. (1977) *Pleasures of Recorded Music*. London: Cassell.

Baskerville, D. and Baskerville, T. (2010) *Music Business Handbook*. Thousand Oaks, CA: Sage.

Bass, B.M. and Avolio, B.J. (1990) 'From Transactional to Transformational Leadership: Learning to Share the Vision'. *Organizational Dynamics*, 18: 19–31.

Baudrillard, J. (1980) 'The Implosion of Meaning in the Media and the Implosion of the Social in the Masses', in K. Woodward (ed.), *The Myths of Information*. Madison: Coda Press, 137–48.

Baudrillard, J. (1983) 'The Ecstasy of Communication', in H. Foster (ed.), *The Anti-Aesthetic*. Port Townsend, WA: Bay Press, 126–34.

Baugh, B. (1993) 'Music for the Young at Heart'. *The Journal of Aesthetics and Art Criticism*, 53(1): 81–3.

Baym, N.K. and Burnett, R. (2009) 'Amateur Experts: International Fan Labour in Swedish Independent Music'. *International Journal of Cultural Studies*, 12(5): 433–50.

Becker, H. (1974) 'Art as Collective Action'. *American Sociological Review*, 39: 767–76.

Becker, H. (1976) 'Art Worlds and Social Types', in R.E. Petersen (ed.), *The Production of Culture*. London: Sage, 41–56.

Becker, S. (1963) *Outsiders*. New York: Free Press.

Benjamin, W. (2002) 'The Work of Art in the Age of Its Technological Reproducibility', in W. Benjamin (ed.), *Walter Benjamin: Selected Writings 3*. Cambridge, MA: Belknap/Harvard University Press, 101–33.

Bennett, A. (1997) 'Bhangra in Newcastle: Music, Ethnic Identity and the Role of Local Knowledge'. *Innovation: European Journal of the Social Sciences*, 10(1): 107–16.

Bennett, A. (1999) 'Rappin' on the Tyne'. *Sociological Review*, 47(1): 1–24.

Bennett, A. (2001) *Cultures of Popular Music*. Maidenhead: Open University Press.

Bennett, A. (2008) 'Towards a Cultural Sociology of Popular Music'. *Journal of Sociology*, 44(4): 419–32.

Bennett, H.S. (1980) *On Becoming a Rock Musician*. Amherst: University of Massachusetts Press.

Bielstein, S.M. (2006) *Permissions*. Chicago: University of Chicago Press.

Black, J. (2009) 'So Who's the Biggest Star?' *The Guardian*, 6 March.

Bourdieu, P. (1984) *Distinction*. London: Routledge.

Bourdieu, P. (1990) *The Logic of Practice*. Cambridge: Polity.

Bourdieu, P. (1993) *The Field of Cultural Production*. Cambridge: Polity.

Bourdieu, P. and Passeron, J.C. (1990) *Reproduction in Education, Society and Culture*. London: Sage.

Brewster, B. and Broughton, F. (2006) *Last Night a DJ Saved My Life: The History of the Disc Jockey*. London: Headline.

Briffault, R. (1965) *The Troubadours*. Bloomington: Indiana University Press.

Burkart, P. and McCourt, T. (2006) *Digital Music Wars: Ownership and Control of the Celestial Jukebox*. Lanham, MD: Rowman & Littlefield.

Burns, J.M. (1978) *Leadership*. New York: Harper & Row.

Campbell, C. (1987) *The Romantic Ethic and the Spirit of Modern Consumerism*. Oxford: Blackwell.

Carrabine, E. and Longhurst, B. (1999) 'Mosaics of Omnivorousness: Suburban Youth and Popular Music'. *New Formations*, 38: 125–49.

Cashmore, E. (1997) *The Black Culture Industry*. London: Routledge.

Castells, M. (1996) *The Rise of Network Society*. Oxford: Blackwell.

Castells, M. (1997) *The Power of Identity*. Oxford: Blackwell.

Castells, M. (1998) *The End of the Millennium*. Oxford: Blackwell.

Castles, J. (1997) 'Madonna: Mother of Mirrors'. *Cultural Studies*, 11(1): 73–92.

Castles, J. (2008) *Big Stars*. Perth: Curtin University of Technology Press.

Caves, R.E. (2000) *Creative Industries*. Cambridge, MA: Harvard University Press.

Cavicchi, D. (1998) *Tramps Like Us*. Oxford: Oxford University Press.

Chambers, I. (1985) *Urban Rhythms, Pop Music and Popular Culture*. London: Macmillan.

Chang, J. (2007) *Can't Stop Won't Stop*. New York: Ebury.

Chapple, S. and Garofolo, R. (1977) *Rock and Roll is Here to Pay*. Chicago: Nelson Hall.

Clarke, D. (1995) *The Rise and Fall of Popular Music*. London: Penguin.

Cloward, R. and Ohlin, L. (1960) *Delinquency and Opportunity*. New York: Free Press.

Cohen, A. (1955) *Delinquent Boys*. Chicago: Free Press.

Cohen, P. (1972) 'Subcultural Conflict and Working Class Community'. *Working Papers in Cultural Studies 2*. University of Birmingham.

Condry, I. (2006) *Hip-Hop Japan*. Durham, NC: Duke University Press.

Cooper, A.F. (2008) *Celebrity Diplomacy*. Boulder, CO: Paradigm.

Corbett, M. (2003) 'Sound Organization: A Brief History of Psychosonic Management'. *Ephemera*, 3(4): 265–76.

Couldry, N. (2000) *Inside Culture*. London: Sage.

Cowell, S. (2003) *I Don't Mean To Be Rude, But . . .* London: Ebury Press.

Csikszentmihalyi, M. (1990) *Flow: The Psychology of Optimal Experience*. New York: Harper & Row.

Cullity, J. (2002) 'The Global Desi: Cultural Nationalism on MTV India'. *Journal of Communication Inquiry*, 26(4): 408–25.

Cutler, C. (2004) 'Plunderphonia', in C. Cox and D. Warner (eds), *Audio Culture: Readings in Modern Music*. London: Continuum, 138–56.

Dannen, F. (1991) *Hit Men: Power Brokers and Fast Money inside the Music Business*. New York: Vintage.

David, M. (2010) *Peer to Peer and The Music Industry*. London: Sage.

David, M. and Kirkhope, J. (2004) 'New Digital Technologies: Privacy/Property,

Globalization and Law'. *Perspectives on Global Development and Technology*, 3(4): 437–49.

Day, T. (2000) *A Century of Recorded Music*. New Haven: Yale University Press.

Denisoff, R. and Romanowski, W. (1991) *Risky Business: Rock in Film*. New Brunswick, NJ: Transaction.

DeNora, T. (2000) *Music in Everyday Life*. Cambridge: Cambridge University Press.

DeNora, T. (2003) *After Adorno: Rethinking Music Sociology*. Cambridge: Cambridge University Press.

DeRogitas, J. (2000) *Let It Blurt: The Life and Times of Lester Bangs, America's Greatest Rock Critic*. New York: Bantam.

Dickerson, J. (2001) *Colonel Tom Parker*. New York: Cooper Square Books.

Dioszegi, V. (1968) *Tracing Shamans in Siberia*. Oosterhout: Anthropological Publications.

Dufrenne, M. (1973) *The Phenomenology of Aesthetic Experience*. Evanston, IL: Northwestern University Press.

Echols, E. (2001) *Scars of Sweet Paradise: The Life and Times of Janis Joplin*. London: Virago.

El-Sawad, A. and Korczynski, M. (2007) 'Management and Music'. *Group Organization Management*, 31(1): 79–108.

Elborough, T. (2008) *The Long Player Goodbye*. London: Sceptre.

Eliade, M. (1964) *Shamanism*. London: Penguin-Arkana.

Eno, B. (2004) 'The Studio as a Compositional Tool', in C. Cox and D. Warner (eds), *Audio Culture: Readings in Modern Music*. London: Continuum, 127–30. (Originally published in *Downbeat*, 50(7), 1983: 56–7; 50(8), 50–2.)

Erlmann, V. (1996) *Nightsong: Performance, Power and Practice in South Africa*. Chicago: University of Chicago Press.

Faulk, B.J. (2004) *Music Hall and Modernity*. Athens: Ohio University Press.

Feld, S. and Keil, C. (1994) *Music Grooves*. Chicago: University of Chicago Press.

Finnegan, R. (1989) *The Hidden Musicians*. Cambridge: Cambridge University Press.

Finnegan, R. (1997) 'Storying the Self: Personal Narratives and Identity', in H.E. Mackay (ed.), *Consumption and Everyday Life*. London: Sage, 58–112.

Fiske, J. (1986) 'MTV: Post-Structural Post-Modern'. *Journal of Communication Inquiry*, 10(1): 74–9.

Fiske, J. (1992) 'The Cultural Economy of Fandom', in L. Lewis (ed.), *The Adoring Audience: Fan Culture and Popular Media*. London: Routledge, 30–49.

Flichy, P. (1999) 'The Construction of New Digital Media'. *New Media & Society*, 1(1): 33–8.

Fowler, D. (2007) 'From Jukebox Boys to Revolting Students: Richard Hoggart and the Study of British Youth Culture'. *International Journal of Cultural Studies*, 10(1): 73–84.

Frank, T. (1998) *The Conquest of Cool*. Chicago: University of Chicago Press.

Friedlander, P. (2006) *Rock & Roll: A Social History*. Boulder, CO: Westview.

Friedman, M. (1989) *Janis Joplin: Buried Alive*. New York: Plexus.

Frith, S. (1996) *Performing Rites*. Oxford: Oxford University Press.

Frith, S. (2001) 'The Popular Music Industry', in S. Frith, W. Straw and J. Street (eds), *The Cambridge Companion to Pop and Rock*. Cambridge: Cambridge University Press, 26–52.

Frith, S. and Horne, H. (1987) *Art into Pop*. London: Methuen.

Fung, A. (2006) ' "Think Globally, Act Locally": China's Rendezvous with MTV'. *Global Media and Communication*, 2(1): 71–88.

Fung, A. and Curtin, M. (2002) 'The Anomalies of Being Faye (Wong): Gender Politics in Chinese Popular Music'. *International Journal of Cultural Studies*, 5: 263–90.

Gallo, P. (2007) 'Digital Sales Boost Music Industry'. *Variety*, January 4.

Garofolo, R. (1997) *Rockin' Out: Popular Music in the USA*. Boston: Allyn & Bacon.

Garofolo, R. (1999) 'From Music Publishing to MP3'. *American Music*, 17(3): 318–53.

Garratt, S. (1998) *Adventures in Wonderland: A Decade of Club Culture*. London: Headline.

Gay, P. (1996) *The Naked Heart: The Bourgeois Experience from Victoria to Freud*. London: HarperCollins.

Gelatt, R. (1977) *The Fabulous Phonograph 1877–1977*. London: Cassell.

Gilbert, D. (1963) *American Vaudeville*. New York: Dover.

Gitlin, T. (1987) *The Sixties*. New York: Bantam.

Gitlin, T. (2002) *Media Unlimited*. New York: Owl Books.

Goffman, E. (1967) *Interaction Ritual*. New York: Pantheon.

Goffman, E. (1971) *Relations in Public*. Harmondsworth: Penguin.

Goldstein, P. (2003) *Copyright's Highway*. Stanford: Stanford University Press.

Goodwin, A. (1991) 'Popular Music and Postmodern Theory'. *Cultural Studies*, 5: 174–90.

Goodwin, A. (1993) *Dancing in the Distraction Factory*. London: Routledge.

Gottschild, B. (2002) *Waltzing in the Dark: African American Vaudeville and the Politics of the Swing Era*. Basingstoke: Palgrave Macmillan.

Gould, G. (1984) *The Glenn Gould Reader*. New York: Knopf.

Gracyk, T. (1996) *Rhythm and Noise: The Aesthetics of Rock*. Cambridge, MA: Harvard University Press.

Gracyk, T. (2007) *Listening to Popular Music*. Ann Arbor: University of Michigan Press.

Gramsci, A. (1971) *Selections from the Prison Notebooks*. London: Lawrence & Wishart.

Greenwood, J. (1986) *Blackpool Entertains the Troops*. Blackpool.

Grossberg, L. (1992) *We Gotta Get Out of This Place*. London: Routledge.

Grossberg, L. (1997) *Dancing in Spite of Myself*. Durham, NC: Duke University Press.

Gurevich, A.J. (1972) *Categories of Medieval Culture*. London: Routledge and Kegan Paul.

Gutman, R.W. (1968) *Richard Wagner: The Man, His Mind and His Music*. New York: Harcourt Brace & World.

Haden-Guest, A. (1997) *The Last Party: Studio 54, Disco and the Culture of the Night*. New York: Quill.

Hall, S. (1968) 'The Hippies'. Occasional paper. Mimeo. Birmingham Centre for Contemporary Cultural Studies, University of Birmingham.

Hall, S. (1980) 'Encoding/Decoding', in S. Hall, D. Hobson, A. Lowe and P. Willis (eds), *Culture, Media, Language*. London: Unwin Hyman, 128–38.

Hall, S. (1996) 'On Postmodernism and Articulation', in D. Morley and K.-H. Chen (eds), *Stuart Hall*. London: Routledge, 131–50.

Hall, S. and Jefferson, T. (eds) (1976) *Resistance through Rituals*. London: Hutchinson.

Halperin, I. (2009) *The Final Years of Michael Jackson*. New York: Simon & Schuster.

Hamilton, M. (2001) *The Sociology of Religion*. London: Routledge.

Hardt, H. (1986) 'MTV: Towards Visual Domination, a Polemic'. *Journal of Communication Inquiry*, 10(1): 64–5.

Hardt, M. and Negri, T. (2000) *Empire*. Cambridge, MA: Harvard University Press.

Hebdige, D. (1979) *Subculture*. London: Routledge.

Hebdige, D. (1987) *Cut 'n' Mix*. London: Routledge.

Hegarty, P. (2008) *Noise/Music*. New York: Continuum.

Hegel, G.W.F. (1949) *The Phenomenology of Mind*. London: George Allen & Unwin.

Hegel. G.W.F. (1977) *The Phenomenology of Spirit*. Oxford: Oxford University Press.

Heidegger, M. (1984) *The Metaphysical Foundations of Logic*. Bloomington: Indiana University Press.

Hesmondhalgh, D. (1998) 'The British Dance Music Industry: A Case Study in Independent Cultural Production'. *British Journal of Sociology*, 49(2): 234–51.

Hesmondhalgh, D. (2002) *The Cultural Industries*. London: Sage.

Hesmondhalgh, D. (2007) 'Audiences and Everyday Aesthetics'. *European Journal of Cultural Studies*, 10(4): 507–27.

Heylin, C. (1993) *From the Velvets to the Voidoids*. London: Helter Skelter.

Heylin, C. (2007) *Babylon's Burning: From Punk To Grunge*. New York: Viking.

Hills, M. (2002) *Fan Cultures*. London: Routledge.

Holmes, S. (2004) '"Reality Goes Pop!": Reality TV, Popular Music and Narratives of Stardom in Pop Idol'. *Television & New Media*, 5(2): 147–72.

Huizinga, J. (1949) *Homo Ludens*. London: Routledge & Kegan Paul.

IFPI (International Federation of the Phonographic Industry) (2010) *Digital Music Report 2010* (http://www.ifpi.org).

Jackson, P. (2004) *Inside Clubbing*. Oxford: Berg.

Jenkins, H. (1992) *Textual Poachers*. London: Routledge.

Jenkins, H. (2006) *Fans, Bloggers and Games*. New York: New York University Press.

Jones, S. and Schumacher, T. (1992) 'Muzak: On Functional Music and Power'. *Critical Studies in Mass Communication*, 9: 156–69.

Juluri, V. (2002) 'Music Television and the Invention of Youth Culture in India'. *Television & New Media*, 3(4): 367–86.

Kalweit, H. (2001) 'Experiencing the Shaman's Symphony to Understand It', in J. Narby and F. Huxley (eds), *Shamans through Time*. London: Thames & Hudson, 178–83.

Kaplan, A. (1993) 'Madonna Politics: Perversion, Repression or Subversion?', in C. Schwichtenberg (ed.), *The Madonna Connection: Representation Politics, Subcultural Identities, and Cultural Theory*. Boulder, Co: Westview, 149–65.

Kaplan, E.A. (1987) *Rocking around The Clock: Music Television, Postmodernism and Consumer Culture*. London: Routledge.

Kealy, E.R. (1979) 'From Craft to Arty: The Case of Sound Mixers and Popular Music'. *Sociology of Work and Occupations*, 6: 3–29.

Keightley, K. (2001) 'Reconsidering Rock', in S. Frith, W. Straw and J. Street (eds), *The Cambridge Companion to Rock and Pop*. Cambridge: Cambridge University Press, 109–43.

Keightley, K. (2004) 'Long Play: Adult Centred Popular Music and the Temporal Logics of the Post War Sound Recording Industry in the USA'. *Media, Culture & Society*, 26(3): 375–91.

Kent, N. (2007) *The Dark Stuff*. London: Faber.

Kent, N. (2010) *Apathy for the Devil*. London: Faber.

Kern, S. (1983) *The Culture of Time and Space 1880–1918*. London: Weidenfeld & Nicolson.

Kohl, P. (1993) 'Looking through a Glass Onion: Rock and Roll as Manifestation of Carnival'. *Journal of Popular Culture*, 27(2): 43–61.

Korczynski, M. (2003) 'Music at Work'. *Folk Music Journal*, 8: 314–34.

Kracauer, S. (1995) *The Mass Ornament*. Cambridge, MA: Harvard University Press.

Kusek, D. (2010) 'Searching for Salvation' (*http://www.futureofmusicnook.com*).

Kusek, D. and Leonhard, G. (2005) *The Future of Music: Manifesto for the Digital Music Revolution*. Boston: Berklee Press.

Lahr, J. (1988) *Sinatra: The Artist and the Man*. London: Phoenix.

Laing, D. (1991) 'A Voice without a Face: Popular Music and the Phonograph in the 1890s'. *Popular Music*, 10(1): 1–9.

Laing, R.D. (1970) *The Politics of Experience and the Bird of Paradise*. Harmondsworth: Penguin.

Laing, R.D. (1995) *Mad to be Normal: Conversations with Bob Mullan*. London: Free Association Books.

Laughey, D. (2006) *Music and Youth Culture*. Edinburgh: Edinburgh University Press.

Lévi-Strauss, C. (1966) *The Savage Mind*. Chicago: University of Chicago Press.

Lévi-Strauss, C. (1970) *The Raw and the Cooked*. London: Jonathan Cape.

Lévi-Strauss, C. (1979) *Myth and Meaning*. New York: Schocken.

Lévi-Strauss, C. (1981) *The Naked Man*. London: Jonathan Cape.

Lévi-Strauss, C. (1997) *Look, Listen, Read*. New York: Basic Books.

Lewis, L. (1992) *The Adoring Audience*. London: Routledge.

Li, K. (2009) 'Sales Help VIAcom Beat Expectations'. *Financial Times*, 4 November.

Lipsitz, G. (2007) *Footsteps in the Dark*. Minneapolis: University of Minnesota Press.

Livingstone, S. (1998) 'Audience Research at the Crossroads'. *European Journal of Cultural Studies*, 1(2): 193–217.

Longhurst, B. (2007) *Popular Music and Society*. Cambridge: Polity.

Lukács, G. (1971) *History and Class Consciousness*. London: Merlin.

MacCannell, D. (1975) *The Tourist*. New York: Schocken.

MacDonald, I. (2003) *The People's Music*. London: Pimlico.

MacDougald, D., Jr (1941) 'The Popular Music Industry', in P. Lazarsfeld and F.N. Stanton (eds), *Radio Research*. New York: Duell, Sloane, and Pearce, 65–109.

McGuigan, J. (2009) *Cool Capitalism*. London: Pluto.

McPhail, T.L. (2006) *Global Communication*. Oxford: Blackwell.

McRobbie, A. (1980) 'Settling Accounts with Subcultures'. *Screen Education*, 34: 37–50.

McRobbie, A. (1991) *Feminism and Youth Culture*. London: Macmillan.

McRobbie, A. (1994) 'Folk Devils Fight Back'. *New Left Review*, 203: 107–16.

Malbon, B. (1999) *Clubbing: Dancing, Ecstasy and Vitality*. London: Routledge.

Mann, C. (2000) 'The Heavenly Jukebox'. *Atlantic Monthly*, September (*http://www.theatlantic.com/issues/2000/09/mann.htm*).

Marcus, G. (1989) *Lipstick Traces*. London: Faber.

Marcus, G. (2005) *Like a Rolling Stone*. London: Public Affairs.

Marcuse, H. (1964) *One Dimensional Man*. London: Abacus.

Marsh, D. (1982) *Elvis*. New York: Rolling Stone Books.

Marsh, D. (2002) 'Colonel Tom Parker (Parker's Death Dark Shadow)' (http://www.elvis.com.au/presley/articles_deathshadow.shtml).

Marshall, Lee (2004) 'Infringers', in S. Frith and L. Marshall (eds), *Music and Copyright*. Edinburgh: Edinburgh University Press, 189–208.

Marshall, Lorna (1962) '!Kung Bushman Religious Beliefs'. *Africa*, 39: 347–81.

Marx, K. (1964) *The Economic and Philosophical Manuscripts of 1944*. New York: International Publishers.

Middleton, R. (2002) *Studying Popular Music*. Milton Keynes: Open University Press.

Miege, B. (1989) *The Capitalization of Cultural Production*. New York: International General.

Miller, D. (2008) *The Comfort of Things*. Cambridge: Polity.

Mitchell, T. (1996) *Popular Music and Local Identity*. Leicester: Leicester University Press.

Morin, E. (1960) *The Stars*. New York: Grove Press.

Morton, D. (2000) *Off the Record: The Technology and Culture of Sound Recordings in America*. Chapel Hill, NC: Rutgers University Press.

Moyn, D. (2005) *Origins of the Other: Emmanuel Levinas between Revelation and Ethics*. Ithaca, NY: Cornell University Press.

Muggleton, D. (2005) 'From Classlessness to Club Culture: A Genealogy of Post-War British Cultural Analysis'. *Young*, 13(2): 205–19.

Napier-Bell, S. (2002) *Black Vinyl, White Powder*. London: Ebury Press.

Nash, A. (1995) *Elvis Aaron Presley: Revelations from the Memphis Mafia*. London: HarperCollins.

Negus, K. (1992) *Producing Pop*. London: Edward Arnold.

Negus, K. (1996) *Popular Music in Theory*. Cambridge: Polity.

Negus, K. (1999) *Music Genres and Corporate Cultures*. London: Routledge.

Nietzsche, F. (1858) *From My Life* (http://www.f-nietzsche.de/musik_eng.htm).

Oakes, S. (2000) 'The Influence of Music-scape within Service Environments'. *Journal of Services Management*, 14(7): 539–56.

Oldenzeil, R. (1999) *Making Technology Masculine*. Amsterdam: Amsterdam University Press.

Olsen, D. (1975) 'Music Alone Can Alter a Shaman's Consciousness, Which Itself Can Destroy Tape Recorders', in J. Narby and F. Huxley (eds), *Shamans through Time*. London: Thames & Hudson, 212–16.

Park, W.Z. (1938) *Shamanism in Western North America*. Evanston and Chicago: Northwestern University Studies in Social Science.

Pettegrew, J. (1995) 'A Post-Modernist Moment: 1980s Commercial Culture and the Founding of MTV', in G. Dines and J. McMahon Humez (eds), *Gender, Race and Class in Media*. Thousand Oaks, CA: Sage, 488–98.

Pinch, T. and Bijsterveld, K. (2004) 'Sound Studies: New Technologies and Music'. *Social Studies of Science*, 34(5): 635–48.

Pinch, T. and Trocco, F. (2002) *Analog Days: The Invention and Impact of the Moog Synthesizer*. Cambridge, MA: Harvard University Press.

Plato (2005) *The Laws*. London: Penguin.

Radano, R. M. (1989) 'Interpreting Muzak: Speculations on Musical Experience in Everyday Life'. *American Music*, 7: 448–60.

Radkau, J. (2009) *Max Weber: A Biography*. Cambridge: Polity.

Rentfrow, J. and Gosling, S. (2003) 'The Do Re Mi's of Everyday Life: The Structure and Personality Correlates of Music Preferences'. *Journal of Personality and Social Psychology*, 84: 1236–56.

Rentfrow, J. and Gosling, S. (2007) 'The Content and Validity of Music-Genre Stereotypes among College Students'. *Psychology of Music*, 35: 306–25.

Rentfrow, J., McDonald, J.A. and Oldmeadow, J.A. (2009) 'You Are What You Listen To: Young People's Stereotypes about Music Fans'. *Group Processes & Intergroup Relations*, 12(3): 329–44.

Reynolds, S. (1998) *Energy Flash*. London: Picador.

Reynolds, S. (2006) *Rip It Up and Start Again: Post Punk 1978–84*. London: Faber.

Reynolds, S. (2007) *Bring the Noise*. London: Faber.

Reynolds, S. (2009) *Totally Wired: Post-Punk Interviews and Overviews*. London: Faber.

Rhodes, C. (2007) 'Outside the Gates of Eden: Utopia and Work in Rock Music'. *Group Organization Management*, 32(1): 22–49.

Rojek, C. (2004) *Frank Sinatra*. Cambridge: Polity.

Rojek, C. (2007) *Cultural Studies*. Cambridge: Polity.

Russell, D. (1997) *Popular Music in England, 1840–1914*. Manchester: Manchester University Press.

Russolo, L. (1986) *The Art of Noises*. New York: Pendragon Press.

Salewicz, C. (2006) *Redemption Song: The Definitive Biography of Joe Strummer*. London: HarperCollins.

Salmon, C. (2010) 'YouTube's Big Billion'. *The Guardian*, 11 March.

Sandvoss, C. (2005) *Fans*. Cambridge: Polity.

Sanjek, R. (1988) *American Popular Music and Its Business*. Oxford: Oxford University Press.

Sassatelli, R. and Santoro, M. (2009) 'An Interview with Paul Willis: Commodification, Resistance and Reproduction'. *European Journal of Social Theory*, 12(2): 265–90.

Saussure, F. de (1974) *Course in General Linguistics*. London: Fontana.

Sayre, S. and King, C. (2003) *Entertainment and Society*. Thousand Oaks, CA: Sage.

Schivelbusch, W. (1988) *Disenchanted Night: The Industrialization of Light in the Nineteenth Century*. Berkeley: University of California Press.

Schmidt-Horning, S. (2004) 'Engineering the Performance: Recording Engineers, Tacit Knowledge and the Art of Controlling Sound'. *Social Studies of Science*, 34(5): 703–31.

Schroder, K.C. (2000) 'Making Sense of Audience Discourses'. *European Journal of Cultural Studies*, 3(2): 233–58.

Schutz, A. (1982) *Life Forms and Meaning Structure*. London: Routledge and Kegan Paul.

Sennett, R. (2007) *The Culture of the New Capitalism*. New Haven: Yale University Press.

Shaw, A. (1968) *Sinatra*. London: Hodder.

Shepherd, J. and Wicke, P. (1997) *Music and Cultural Theory*. Cambridge: Polity.

Shusterman, R. (2000) *Performing Live*. Ithaca, NY: Cornell University Press.

Simmel, G. (1971) *On Individuality and Social Forms*. Chicago: University of Chicago Press.

Simmel, G. (1978) *The Philosophy of Money*. London: Routledge.

Steen, A. (1996) *The Long March of Rock 'n' Roll: Pop and Rock Music in the People's Republic of China.* Münster: LIT Verlag.

Stein, C. (1983) *American Vaudeville as Seen by Its Contemporaries.* New York: Da Capo.

Stevenson, N. (2006) *David Bowie.* Cambridge: Polity.

Stokes, M. (1997) *Ethnicity, Identity and Music.* London: Berg.

Strauss, N. (2002) 'Behind the Grammys, Revolt in the Industry'. *New York Times,* 24 February.

Straw, W. (1990) 'Popular Music as Cultural Commodity: The American Recorded Music Industries 1978–85'. Unpublished Ph.D. thesis. Montreal: McGill University.

Straw, W. (1991) 'Systems of Articulation, Logics of Change: Communities and Scenes in Popular Music'. *Cultural Studies,* 5(3): 368–88.

Strawson, P. (1966) *The Bounds of Sense.* London: Methuen.

Sylvan, R. (2002) *Traces of the Spirit.* New York: New York University Press.

Tagg, P. (1987) 'Musicology and the Semiotics of Popular Music'. *Semiotica,* 63(1/3): 279–98.

Taraborrelli, J. (2004) *Michael Jackson.* New York: Pan.

Taylor, C. (2004) *Modern Social Imaginaries.* Durham, NC: Duke University Press.

Terranova, T. (2000) 'Free Labour: Producing Culture for the Digital Economy'. *Social Text,* 18(2): 33–58.

Terranova, T. (2004) *Network Culture: Politics for the Information Age.* London: Pluto.

Tetzlaff, D. (1993) 'Metatextual Girl: Patriarchy, Postmodernism, Power, Money, Madonna', in C. Schwichtenberg (ed.), *The Madonna Connection: Representational Politics, Subcultural Identities, and Cultural Theory.* Boulder, CO: Westview, 239–64.

Théberge, P. (2004) 'Technology, Creative Practice and Copyright', in S. Frith and L. Marshall (eds), *Music and Copyright.* Edinburgh: Edinburgh University Press, 139–56.

Thompson, B. (2009) 'The State of the UK's Pop Music Industry'. *Financial Times,* 13 February.

Thompson, E.P. (1963) *The Making of the English Working Class.* Harmondsworth: Penguin.

Thompson, E.P. (1991) *Customs in Common.* London: Penguin.

Thornton, S. (1995) *Club Cultures.* Cambridge: Polity.

Topping, A. (2010) 'Summer Festivals Help Boost UK Music Industry Revenues'. *The Guardian,* 13 May.

Toynbee, J. (2000) *Making Popular Music.* London: Arnold.

Turner, C. (2004) *Modern Social Imaginaries.* Durham, NC: Duke University Press.

Vogel, H. (1998) *Entertainment Industry Economics.* New York: Cambridge University Press.

Waksman, S. (1999) *Instruments of Desire: The Electric Guitar and the Shaping of Music.* Cambridge, MA: Harvard University Press.

Waksman, S. (2004) 'California Noise: Tinkering with Hardcore and Heavy Metal in Southern California'. *Social Studies of Science,* 34(5): 675–702.

Wall, T. (2003) *Studying Popular Music Culture.* London: Hodder Arnold.

Weber, M. (1922) *The Sociology of Religion.* Boston: Beacon Press.

Weinstein, D. (2000) *Heavy Metal: The Music and Its Culture,* 2nd edition. New York: Da Capo.

Weitzer, R. and Kurbin, E. (2009) 'Misogyny in Rap Music: A Content Analysis of Prevalence and Meanings'. *Men and Masculinities*, 12(1): 3–29.

Williams, R. (1961) *The Long Revolution*. Harmondsworth: Penguin.

Williams, R. (1976) *Keywords*. London: Fontana.

Williams, R. (1977) *Marxism and Literature*. Oxford: Oxford University Press.

Williams, R. (1980) *Culture and Materialism*. London: Verso.

Willis, P. (1978) *Profane Culture*. London: Routledge and Kegan Paul.

Willis, P. (2000) *The Ethnographic Imagination*. Cambridge: Polity.

Wilson, B. (1975) *The Noble Savages*. Berkeley: University of California Press.

Wilson, O. (1985) 'The Association of Movement and Music as a Manifestation of a Black Conceptual Approach to Music Making', in I. Jackson (ed.), *More Than Dancing*. Westport, CT: Greenwood Press, 9–23.

Witkin, R. (2003) *Adorno on Popular Culture*. London: Routledge.

Woolgar, S. (1997) *Virtual Society? Technology, Cyberbole, Reality*. Oxford: Oxford University Press.

Wouters, C. (2007) *Informalization: Manners and Emotions*. London: Sage.

Zuckerman, P. (2003) *An Invitation to the Sociology of Religion*. London: Routledge.

Subject Index

Author Index